European Armies and the Conduct of War

European Armies and the Conduct of War

HEW STRACHAN

London
George Allen & Unwin
Boston   Sydney

George Allen & Unwin (Publishers) Ltd,
40 Museum Street, London WC1A 1LU, UK

George Allen & Unwin (Publishers) Ltd,
Park Lane, Hemel Hempstead, Herts HP2 4TE, UK

Allen & Unwin, Inc.,
Fifty Cross Street, Winchester, Mass 01890, USA

George Allen & Unwin Australia Pty Ltd,
8 Napier Street, North Sydney, NSW 2060, Australia

First published in 1983
Second impression 1984

British Library Cataloguing in Publication Data

Strachan, Hew
  European armies and the conduct of war.
1. Military art and science – Europe – History
2. Military history, Modern
3. Europe – History, Military
I. Title
355'.02' 094   D215
ISBN 0-04-940069-X
ISBN 0-04-940070-3 Pbk

Library of Congress Cataloging in Publication Data

Strachan, Hew
  European armies and the conduct of war.
Bibliography: p.
1. Military art and science – Europe – History.
2. War. 3. Military history, Modern. I. Title.
U43.E95S76   1983   355'.0094   83–8787
ISBN 0-04-940069-X
ISBN 0-04-940070-3 (pbk.)

Set in 10 on 11 point Times by Red Lion Setters, London
and printed in Great Britain
by Mackays of Chatham

Contents

List of Maps and Figures

Acknowledgements

We wish to thank the following publishers for their kind permission to reproduce the maps which appear in this volume: Batsford (BT) Ltd., for Map 1 from *Marlborough as Military Commander* by David Chandler; Map 6 from *The Art of Warfare in the Age of Napoleon* by Gunther E. Rothenberg and Map 8 from *Napoleon* by James Marshall-Cornwall. Arms and Armour Press for Map 2 from *Atlas of Military Strategy* by David Chandler. David & Charles Ltd., and Christopher Duffy for Map 3 from *The Army of Frederick the Great* by Christopher Duffy. Oxford University Press for Map 4 from *The Defence of Piedmont* by Spenser Wilkinson. Faber & Faber Ltd., for Map 14 from *A History of the World War, 1914–18* by B. H. Liddell Hart. Eyre Methuen Ltd. (London), for Map 10 from *The American Civil War* by Peter J. Parish. Cambridge University Press for Maps 7 and 13 from *Supplying War* by Martin Van Creveld. Davis-Poynter Ltd., for Map 16 from *France and Belgium 1939–1940* by Brian Bond. Weidenfeld & Nicolson Ltd., for Maps 5 and 9 from *The Campaigns of Napoleon* by David Chandler; Map 11 from *The Art of War* by William McElwee; Map 15 from *Recent History Atlas, 1860–1960* by Martin Gilbert and Map 17 from *The German Army 1933–1945* by Albert Seaton.

For C. B. R.

'Quiconque aujourd'hui réfléchit sur les guerres
et sur la stratégie, élève une barrière entre
son intelligence et son humanité'

Raymond Aron, *Penser la Guerre, Clausewitz*, vol. 2, p. 267.

Introduction

This is a book about the theory and practice of war. It is not primarily an account of the campaigns fought in the last two or three hundred years; it is more an attempt to consider how European armies rationalised their experience of those campaigns and so prepared their plans and doctrines for the next. It is also a book about social and technological change. Therefore, it begins with the eighteenth century, and thus aims to set its subject matter in the context both of the Industrial and of the French Revolutions. Geographically, it takes a broad swathe through Central and Western Europe. It tends to neglect the Scandinavian and Mediterranean peripheries, and at points it focuses exclusively on the leading and most innovative nation of the day. The attention given to the military experience of the United States, and the consideration of airpower, may both seem extraneous elements. By the end of the book, I hope it will be clear why they have been included. A chapter has been devoted to colonial warfare, but guerrilla and counter-insurgency operations have not been treated.

A book like this is a work of synthesis. I have leant heavily on the research and writing of others, and in particular – like many other military historians – I have been inspired by the work of Michael Howard and Peter Paret. The Guides to Further Reading at the end of each chapter (while not revealing the full range of my obligations) are intended to suggest a number of reasonably available works, preferably in English, with which to begin further study. They refer to books by the author's name (and, if necessary, by the date of publication): the full bibliographical details of each are contained in the Select Bibliography at the end. Bibliographical comments of a general nature are to be found in the Guide to Further Reading at the end of chapter 1.

The bulk of this book first took shape in lectures and seminars at Cambridge and Sandhurst. I am therefore indebted to my colleagues and pupils in both places. Over the years I have learnt much from Clive Trebilcock, Brian Bond and Dr Christopher Andrew. More specifically, Dr T. C. W. Blanning, Dr C. A. Bayly and Dr D. Stevenson have read and commented on portions (or, in the latter case, all) of the work. Their advice was invaluable. Professor Paul Kennedy has played a vital, if fortuitous, role. Finally I must thank the Master and Fellows of Corpus Christi College, Cambridge, for a number of research grants and for providing such a congenial environment in which to work.

HEW STRACHAN

Chapter 1

The Study of War

'The moderns, who have undertaken to write the history of different wars, or of some renowned Commanders, being chiefly men of learning only, and utterly unacquainted with the nature of military operations, have given us indeed agreeable, but useless productions.' Thus did Henry Lloyd, a Welshman who had achieved general's rank in Russian service, commence his *History of the Late War in Germany*, published in 1766. What Lloyd was anxious to do was to point to the distinction between the didactic function of the study of warfare and the purely historical. For him the pre-eminent examples of the first category were the ancients, Xenophon and Caesar, but it has remained the dominant trait in military historical writing up until our own times. In 1925 another major-general, J. F. C. Fuller, concluded from his study of light infantry in the eighteenth century that 'Unless history can teach us how to look at the future, the history of war is but a bloody romance.'

The argument for the didactic use of military history does not therefore simply spring from a liberal horror of a subject outwardly so obscene. It is also profoundly utilitarian. The permutations of war are infinite, but each soldier's personal experience of combat is likely to be very limited. For every *grognard* who marched from Rivoli to Waterloo, for every Thomas Atkins who fought from Dunkirk to Berlin, there have been many more whose military service has coincided with long periods of peace or with little more than a brief period of bush-fighting. Real soldiering for some professionals in the Second World War was the return to coping with the boredom of cantonment life in India. So, if the potential warriors of the future are to gain any knowledge of war before they encounter the reality or if they are to enlarge on their limited stock of actual experience, the only means available for them to do so is vicarious. They must perforce read military history.

The profession to which they belong is not, however, primarily a literate or an academic one. Its attraction to a young man is the challenge of outdoor life not that of desk-bound theory. Thus wide reading must be replaced by succinct and readily assimilable analysis. To this end the didactic tradition in military history has endeavoured to establish a number of immutable principles of war. They serve as a check-list for a subaltern suddenly faced with the command of a company or as a vade-mecum for the staff college candidate battling his way through seemingly irrelevant detail in campaign histories. A rough check-list would include the following:

1 *The object*, the need to select the primary target and not to be deflected from that aim.
2 *The offensive*, which is the stronger form of warfare as it affirms

morale and only it can lead to victory. The defensive is weaker because it disperses resources, yields the initiative to the enemy, and is therefore acceptable only as the prelude to a counter-attack.

3   *Security of forces*, the importance of keeping up a guard while delivering the blow, of protecting one's own communications while falling on those of the enemy.

4   *Surprise*, whether physical or psychological, in order to ensure moral superiority over the enemy. This is clearly related to the second principle.

5   *Concentration*, or bringing the mass of troops to bear on the decisive point.

6   *Economy of effort*. Notwithstanding the fifth principle, the commander must also judge the upper limit required, since there is little point in taking a sledge-hammer to swat a fly.

7   *Flexibility and mobility*, which are important elements in attacking with surprise, in concentrating decisively, and with no more effort than is requisite.

8   *Simplicity of plan*, since excessive complexity may overtax the training, capability and command structure of the forces and thus carry its own risk of breakdown.

9   *Unity of command*, thus ensuring the co-operation of the various parts of the army.

10   *Morale*, without which no troops will carry out even the best plans.

These maxims are designed for the purpose of training soldiers, but it remains important that the historian should be aware of them. In the first place, although there are innumerable exceptions to each one, used with judgement they can aid an understanding of war. It is their slavish application that is dangerous. Secondly, and more to the point for the purposes of this book, their establishment and reinforcement have been a primary purpose of many of the great theorists of war. Thus at the very least they provide an insight into the military brain.

Most writers on strategy have looked for general principles, trying to establish broad theories of universal application. But this is where the didactic use of military history begins to present problems. In many countries, particularly before 1914, the research and writing of military history were in the hands of specialist sections of the general staff. Although in some cases this arrangement did serve the purposes of scholarship, its justification was unashamedly didactic. As members of an organisation that needed to reinforce its own institutions and *esprit*, such historians inevitably started with more than the average number of preconceptions. As General Bronsart von Schellendorf pointed out, 'It is well known that military history, when superficially studied, will furnish arguments in support of any theory or opinion.'

This tendency to systematise, or to try to fit the facts into a preconceived and universally applicable explanation, reached its most idiosyncratic and damaging levels not in the works by teams of general staff historians but with those of individuals. Jomini, whose *Précis de l'art de la guerre* (1838) will be discussed in more detail later in this book, was on the whole accurate in his observation of the campaigns of Napoleon, but, because he wished to fit them into an eighteenth-century model of limited warfare, completely misunderstood their spirit. Furthermore the uncritical adoption of his rules – in the erroneous belief that they were also Napoleon's – to totally different conditions, could result only in disaster. The predecessors of Ulysses S. Grant in the commands of the Union armies in the American Civil War had received a full diet of Jomini at West Point. Grant said of them that 'They were always thinking about what Napoleon would do. Unfortunately for their plans the rebels would be thinking about something else . . . . If men make war in slavish obedience to rules, they will fail . . . . While our generals were working out problems of an ideal character . . . practical facts were neglected.'

Similarly Sir Basil Liddell Hart's *Strategy. The Indirect Approach* was a conscious reaction to the excessively direct approach of the western front in 1914–18. He influenced a later generation of soldiers as profoundly as had Jomini. He argued that by attacking on the line of so-called 'least expectation', the general will always succeed and probably do so at little cost in lives. But the line of least expectation may in fact be that of supposed *greatest* expectation. For example, a direct assault could be mounted after the enemy has been temporarily distracted by a diversionary attack to his flank and rear. Or again, the line of least expectation may be just that because it does not threaten any object of decisive importance for the enemy. Not only is Liddell Hart's argument tortuous in its logic; it is also selective in its history. Sherman's Atlanta campaign of 1864 was taken as a classic example of the indirect approach, with its succession of turning movements in a fresh theatre of operations. But it was also total war, involving the destruction of crops and Southern farmsteads. Liddell Hart found difficulty in accepting that the indirect approach could by its attack on the civil population thus be even more horrific than any conventional military operation.

For not only he and Jomini, but also a host of other systematisers, have been drawn into attempts to rationalise war because they find difficulty in accepting the elemental forces at its centre. They have attempted to argue that war can be limited of itself, that its conduct can be moderated. At first sight this seems puzzling. There is nothing inherently limitable in violence. For an individual killing and maiming are extremes, and even for a state to pull its punches is to court that one thing more terrible than victory – defeat.

The influence of their general theories has coincided with periods of so-called limited war, or eras when Europe has drawn breath and taken stock after punishing and exhausting campaigning. Historically, three periods of limited war are normally identified in modern times. The first runs from 1648, the Peace of Westphalia and the end of the Thirty Years' War, to 1792 and the onset of the Revolutionary Wars. Europe in the eighteenth century is taken to have an advanced international system, bound together on the one hand by dynastic monarchies, which respected each other's constitutional positions, and on the other by nobilities, affiliated to these royal courts, and united by the spirit of reason, by the Enlightenment and by the international dominance of the French language.

Religion ceased to be a *casus belli*, and thus an incentive for extremism was removed. There had been no logical limits when a man was fighting for his beliefs, convinced that he possessed a monopoly of the truth. But now violence became socialised: man fought as a member of a nation state. During the seventeenth century the central administration of armies took hold – military secretariats were established in France in 1635, in Austria in 1650, in Britain in 1661 and in Piedmont in 1717. War therefore became an activity regulated by the state. *Raison d'état* could act as a moderating influence. But in 1789 the French Revolution transformed the state from within and released the violent feelings of nationalism. Between 1792 and 1815 forces from outside the existing equation broke down the balance and inaugurated a period of total war. In 1815, at the Treaty of Vienna and by the Concert of Europe, Metternich and his ilk attempted to re-establish the old European order. So successful were they that although there were signs of breakdown after the 1848 revolutions – manifested in a number of European wars – it was not until 1914 that the old order of interrelated monarchies was swept away in a fresh bout of total war. The defeat of Germany in Hitler's war inaugurated the third period. The world since 1945 has boasted some successes for the United Nations and has constructed an international system, which, although based on superpower rivalry and the threat of appalling devastation, has contrived to avert total war. But equally, like its predecessors, its strengths rest in the status quo. It is most vulnerable to forces from without, to the proliferation of nuclear weapons in the hands of those not aligned to the balance of East/West politics.

Even a chronology as superficial as the one given here suggests that it is not the theories of war that have limited the horrors of combat, but factors far more compelling, be they social, economic or political. A principal theme therefore of this book will be to examine the works of the better-known theorists of war and to explain their popularity in the context of the external constraints that have operated on war. To achieve this we must escape from the didactic tradition in military history and put war in its historical context. The development of war cannot be understood, as Jomini attempted to understand Napoleon, simply as a continuous, independent, self-generating growth, unaffected by external phenomena. Napoleon was a product of revolutionary France, and his methods of warfare were rooted in political and social change. Those origins gave his conduct of war a validity for his times only, and meant too that his campaigns can best be understood in their own chronological context. To approach the truth we must discard the military, telescopic perspective, which excludes extraneous factors, and instead think laterally.

In addition to a desire on the part of many theorists of war to rationalise and thus to limit, they have also agonised at length over whether the conduct of war constitutes an art or a science. Broadly speaking, at a tactical level, war needs to be as precise a science as possible. If a battalion, when it comes under fire, has a clear and exact procedure to follow, one in which all its constituent parts have been thoroughly trained, then it will gain time for the commander to take his decisions and it will give confidence to the men in their actions. The fact that Machiavelli in the sixteenth century and most military writers down to the eighteenth century reckoned warfare could be reduced to a science is not therefore simply a reflection of the age of reason. It also denotes the dominance of tactics in military thought, and in particular the importance of siegecraft, in itself one of the most exact procedures in battlefield techniques. But by the end of the eighteenth century, views were changing. Lloyd's assertion that the art consisted in how to apply the rules of war in their correct combinations has found echoes ever since. The contribution of Behrenhorst (writing in 1797) and Clausewitz (whose *Vom Kriege* first appeared in 1832) may have been to stress the uncertainties and contradictions inherent in war, but they did not depart from the basic assumption that science provided the framework or the grammar of war, and art the genius of inspired command.

The evolution of the scientific aspect of war during our period has been affected by two interacting pressures. Both of them are major themes in this book. The industrial revolution and the advance of technology have transformed the mechanics of warfare. At the same time the bearing of arms in civilian life has all but disappeared, and thus the skills of the soldier have become more distinct. Professional armies prepare and train for war in peacetime. Their approach to these preparations is itself scientific, and the acquisition of the techniques of fighting widens the division between the bulk of society and the long-service regular soldier. Therefore, at this point the theorists' semantic question as to whether warfare is a science begins to shed light on their concern with war's limitation. A war fought by professional soldiers, because they are more costly to train and maintain, will in all probability be a war between smaller armies, with fewer consequent casualties and less impact on society as a whole. Therefore, writers like Liddell Hart have averred, a professional army is the desideratum because it will limit war. Such attitudes of course neglect the nature of the society from which the army is recruited, and the type of mission which its nation's foreign policy is likely to require it to undertake. But if war is conducted by professionals in accordance with this thesis, it will also be more scientific because the level of military expertise will be higher and it will be more amenable to rational influences. Both Fuller and Liddell Hart embraced the mechanisation of armies after 1918 because it would reduce the element of chance. 'Tactically', Fuller wrote, 'the soldier is simply a weapon-mounting of about one-eighth h.p. energy.'

During our period, the direction of war at the level of art has been vested in commanders ever more removed from the battlefield. Marlborough contrived a remarkable independence of his political masters, but was eventually recalled. Today the major strategic decisions facing NATO to all intents and purposes lie with the President of the United States, a civilian politician. Generals, however senior, are excluded from a directing function at this level, and instead act in a merely advisory capacity. They are back to a position where the science of war, what is technically feasible, has become the prime military role. The art of war is a civilian task, not least because only thus will the political causes of war, and the political consequences that accrue from it, remain constant factors in its conduct. The relationship between politics and the waging of war is therefore another broad theme in this book.

As a technician, the soldier's function is to warn of the enemy's capabilities rather than his intentions. His professional role is in a sense a pessimistic one, to present a worst-case analysis which will ensure sufficient preparation to avert defeat and – ideally – to deter war altogether. But military preparations have been the most costly of state activities since budgets were first centralised. There is thus a conflict between what is strategically desirable and what is economically feasible. Decisions about enemy intentions have to be made if any check is to be enforced on the expenditure which their capabilities would seem to warrant. Strategy therefore concerns not only the relationship between war and politics but also that between war and cash. This is perhaps a subdivision of politics, since the revenue is raised by taxation, in its turn probably voted by a house of representatives. But it remains helpful to consider the economic constraints on military policy as a distinct pressure on the development of war's conduct.

Mention has just been made of Clausewitz, and what has been written in this introduction reflects his influence. His contribution will not be analysed in detail until chapter 7, but what he wrote has provided a far more valuable framework for approaching the study of war than any comprehensive theories or list of principles. It is one of the greatest condemnations of the quality of military studies that, despite his imperfections and his inconsistencies, Clausewitz still stands unassailably supreme in military literature. Furthermore, this judgement applies not merely to what he had to say about the relationship between war and politics, but also to his view of the function of military history. 'Theory', he wrote,

> cannot equip the mind with the formulas for solving problems, nor can it mark the narrow path on which the sole solution is supposed to lie by planting a hedge of principles on either side. But it can give the mind insight into the great mass of phenomena and of their relationships, then leave it free to rise into the higher realms of action. There the mind can use its innate talents to capacity, combining them all to seize on what is *right* and *true* – as though it were a response to the immediate challenge more than a product of thought.

The theory thus applied must be developed from military history, and the latter must therefore be as detailed and accurate as possible. The first step, then, in Clausewitz's development towards an understanding of war is a historical study that accords with the untrammelled demands of scholarship. If uncomfortable facts do not accord with theories, then it is not the facts that must be suppressed but the theory that should be revised. A purely academic approach to military history is therefore not only the key to Clausewitz's arguments but also in fact the basis for its didactic use. Rigorous, honest and accurate reporting will provide a surer base for didactic military history than will the selective use of facts to buttress preconceptions. Thus, although the purpose of this book is purely academic, to seek greater understanding, it is not illogical to argue that, if the picture it presents contains an element of truth, it is also didactic.

Guide to Further Reading

The best history of war in Europe is Howard (1976): its only fault is its brevity. Other good general accounts are Ropp, and Preston, Wise and Werner. They too cover a wide span in a short compass. Delbrück's magisterial work is now being translated: unfortunately it stops short of the First World War. Earle is still the best book on its subject, although some of the later chapters (particularly that on Liddell Hart) are now dated. For factual summaries of campaigns, go to Dupuy. Fuller (1972) is polemical.

The relationships between armies and their parent societies are covered by two excellent works, Corvisier for the period before 1789 and Gooch (1979) for the period after. *The Fontana History of War and European Society* promises to have a broader and more general remit, but so far only the volumes by Best (1982) and Kiernan (1982) have appeared. Many of the works Gooch cites in his full bibliographical guide have been of value in the writing of this book. But there has been no attempt in the Guides to Further Reading or in the Select Bibliography to give full coverage to the same ground, and the interested reader should therefore refer to Gooch.

In any case, the plea to put military history in its social context has been so successful that many histories of individual armies do not give adequate coverage to tactical and operational problems. The works of Carrias on the French and Germans are therefore still important, and Andolenko has proved helpful on the Russians. Splendid examples of what might be achieved are provided by Weigley (1968 and 1973) for the United States, and Papke and Petter for Germany.

The themes of militarism, the mass army and war's relationship to economic development have been given general treatments by Vagts, Nickerson and Nef respectively. All three are somewhat dated, but Vagts and Nef in particular repay reading. William H. McNeill, *The Pursuit of Power; Technology, Armed Force, and Society since AD 1000* (Oxford, 1983) and Maurice Pearton, *The Knowledgeable State: Diplomacy, War and Technology since 1830* (London, 1982) provide sophisticated discussions of war and technology. Van Creveld (1977) has dealt with supply, but he tends at times to overstate his case. Shaw, although old, has some interesting but very different things to say on the same question. The behaviour of the individual under fire is covered in two beautifully written and highly suggestive works – one more general (Keegan, 1976), and the other specific and autobiographical (Gray). The ethical and legal problems of war are covered by Best (1980), Howard (1979) and – in a more purely philosophical vein – Paskins and Dockrill.

Chapter 2

The Age of Marlborough and Frederick

The eighteenth-century systems of war, wrote Marshal Foch, 'tried to achieve their objectives by stratagems, threat, negotiation, manoeuvre, partial actions, occupation of hostile territory and the capture of fortified places.' The marshal accepted the oft-held view that war in the Age of Reason was limited because its exponents wished it to be so, that generals earned their reputations by ponderously moving their armies round the Low Countries, deliberately avoiding battle.

However, a number of other constraints operated on the conduct of war, irrespective of any limitation as to the choice of means. Europe was exhausted by the duration and intensity of the Thirty Years' War; certain areas had been virtually depopulated, and their economic and social life had been fundamentally disrupted. During the course of it, in 1625, Grotius had published his *De jure belli ac pacis*, arguing for the protection of the rights of the individual against the evils of war, and grounding his argument in the enlightened self-interest of states. Vattel's *Droit des gens* (1758) underscored the point. The prevailing economic orthodoxy of mercantilism stressed the need for countries to sell more than they imported. Thus national strength depended on a trading surplus, and import controls – in Britain, the Navigation Acts (1651 and 1661) – checked the flow of specie abroad, particularly by ensuring that goods were only carried in national vessels. War moved to the peripheries of Europe, to the control of sea-lanes and to the dominance of fresh markets. Trade wars, such as the Anglo-Dutch Wars of 1652–4, 1664–7 and 1672–4, followed, but their justification was economic not humanitarian. Because they were fought at sea, such wars were limited in their impact.

Economic considerations also played their part in curtailing the value of land warfare as an instrument of policy. Protection for nascent industries was incompatible with a war of exhaustion. During the Seven Years' War (1756–63), Prussia expended 82 million pounds of gunpowder, but her own annual production was only just over half a million pounds. In consequence she had to import supplies from Holland and Britain, and bring in saltpetre from India to supplement her domestic production. To Frederick, the outward flow of gold to pay for this could only jeopardise the shaky industrial base which Prussia was forging.

Even more dramatic was the relationship between economic demands and the size and composition of armies. Broadly speaking, a monarch had to balance the competing claims of productivity and military efficiency. With great tracts of Europe not yet even under cultivation, let alone producing a surplus, a growing population was thought to be the *sine qua non* for economic growth. But in the Seven Years' War, the Prussian army lost three times its own strength in men, suffering 180,000 deaths. Prussia, like most other European countries, employed mercenaries in order to lessen the impact of unproductive labour on her economy. About a fifth of the Austrian army and up to a third of the French army came from abroad. As one French general said, each foreign soldier was worth three men, one more for France, one less for the enemy, and one Frenchman left to pay taxes. In peacetime, therefore, the military ethos was predominantly that of the mercenary. At the end of the War of Austrian Succession (1745), two-thirds of the Prussian army was composed of Prussian nationals, but by 1751 only one-third of it was. The outbreak of war in 1756 saw the nationals return to the colours and by 1763 the two-thirds proportion was restored. In 1786, half the army was again composed of foreigners. At the same time, the officer corps became more aristocratic. The purpose was to link and subordinate the nobility to the Crown and increasingly to the idea of the state. In Russia noble rank was conferred by service in the monarch's army rather than by the independent ownership of land. Elsewhere the aristocracy's relative loss of independence is well-illustrated by the ending of the colonel's proprietorial rights in his regiment – carried through as late as 1769 in Austria and not completed in France even by 1789. But the more noble the officer, the fewer the ties he had with the mercenary. The status of the private soldier declined. The 'gentleman' soldiers, who provided their own equipment and who still formed the nucleus of the British Horse Guards in 1660, were ousted by men from lower social orders. Desertion became rampant. One in four Frenchmen deserted from the army in the War of the Spanish Succession, and from 1717 to 1728 there were 8,500 deserters for every 20,000 men in the Saxon infantry. In the Seven Years' War, 80,000 men absconded from the Prussian army, 70,000 from the French and 62,000 from the Austrian. An incident from that war graphically illustrates the unreliability of the troops. In 1758, a convoy destined to help the Prussian besieging force at Olmütz was attacked by the Austrians, and 200,000 thalers were lost; 70,000 thalers were later recovered from the escorting Prussian troops, who had taken the opportunity to join in the plunder. The monarch had a choice. If he had a well-motivated army, home production would be neglected and, in the words of Frederick William's political testament of 1722, 'the tax returns will be reduced to less than a third; prices will fall, rents will not be fully paid, and there will be total ruin.' The alternative was to place greater weight on home production and so accept the inevitability of an army whose social characteristics would place distinct limitations on its performance.

The latter option was more appealing because, by using mercenaries and nobles, military affairs were removed from the ken of the emergent bourgeois classes. If either they or their employees were taken from their more productive roles, then the national economy would suffer, and so too would their ability to pay the taxes which kept the army in the field. A protracted and costly war was therefore additionally undesirable because it could force the monarch, in raising the money to pay for it, to have to secure the approval of representative institutions for his proposed taxation.

War was the principal and most costly state activity in the eighteenth century, and it was this above all that triggered the emotive cry of 'no taxation without representation'. The American War of Independence was a case in point. The colonists rebelled not least because they objected to meeting the costs of the British garrison. France financed her involvement in the war by extravagant borrowing which trebled the annual cost of servicing the debt. Fiscal organisation remained rudimentary and its administrative problems were heightened by noble and ecclesiastical resistance to centralisation. The attempt in France to subvent such opposition in 1787 by proposing to tax all land was thwarted with the cry that only the Estates General could sanction new taxes. Eventually, two years later, the demand was met, the Estates convened and the first stage of the French Revolution inaugurated. Thus the cost of war could drive a wedge between the Estates and the Crown, and, through the growth of representative institutions, weaken absolutism.

The economic constraints on going to war were compounded by equally powerful brakes on the formulation of strategy after the war had begun. The seventeenth and eighteenth centuries had witnessed the assertion of monarchical power over the particularism of the nobility. The consequent growth in central authority had allowed an increase in the size of armies, from an average of 40,000 in the mid-seventeenth century to 100,000 by 1710. But there had been no proportionate population growth, no concomitant increase in the food supply to feed these armies and no consequent improvement in communications to hasten their marches. Only five areas in Europe at the beginning of the eighteenth century possessed sufficient population (thirty-five inhabitants per square kilometre) to be able to produce enough to provision an army without magazines. They were parts of France and the Rhineland, Westphalia, the Spanish Netherlands and Lombardy. As an army on the move normally subsisted by requisition, once it was concentrated it went abroad, so that it could burden a countryside other than its own. This was one reason why, at the start of the Seven Years' War, Frederick the Great promptly moved into Saxony rather than stay in Prussian Silesia. But even if the army found itself in fertile country, it still had to maintain a train for its artillery and ammunition. The roads were few and poor, and the threat of enemy cavalry would force the column together for mutual support. Thus progress was slow. But the slower the movement, the more difficult were the problems of requisitioning, since the army could not move into fresh areas fast enough. And so it had to carry at least a part of its own food and fodder with it. In consequence the train grew and the army's movements were further curtailed. The Russian army was so used to campaigning in the wastes of the Ottoman empire (where there was nothing to requisition) that in the battles at the outset of the Seven Years' War it required a quarter of its combatant strength to protect its baggage. By the 1790s, a Prussian infantry regiment of 2,200 men was accompanied by 2,400 non-combatants and 1,200 draft horses. Therefore, although requisitioning continued to play a role in eighteenth-century warfare, the lack of an available surplus and the difficulties of rapid movement meant that the magazine system, pioneered by Louvois in France in the mid-seventeenth century, assumed ever-increasing prominence. In 1776, the Berlin and Breslau magazines alone contained enough grain to feed an army of 60,000 men for two years. In the Seven Years' War bread was actually baked from flour forty years old. Tempelhoff, the historian of that war, averred that sixty miles was the maximum distance which field ovens could advance from the magazines in order to bake, and the bread wagons could cover another forty miles. As a result, in theory (although of course an army could always forsake its communications temporarily), a 100-mile limit existed on an advance into enemy territory unless an intermediate magazine was formed.

Adequate communications were therefore vital. In the absence of good roads, waterways were the crux. It was no coincidence that the Low Countries, with their network of canals, and Saxony-Silesia, with the Elbe and Oder running south-east/north-west to Prussia, were the principal campaigning areas of the age. Communications became like funnels, through which the army had to pass, and which revealed to its enemy its likely course of advance. In peacetime, therefore, a state could take precautions by the erection of forts at the confluences of rivers, at defiles and junctions. The bastion system of fortification, a product of the Italian Renaissance developed by Louis XIV's great engineer, Vauban, greatly strengthened the powers of the defensive. Its projecting fronts, with their numerous refinements, broke up the attack and exposed it to flanking fields of fire. As a result the besieger had to add a large battering train to his convoy and so hamper even further his already slow progress. In 1708, Marlborough's train of eighteen heavy guns and twenty siege mortars required 16,000 horses and 3,000 wagons to move it and covered thirty miles of highway. Thus although Marlborough was pre-eminently a seeker of battles, in ten campaigns he conducted thirty sieges and fought only four major actions in the open field.

The dominance of forts in the eighteenth century was well-nigh crippling to the offensive. Even as he marshalled his army for the invasion, the commander used existing border-forts and magazines as jumping-off points, and therefore displayed in advance his likely lines of operation. If the defence's forts were placed well back from the frontier, his line of communications would lengthen and become more vulnerable. The example already cited, of the Austrians harrying the Prussian convoys destined to aid the besiegers of Olmütz in 1758, illustrates the consequences. Frederick planned to open the way into Austria but was foiled by his inability to sustain the siege which would clear his communications. Sedentary operations made requisitioning daily more difficult as the surrounding produce was eaten up. And the army had to be a big one, because, while half invested the fort, the remainder had to be strong enough to cover it from any relieving or roving forces without. All the defenders had to do was to avoid battle, maintain the threat of the army in being, harry the enemy's convoys and occasionally alarm his covering army. The dictates of strategy, therefore, rendered the defensive supreme, without battle ever being joined. War was in consequence limited by its means, but this was in spite of its practitioners, not because of them.

The objectives of warfare had to be moderated accordingly. Grand designs were quite simply incapable of fulfilment. The conquest of a province was a lengthy process, and its reconquest even more costly. In the First Silesian War (1740–2), Frederick stopped at the acquisition of Silesia, and the country he had deprived, Austria, had, at least temporarily, to accept the loss. Furthermore this sort of war was for Lloyd the highest category of endeavour: frequently objectives were even more modest – the raising of contributions, the destruction of magazines, or the creation of a diversion for another army. Frederick, who cannot be interpreted as anything other than a determined general seeking decisive victory, saw clearly the dangers of an over-ambitious plan, and was wont to cite the disaster that overtook Charles XII of Sweden at Poltava (1709) in order to illustrate the dangers of a campaign of deep penetration. Peter the Great of Russia had refused to give battle to Charles XII's advancing Swedes, until their army had been shattered by the problems of supply and movement.

Even if the means had allowed more exalted objectives, it is doubtful whether they were desirable or practicable. The balance of power did command an element of universal respect, and warfare was in a sense a form of negotiation over towns and frontiers within that overall framework. To destroy the machinery of another state, to remove its king, implied a threat to other crowns. Self-interest dictated a mutual acknowledgement of the continuity of monarchy. And, in any case, few other targets existed. Backward countries, with agricultural economies, cannot be conquered in the same way as modern, industrialised and centralised states. In October 1757, the Austrians rode into Berlin but Prussia did not surrender. This was still true of Russia in 1812. The fact that Marlborough planned to invade France after the battle of Oudenarde (1708), masking the border forts as he did so, is an indication of France's relative economic maturity. For most countries, the army in the field was not only the greatest manifestation of its power as a state but also the only reasonable objective.

The problems of manoeuvre and communication were therefore paramount if an offensively minded army was going to bring its opponent to a decisive battle. Strategy was a word rarely used in the eighteenth century, and, if it was, it denoted the organisation of supplies and marches. The genius of the great commander – and in particular of the French general, Turenne, and of his pupil, Marlborough – lay therefore in overcoming the inherent difficulties in the movement of armies.

Turenne's campaign of 1674 can serve as an illustration. His opponents, the German princes of the Holy Roman Empire, had gone into winter quarters in Alsace. Turenne took up a position to the north, but then marched south, screened from Alsace by the Vosges, to Epinal and Belfort. When he met the Imperialists on 5 January 1675 at Turkheim, they had only half their army assembled. A daring and rapid march at an unexpected time of the year had achieved complete strategic surprise.

Marlborough fought under Turenne and it is tempting to see the latter's influence in the Blenheim campaign of 1704 (see Map 1), which even today is impressive for its strategic insight and which in the eighteenth century must stand supreme. Marlborough's army was stationed in the Low Countries, and the Dutch were extremely anxious that it should stay there,

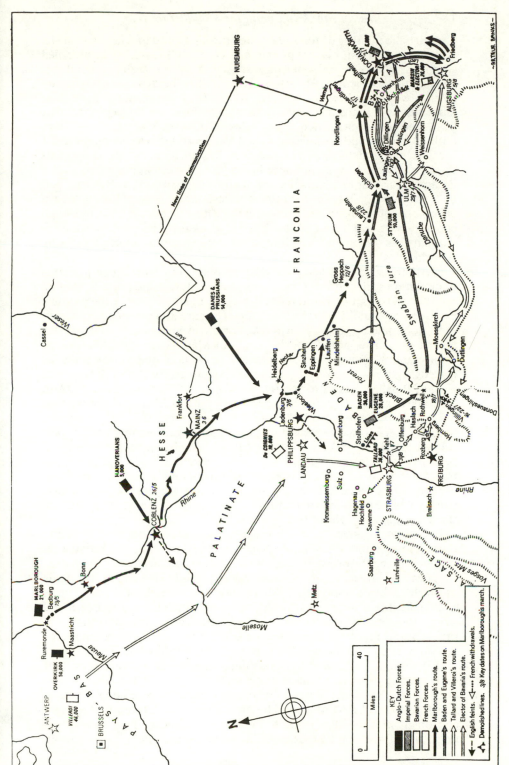

Map 1 *The Blenheim campaign, 1704*

although the number of forts precluded the likelihood of a decisive battle. At the end of April, his troops began to cross the Meuse. As he marched south, so he left his flank open to France, and it was therefore crucial that he maintain the element of surprise and rapidity, because only thus could he ensure that the French's concern for his intentions and for their communications continued to prevent them from implementing a plan of their own. The advance threatened a number of different objectives. At first, both the enemy and his allies assumed Marlborough was heading for the Moselle. After he was across the Moselle, the French feared a thrust through Alsace. It was only once he had let all these options pass that it became clear that he planned a union with the Austrians in Bavaria, and by then it was too late for the French to respond. Even had his bluff been called, the fact that he was following the Rhine meant that Marlborough could at any stage have doubled back to Holland. The result was a decisive battle at Blenheim, which resulted in the annexation of Bavaria by Austria.

Marlborough clearly had great strategic ability that transcended theatres of operation and embraced the elements of seapower and politics. He had too the will to battle. Yet in ten campaigns, Blenheim − with the possible exception of Ramillies − stands unique. The caricature of generals avoiding battle could by gross distortion be applied even to him. This image has tended to gain support from the words of Maurice de Saxe, Marshal of France and a commander at Fontenoy (as well as one of 354 acknowledged illegitimate children of Frederick Augustus, Elector of Saxony and King of Poland). Saxe's *Reveries upon the Art of War*, written in 1732, in great haste and, Carlyle maintained, under the influence of opium, was published posthumously in 1757. In it he wrote, 'I do not favour pitched battles, especially at the beginning of war, and I am convinced that a skilful general could make war all his life without being forced into one.' Similarly, to reinforce the point, Lloyd concluded that 'The great and important parts of war, as well in the formation, as in the execution, depend on the knowledge of the country; and wise generals, will always chuse to make them the foundation of their conduct, rather than trust to the uncertain issue of battle'.

But it is a long step − and a misguided one − to conclude that therefore the will to fight did not exist. Principally, of course, Saxe and Lloyd were acknowledging the decisive effects of a defence conducted without battle. Practical requirements, not abstract theory, dictated the choice. Even one of Marlborough's opponents, Villars, delivered himself of the opinion in 1709 that: 'My principle is that saying of Turenne's . . . , that the general who is absolutely determined to avoid a battle delivers himself over to him that seeks it.' Frederick construed the Seven Years' War as one fought for the survival of Prussia, and felt that he must fight the battle of Leuthen (1757) 'or all is lost'. 'War', he concluded, 'cannot be conducted without encountering decisive battles that determine the fate of the kingdom.'

The desire to force the issue was reinforced by the economic pressures which demanded a short war. The means were not limited if they were consonant with the objectives. In these circumstances, the arguments of Grotius and Vattel for moderation in war's conduct held little sway. In

1704 Marlborough burnt farms in order to bring the Elector of Bavaria to terms. In 1760, at the siege of Breslau, the Austrians demanded its surrender or, they said, they would pluck the babies from their mothers' wombs. The Prussian commander replied, 'I am not pregnant, nor are my soldiers'. In the war in Piedmont (1742–8), the French soldiers' harshness to the inhabitants provoked guerrilla operations against their communications, and this was always a danger when the troops had to requisition. As the militarist Joseph II of Austria admitted, when faced with his first real campaign in 1778: 'War is a frightful thing, what with the destruction of the fields and villages, the lamentation of the poor peasants, the ruin of so many innocent people and, for myself, the disturbances I experience for days and nights on end'.

Attitudes to war and to battle were therefore no more humanitarian than in any other age. If the effects of battle were limited, this was due to the practical constraints of the times and not to design. We have already seen the advantages to the defence in not joining battle. Furthermore, even for the attacker there were powerful disincentives. The problems of supply and transport – in addition to the cost of maintaining professional, standing armies – favoured keeping armies small. The difficulties of moving and feeding large formations led Lloyd to conclude that 'Numbers, beyond a certain point, can add nothing to the force of an army, unless they can be made to act together; they increase its inactivity and render it altogether unmanageable'. Saxe, who had beaten the Turks with considerably smaller forces, maintained that the maximum size of an army should be 34,000 infantry and 12,000 cavalry. The casualties inflicted in battle were great, and proportionately more severe because of the initial size of the force. At Malplaquet, Marlborough lost 33 per cent of the troops he committed to the fight, and at Zorndorf (1758) the Russians suffered 50 per cent casualties and the Prussians 38 per cent. Not only were armies so stricken useless for the rest of the campaign, but in addition the gaps in the ranks of trained men were both hard and costly to fill.

Economic as well as military sense therefore dictated that generals should be very cautious about engaging in battle unless they were sure of the outcome. Frederick never committed his full force until he was certain of success, and it was axiomatic – as Napoleon told Joubert in 1797 – that for an inferior army the art of war was not to come to battle. Conversely, when both sides felt certain of victory – as was the case when the French smashed the Spanish *tercios* at Rocroi in 1643 – then the clash was rapid.

The whole drift away from battle – be it strategic or economic – was confirmed by the difficulties of eighteenth-century tactics. The declining reliability and the consequent harsh discipline of armies meant that the fear of desertion circumscribed reconnaissance. It was therefore often hard to establish contact with the enemy. Even if this vital preliminary was achieved, the time taken to deploy gave the enemy plenty of opportunity to withdraw. It took from 7 a.m. to 1 p.m. for the British army to distribute itself before the battle of Blenheim. The conventional formation adopted was for the infantry to form line, with the cavalry on the flanks and the artillery arranged among the regiments of foot in order to cover their deployment.

The cavalry was still the decisive arm at the end of the seventeenth century. It alone retained mobility and flexibility, and it alone was capable of a flank attack. By contrast the infantry was ponderous, too slow to form square to repel cavalry, and considered incapable of independent operations. At Ramillies, Marlborough, rather than exploit the breakthrough of Orkney's infantry, recalled them, as they had no cavalry to support them. In the 1674 campaign, Turenne had 10,000 cavalry and 12,000 infantry, and his opponents, the Imperialists, had more cavalry (19,000) than infantry (18,000). But from 1680 to 1750, the proportions of cavalry declined dramatically: from between a third to a half of any army they dwindled to a quarter.

This trend is in part to be accounted for by the cost both of the horse and of his fodder. In the Seven Years' War, the price of horses in Prussia doubled with the result that the army was short of 3,400 of them by the spring of 1761. Austria imported her heavier breeds from Holstein and Hanover, but the costs forced her to disband seven regiments of cuirassiers between 1769 and 1775. Russia's employment of heavy cavalry was continuously curtailed by her lack of a sufficiently strong native breed of horse. For France the main problem was feed, and in the winter of 1758–9 the army sent 20,000 horses and 6 cavalry regiments home in order to lessen the consumption of dry forage, although simultaneously incurring a loss of mobility. In the 1730s Santa Cruz reckoned that 2,500 infantry could be put into the field for the same price as 1,000 cavalry, and for this reason as early as 1688 Prussia, a poor state, had 21,000 infantry but only 4,800 cavalry.

However, the principal reason for the cavalry's decline was the comparative improvement of the infantry, and in particular its development of firepower. At the battle of Killiecrankie (1689), the Highlanders had fallen on the regular infantry in the interval between their firing and their fixing bayonets. At that date the bayonet was plugged into the muzzle of the musket and thus, when fixed, prevented any further firing. From 1700, the socket bayonet was adopted – a weapon which had a sleeve to fit over the barrel and could therefore be fixed while fire was maintained. In consequence all infantry could now boast the attributes of shock and firepower, the pike could be abolished, and the same numbers of men could double their effectiveness in either form. Simultaneously, by the time of the outbreak of the War of the Spanish Succession, the musket had been made lighter and the matchlock had been replaced by the flintlock. The former required forty-four movements to load it and the latter twenty-six. The rate of fire was in consequence doubled, to one round a minute, and a well-drilled exponent could achieve two rounds. From the 1720s and 1730s iron ramrods were issued, and so facilitated loading as to make possible a rate of fire of up to three rounds a minute. Indeed at Mollwitz (1741), the Austrians, still using beech ramrods, reckoned the Prussian rate of fire to be five rounds per minute in contrast to their two. The adoption by the Prussians in the 1770s of a ramrod with a top as broad as its bottom obviated the need to reverse the ramrod in the loading process. The action of ramming automatically primed the weapon, as it funnelled some of the main powder charge through the touch-hole and into the pan.

But it is hard to accept the claim that some men could now achieve a rate of six rounds per minute. A more normal performance remained two or three rounds.

Casualty figures reflected the dominance of the musket: only 9 per cent of the wounded admitted to the Invalides in Paris in 1762 were suffering from injuries inflicted by the bayonet but 80 per cent from those of fire-arms. However, the emphasis in shooting was on speed rather than accuracy. The maximum effective range of smooth-bore musketry was about 200 yards, and between 10 and 20 per cent hits at ranges below this was a reasonable performance. In consequence, although in truth a revolution in firepower had been carried through, there continued until the end of the smooth-bore era advocates for the restoration of the pike. These included Saxe and Lloyd, and Frederick himself – while cultivating the musketry of his infantry – remained curiously ambivalent about its priority over shock. They seem not to have fully realised that the close-range volley was the agent of disorganisation, and the advance with the bayonet simply its confirmation.

The concomitant cause of the rise of the infantry was the improvement in drill which professional and centralised armies permitted. In 1700, a regiment marched onto the battlefield out of step and in column. It then deployed into line in order to give fire. All this took time. In Britain, Marlborough encouraged the development of platoon fire, whereby a battalion was divided into eighteen platoons, broken into three 'firings' of six platoons each. Every third platoon fired together, thus giving continuous fire along the whole length of the line, while at the same time maintaining a reserve and ensuring reasonable control. But until 1728, the company was the prime administrative unit, and the reorganisation into platoons was done on the battlefield itself. Once in position, changes were difficult, particularly since they might be interrupted by the enemy. Good drill, therefore – at which of course the Prussians became the past masters – eased the springs of the machine, giving it more flexibility and more rapidity.

It could, however, do little more than allay the inherent problems. The pattern of a long line of infantry meant that the ability of cavalry to support infantry, and vice versa, was reduced simply by the physical distance between them. Fire and shock were thus badly combined. The decisiveness of battle was further hampered by the difficulty of forming column again, in order to pursue the vanquished foe from the field. The delays in starting the action meant that evening would already be nigh, and even if left in possession of the field the general might have achieved little else.

He was therefore reluctant to undergo the trial of battle. In manoeuvring he retained control, but once in position before the enemy he had forfeited many of the advantages his ability might have vouchsafed him. An encounter battle – when two armies met each other on the march – could prove the only means for an engagement to take place. Furthermore, it allowed a good general scope to display his powers of maneouvre on the battlefield itself. Examples in this period are Oudenarde and Leuthen, and the successful commanders on both those occasions, Marlborough and Frederick, demonstrated that perfection in eighteenth-century tactics was achieved by the successful combination of infantry and cavalry, by the ability to retain the power of manoeuvre even when on the battlefield, and by the use of terrain to maximum advantage. In other words, they accepted the existing system but so resolved its limitations and perfected its techniques as to gain the tactical advantage.

At Blenheim Marlborough drew his army up, not with the cavalry on the flanks, but in four lines – infantry in front, two lines of cavalry, and infantry to the rear. The infantry fire checked the French cavalry, who were then hit by the allied cavalry, who passed through the infantry line and charged, relying on the sword alone. The French still practised the seventeenth-century tactic of riding up, firing their pistols, and then charging or retiring to reload. By integrating horse and foot, Marlborough allowed the former to concentrate on shock effect, leaving the development of fire to the infantry.

Marlborough's use of ground is best demonstrated by Ramillies (1706) (see Map 2). The allied armies rested their left flank on the Mehaigne river, and then described an arc, with the right flank drawn back. In the centre of the French position was the fortified village of Ramillies. But the ground north of Ramillies, between the allied right flank and the French left, was boggy and hard to cross. Marlborough was therefore able to move troops on a short chord across the field in the course of the battle, and bring them into the main fight before the French could redeploy their regiments from the same sector. In other words, Marlborough had, by his astute use of ground, retained mobility in the battle, and, it has been argued, had anticipated the oblique order of Frederick with a holding attack all along the line but bringing the main weight against the decisive point.

Frederick's first battle was Mollwitz (1741), where the Austrian cavalry caused things to develop so badly for the Prussians that the young king was fifty miles from the field before he heard that he had in fact won the day. The direct consequence of his mortification was scrupulous attention to the improvement of Prussia's cavalry, which poverty had so far led her to neglect. As had Marlborough, Frederick emphasised the *arme blanche* and the speed of the charge. He achieved its combination with the infantry by placing it not on the wings but in the third rank, ready to pass through the intervals in the front two lines and to exploit the destruction wrought by the fire of the foot. Its great commander, Seydlitz, employed cavalry columns to increase the impact, and would obscure his movements from the enemy's gaze and consequent fire by the use of ground. Thus at Rossbach (1757), Zorndorf (1758) and Hochkirch (1758), the Prussian cavalry earned a reputation for decisive, shock action.

Arguably, however, Frederick's greatest contribution to the conduct of war was his attention to mobility on the battlefield, motivated above all by his quest for a successful flank attack. Proceeding from a number of strategic axioms – the principle of always attacking the enemy where he is weakest and of bringing strength against the decisive point – his battles are hallmarked by his choice of ground. Well-chosen terrain covered much of the position, allowing it to be weakly held and releasing troops to fall on the flank. At Kolin (1757), the Austrian army was formed up on

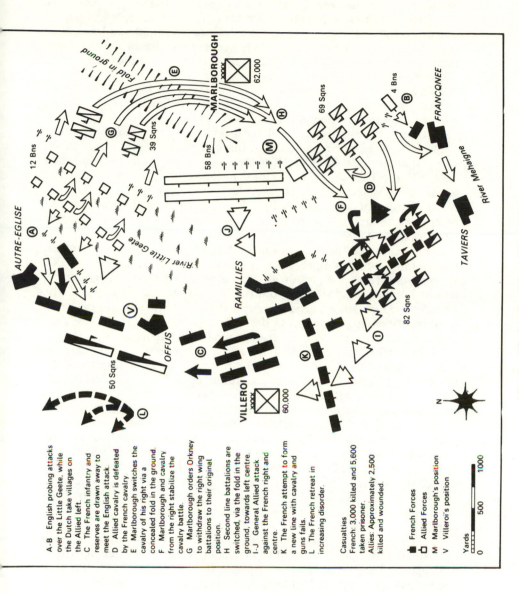

A-B English probing attacks over the Little Geete, while the Dutch take villages on the Allied left.
C   The French infantry and reserves are drawn away to meet the English attack.
D   Allied cavalry is defeated by the French cavalry
E   Marlborough switches the cavalry of his right via a concealed fold in the ground.
F   Marlborough and cavalry from the right stabilize the cavalry battle.
G   Marlborough orders Orkney to withdraw the right wing battalions to their original position.
H   Second line battalions are switched, via the fold in the ground, towards left centre
I-J General Allied attack against the French right and centre.
K   The French attempt to form a new line with cavalry and guns fails.
L   The French retreat in increasing disorder.

Casualties
French: 3,000 killed and 5,600 taken prisoner.
Allies: Approximately 2,500 killed and wounded.

■□ French Forces
□   Allied Forces
M   Marlborough's position
V   Villeroi's position

Yards
0   500   1000

Map 2   *The battle of Ramillies, 1706*

two hills, and the fact that it was therefore inaccessible to a frontal attack permitted Frederick to plan to refuse his right flank entirely and put his weight on the left, where the ground was approachable and where he could turn the Austrian position. If the enemy was drawn to the refused flank, the advanced Prussian flank could still turn in on the enemy flank which would thus be even more exposed.

This degree of flexibility was achieved above all by drill, by highly trained professionals marching in cadence. Frederick's most famous manoeuvre was the oblique order, that is to say placing his line across the extremity of his adversary's either by extending one flank beyond the enemy's or by advancing with battalions in echelon to strike beyond the enemy flank with the foremost. The idea was not new. It had originated at least with the Theban, Epaminondas, in the fourth century BC. But the quality of its execution was. At the battle of Campo Santo in 1743, the Austro-Sardinian army attacked the Spanish right, but in preserving its order in an oblique march over broken ground it took two hours to cover a thousand yards.

Contrast this performance with Frederick's *chef d'oeuvre*, Leuthen, fought only fourteen years later (see Map 3). The Austrians (65,000 strong) were drawn up in line, with dead ground to their front, and the village of Leuthen itself situated towards the left of their position. As the Prussians (33,000) approached, their first and second columns deployed in front of the Austrians and so drew in their reserve. But the rest then turned right, passed behind the dead ground, and fell on the Austrian left flank in echelon. The battalions were fifty paces behind each other, so that the right of the Prussian line was a thousand yards in advance of the left and each battalion could engage without specific orders. This formation put the Prussian line round and to the rear of that of the Austrians. The Austrians endeavoured to retrieve the situation by forming a new line at Leuthen, at right angles to their first. But Seydlitz's cavalry charged as they were deploying. Frederick captured the bridge at Lissa and so forestalled the Austrian retreat. In the actual battle his casualties (5,978) were not much less than those of the Austrians (7,400) but the pursuit brought in 21,000 prisoners of war and rendered the success a decisive one. It was a victory for the oblique order, for drill, for firepower (some men fired 180 rounds in the battle), for the combination of arms and for the use of terrain.

The danger inherent in a masterpiece is its slavish imitation, its over-rigid systematisation. Not only his inferiors but even Frederick himself — although on his own admission surprised by the extent of his success — tried too often to repeat Leuthen. As a result a ready adaptation to the development of the battle in hand was sacrificed. At Kolin, the refused wing attacked contrary to orders. Conversely, at Zorndorf the right wing hung back so well that it allowed the left to be destroyed. What Frederick had done was to complete an evolution in infantry drill started by Maurice of Nassau and Gustavus Adolphus at the beginning of the previous century. He accepted the limitations which the circumstances of eighteenth-century war imposed, and then, with the machinery perfected, he exploited them as best he could. But even as he did so a revolution in tactical doctrine

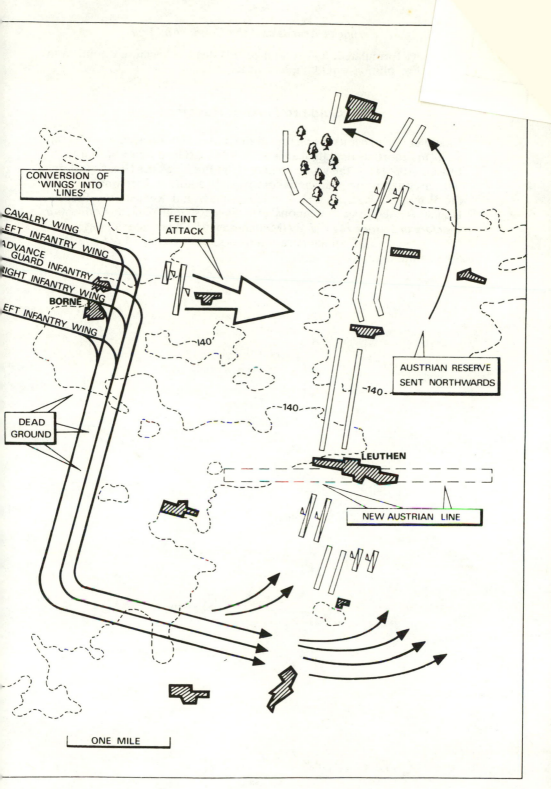

CONVERSION OF
'WINGS' INTO
'LINES'

CAVALRY WING

EFT INFANTRY WING

ADVANCE
GUARD INFANTRY

IGHT INFANTRY WING

BORNE

EFT INFANTRY WING

FEINT
ATTACK

140

140

140

140

DEAD
GROUND

AUSTRIAN RESERVE
SENT NORTHWARDS

LEUTHEN

NEW AUSTRIAN LINE

ONE MILE

Map 3   *The battle of Leuthen, 1757*

was being formulated, and soon after his death a social, economic and political revolution would implement it.

Guide to Further Reading

Chandler (1976) paints the picture at the outset of our period, but his concerns are more tactical than strategic. Read Atkinson on Marlborough. Luvaas (1966) is on the whole content to let Frederick the Great speak for himself, but has some judicious comments in addition. Duffy has covered the Prussian, Austrian and Russian armies, and Kennett the French. Hughes is interesting on weapons' effectiveness. John Childs, *Armies and Warfare in Europe 1648–1789* (Manchester, 1982) provides a brief, wide-ranging survey. Of contemporary authors, both Henry Lloyd and Saxe are stimulating.

Chapter 3

The Eighteenth-Century Revolution in Tactics

During the course of the eighteenth century, major tactical developments occurred in four main areas. The infantry began to use the column for battle as well as for manoeuvre, light troops were employed with increasing frequency, the artillery emerged as an arm to rival the cavalry and the infantry, and armies separated into divisions to fight as well as to march. All these innovations were to be exploited by the armies of Napoleon. Their antecedents, however, lay in the previous hundred years.

The principal problem that faced the eighteenth-century tactician was the need to find forms and evolutions best suited to the flintlock and bayonet. The latent superiority which the new armament conferred on infantry was forfeit to its slowness in movement. While infantry marched onto the field in column and then deployed by executing a quarter turn to the right, so creating a long, continuous line, an army remained predictable in its intentions. The chance of decisive victory was rendered remote by the fact that 70,000 men might constitute a column five miles long and therefore take the best part of the day to achieve such a formation. Furthermore its vulnerability to cavalry meant that the latter could continue to prevent the full exploitation of firepower by forcing the foot to expend its energy forming square in order to protect itself.

Infantry drill started from the basic premiss that the line was the best means to deliver fire. In 1703, the French army still formed in a line five ranks deep, but four were generally adopted in the War of the Spanish Succession and three were the norm by mid-century. In 1763, the Russians settled for two ranks. The line allowed as many men as possible to level their muskets but it did not permit them to manoeuvre. Its extended front made it hard to advance, and the onset had to be deliberate in order to keep the formation and was even then likely to be disjointed on its arrival. Broken country could easily disrupt it and a counter-attack would have little difficulty in smashing its serried ranks.

The Prussians contrived to work efficiently within this framework by virtue of their high standards of drill. But it was the French, their military prowess stung by the successive defeats of the War of the Spanish Succession and then of the Seven Years' War, who began to think through the tactical problems from first principles. Another motivation for the French was the belief – to emerge again in later generations – that nature had suited them for the offensive. Saxe subscribed to this view, and Lloyd wrote that the French 'are impetuous, and dangerous in their attacks; all the animal spirits seem united, and produce a sort of furious convulsion'. The line, with its complications of manoeuvre, appeared therefore to hinder the French from self-expression in the manner which became them best. The desideratum was a form of evolutions that could allow the development of firepower to be combined with shock action.

In 1727, the Chevalier Folard began to publish his commentaries on Polybius. As befitted an eighteenth-century rationalist, he was impressed by the precepts of the ancients, and therefore espoused the phalanx as the ideal infantry formation. He added in its support two occasions, at Speyer (1703) and Denain (1712), when the French had not deployed from their marching columns but had advanced with the bayonet. His updated version of the phalanx was therefore a closely packed column, formed of from one to six battalions, and ranging from twenty to sixty files across. Half its strength was made up of pikemen. He contended that it was a formation which could be easily moved over all types of ground, that had resilience in all directions, and which allowed the use of cavalry close in with the infantry rather than confined to the flanks. However, his main supposition was proved in practice to be false. He believed that the weight and depth of the column would be decisive, since the pressure of the men in its rear would force the advance and fill the gaps to the front. In fact the impulse derived from the head of the column, and the men in the rear could not see, became confused and frightened, and eventually began to fall away. The process of disintegration was hastened by the exposure of such a massive formation to artillery and infantry fire, while it itself lost much of its firepower by placing so many muskets out of the front line. Folard had in a sense failed to perceive the nature of the problem. He saw a straight choice between shock or firepower and had opted for the former. The column was undeniably better for manoeuvre but it was not necessarily the formation for attack. At Rossbach (1757) the column of march became a column of attack, but it was checked by Prussian fire.

Saxe, writing in 1732, realised that the need to regain mobility should be the prime concern. In condemning columns, he moved on to Roman examples for his inspiration. He favoured doubled battalions in maniples, eight ranks deep, their front covered by skirmishers and with gaps between them to allow the cavalry to pass through. The line was thus flexible, combined mobility without too great a loss of firepower, and the shock element was provided by the arm still best enabled to furnish it – the horse.

The doubts about the qualities of the musket meant, however, that arguments such as these would not sweep the field unopposed. Saxe himself wanted half his infantry armed with pikes and argued that delivering fire both slowed the onset of the infantry and 'causes more noise than harm'. Lloyd held similar views: 'The musket is by no means so dangerous and fatal as the sword and pike'. And Suvorov, the Russian general, succintly stated, 'The bullet misses, the bayonet does not'. As a result the theories of Mesnil-Durand, published in 1755, commanded more credence than they deserved. He too was enamoured of the pike and spurned musketry. But he also held it as axiomatic that troops in deep formations cannot be broken by those in less deep, that such formations had no vulnerable flanks and that their mobility would reduce the casualties they would otherwise suffer. His column – or *plésion* – was twenty-four men across and a massive thirty-two deep.

The most helpful directions taken by the debate were the compromises, of which Saxe's maniples were one. Another – and a related one – was the chequer formation allowed by Frederick. The first line of infantry would form, leaving gaps between the battalions, and the second line would cover the gaps. Either the second line could give immediate support to the first in the attack, or in defence the first could withdraw through the intervals, leading the enemy onto the fire of the second. By the mid-century, some Frenchmen were advocating the *ordre mixte*, one battalion per brigade in column and the rest in line, and this was adopted at Minden (1759).

But the crucial development was the arrival in the French army in about 1766 of a system of deployment which allowed a rapid switch from column to line and back again. The order of battle could be formed ahead of the line of march, and so it permitted deployment nearer the enemy and, above all, it enabled manoeuvre to be carried out during the course of battle. This was the true solution to the problems of mobility and flexibility which had faced the generation of Marlborough.

Its author was the comte de Guibert, a French noble and a romantic versifier, who at the age of 29 produced in the *Essai général de la tactique* (1772) the most important work on military theory of the eighteenth century. He was too a product of the Enlightenment, admired by Voltaire and himself influenced by Montesquieu. He stressed the relationship between war and politics, arguing that the nature and composition of an army should not reflect the attributes of those of its neighbours but should be rooted in the customs and constitution of its own nation. Its foreign policy reflected its domestic policy, the cohesion and direction of its peoples would guide it in its behaviour abroad. Therefore his first observations on the conduct of war were on France's constitution, arguing for an army of citizens, members of a nation, whose patriotism would motivate them in action.

Such an army depended on a social revolution for its existence, but it would be capable of implementing a revised system of tactics. Infantry lay at the centre of Guibert's thinking. Its firepower was more important than shock action since, before making contact, musketry first disordered the enemy's formation. Each soldier should be thoroughly instructed and practised in target-shooting. The three-rank line was therefore best as it allowed the most efficient management of arms. Indeed a deeper order did not necessarily add to the shock effect, since a group of men was not a contiguous mass but a number of individuals. If the column was to be employed in the attack, it should be in the form of several small columns, capable of moving at speed, and yet always under the direct control of their officers. Ahead of them should be a line of skirmishers to give and draw fire. But Guibert distinguished this function of the column from its primary one, that of manoeuvre. When passing through narrow ground, when withdrawing in the face of hostile cavalry, when moving before deploying into line, on all these occasions the column was indisputably required. The important asset was to be able to switch from one formation to another, even during the course of an action, thus allowing redeployment on a more threatened point. Instead of the column of manoeuvre

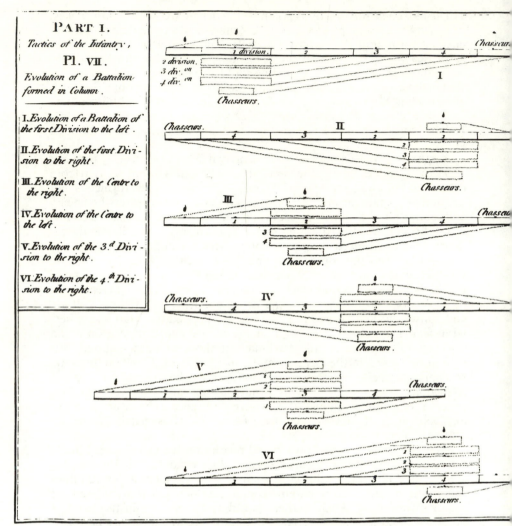

Figure 1   *Guibert's system of deployment*

marching onto the battlefield, wheeling along its frontage, and then turning to face its enemy, Guibert proposed that battalions should deploy to their front on the second leading battalion, as the whole column continued to march forward (see Figure 1). A multiplying number of columns could thus form line simultaneously and ground continue to be gained as they did so. Guibert eventually advocated an increased rate of 120 paces to the minute – as opposed to 60 – and thus his method of deployment was four to six times as rapid as that which it bidded to supplant.

Guibert's book did not have the initial impact it might have expected, partly because its author shared the contemporary respect of Frederick. The fact that he was a self-confessed admirer of the Prussian king obscured

Guibert's own originality. Indeed the 1776 French ordinance reflected the formalism of Prussian infantry tactics. But finally, two years later, in 1778, these extreme linear tactics and their opposite pole, Mesnil-Durand's battering-rams, were both seen from the field by Guibert. The effect of a camp of instruction at Vaussieux was to vindicate Guibert, and in 1779 in his *Défense* the count confirmed his contempt for massive columns by his advocacy of the *ordre mixte*.

But in other European countries, Frederick's influence took form in the worship of regularity in tactical evolutions. In particular Saldern, the Magdeburg infantry inspector from 1763 to 1785, institutionalised and perfected the alleged secrets of Prussian success in the Seven Years' War, much to the gratification of a succession of European visitors. Behrenhorst might fancy the great seventeenth-century tacticians, Montecuccoli and Gustavus Adolphus, asking Saldern in heaven 'whether since their time the surface of the globe had been planned flat'. But what Saldern taught and wrote was adopted in Spain and Russia, became a model for Austria and even found its way to Britain. David Dundas's *Principles of Military Movements* (1788) were influenced by Saldern and, when they were accepted as the official *Rules and Regulations* in 1792, they gave a uniformity and standardisation that had hitherto been sadly lacking. Indeed the armies of Europe through the influence of Prussia became more highly organised and more manageable in the field.

Only in France, however, did the results throw up something radically different. The eventual product of the debate was the ordinance of 1791, which was a model of flexibility. It encouraged the use of the formation best suited to the circumstances – be it line, column of attack or column of manoeuvre – and it could do this because, by embracing Guibert's system of deployment, the switch from one to the other was rapid. It allowed platoons to invert – to get out of their prescribed order – and it stipulated independent fire after the first discharge. Equipped with this degree of tactical adaptability, the French army absorbed the impact of the Revolution and then fought so triumphantly under Napoleon.

In discussing the theories of Saxe and Guibert, mention has already been made of the use of skirmishers to screen the main infantry formation. Their appearance was novel because by 1700 the distinction between light infantry (missile troops formed in open order) and heavy infantry (the pikemen in close order) had been supplanted by a universal infantryman, capable, by virtue of the bayonet, of both forms of warfare. In practice, however, the neglect of musketry and the emphasis on preserving the cohesion of the line meant that only the close-order formations of the battlefield were practised by most infantry. The role of light troops was not that of skirmishing and covering the main body, arguably an unnecessary role in any case since the line provided its own firepower, but the operations of petty war, such as reconnaissance, ambushes, patrolling and fighting in broken ground. Furthermore, these were tasks which demanded very different qualities from those imbued by the harsh discipline imposed on mercenaries prone to desertion. The soldier of petty war needed to be intelligent, self-reliant and well-motivated – in short, Guibert's citizen.

On 8 July 1755, a British force under General Braddock, instructed to take the French Fort Duquesne on the Ohio river, was ambushed after fording the Monongahela river. Braddock failed to use adequately the light troop tactics of European petty war: he kept the scouts and local militia of his advance and flank guards too close in, and he himself immediately brought up the main body while it was still in column, thus preventing the development of its fire. But the subsequent accounts glossed over Braddock's faults as a commander and instead stressed the tactics of his opponents. The French and their Indian allies did not close for a conventional Frederickian battle, but hung back, protected by the undergrowth, unleashing a hail of fire without exposing themselves to the sight of British eyes. The French force of 900 suffered 5 per cent casualties in repelling 1,450 Englishmen, who lost 70 per cent of their force, including 60 out of 86 officers. This was a new experience. It was the tactics of petty war applied to the battlefield itself.

Braddock's defeat had favourable consequences for the British army in America, principally because the broken and wooded terrain of the colonies demanded that petty war be the norm. Furthermore it was an army that did not suffer so acutely from the problems that beset the other armies of Europe. In the colonies, the regiment was turned in on itself, the officers were cut off from the blandishments of home society and devoted their paternalistic attentions to the welfare of their men. Moreover, the effect of local troops, in particular the militia, was to bring in individuals of higher intelligence used to local ways. The rapidity with which all these strands were pulled together is highly creditable. For on Christmas Day of the very same year in which Braddock was defeated, the first steps were taken to raise four battalions of American provincials, to combine the qualities of the scout with the discipline of the trained soldier. Many of them were Swiss and German *émigrés*, brought up to the use of the rifle (rather than the smooth-bore musket) and trained in the ways of the woods from their earliest days.

The training of the 60th Royal Americans, as the regiment was called, reflected in particular the thinking of Henri Bouquet, who commanded the 1st battalion. The men were inspired by kindness and emulation, by the award of prizes rather than the lash. They were instructed in shooting, swimming and running rather than in the formalism of Prussian drill. When attacked by Indians, Bouquet would form his column into square. His light troops would then push out towards the circle of Indians, forcing them back so that their fire could no longer take effect on the square. Simultaneous charges on a number of points would puncture the Indians' cordon, and expose them to attack on the flanks.

Because the Seven Years' War broke out in the year following Braddock's disaster, British light infantry developments continued to be stimulated by North American experience. In addition in the years 1757–9 the army profited from the foresight of a number of highly intelligent officers – Howe, Gage, Amherst and Wolfe. But without such practical reminders, peacetime practice reverted to Prussian norms, and the light infantry sacrificed the central position it had occupied. Thus, although in 1770 a light company was established in every battalion of British foot, they were used at Bunker Hill (1775), on the outbreak of the American War of Independence, as conventional infantry. In other words the notion that light troops might have a distinct role in the main battlefield had not yet supplanted or supplemented their principal use in petty war. The renewal of fighting in America helped rectify the position. In 1774, Howe held a camp of instruction for the light companies and in 1776 organised them into independent battalions. Local influences were incorporated through the service of Loyalists, and notable leaders of irregular troops – Simcoe, Tarleton and Ferguson – left their mark on the British service. Indeed Ferguson developed an early, if flawed, breech-loading rifle, theoretically the ideal weapon for light infantry in that it had the accuracy imparted by a rifled barrel with the ease of loading associated with a breech-mechanism. In America, the British had under-gone the three developments that were to redefine infantry tactics. Irregu-lar light troops were increasingly employed with the line, skirmishing specialists had been added to each battalion, and the élite regular units – chasseurs or *Jäger* – found their embodiment in the 60th. The action at Vignie, in St Lucia, in 1778, when light infantry tactics were employed in regular fighting, shows what the British had learned. Outnumbered by four to one, they skirmished, using cover, and kept the French under a continuous and destructive fire. If the French extended, they threatened to charge with their bayonets. If the French advanced, they withdrew and opened fire from a fresh direction. The British suffered 13 deaths and 158 wounded; the French lost 400 killed and 1,200 wounded.

The difficulties the British had in absorbing light infantry tactics can be appreciated even more fully when contrasted with the experience of the American rebels. Here was an army put into the field by men who breathed the spirit of the Enlightenment and by a population brought up to the use of arms. In their midst was a former British officer, Charles Lee, who was well-versed in Locke and Rousseau and who argued in terms similar to those employed by Guibert. Guided by his political radicalism, he con-tended that American tactics and strategy should be in accordance with the dictates of the American genius. Rather than meet the British regi-ments in the conventional operations for which they were trained, America's military effort should be centred on the militia, local troops who knew the ground, and who could thus harry and skirmish, exhausting the British, and elevating the operations of petty war to the status of the main action. Although the militia was already formed and the option therefore immediately available, Washington spurned Lee's proposal and preferred to create the Continental Army on lines similar to those of the European states. The terrain round New York perhaps justified his deci-sion, but in the south the rivers and swamps forced Nathanael Greene to disperse his slender forces in order to subsist. The British, hoping to base their counter-revolution on Loyalist support, exacted too great a venge-ance on the rebels. Thus they fomented local support for Greene. Corn-wallis, anxious for battle, cut himself off from his supplies and at times marched thirty miles a day, but all in vain. The same strategic constraints operated on him in America as in Europe, and the tactical superiority of his troops could not gainsay them. Arguably it was Greene's partisan warfare that played the principal role in forcing the surrender at York-town. Furthermore, in the north, Washington too had been forced to place his Continental Army on the defensive, and limit its attacks to raids on detachments and communications. It was not tactically but logistically that the British were defeated. None the less for Washington the Euro-pean mode of fighting remained the ideal. Perhaps he feared the econo-mic consequences of protracted, guerrilla war, with its dislocation of society and its potential loss of central political control. Certainly the rebels enjoyed the advantages of self-reliant and well-motivated soldiers, capable of independent action, but they did not make this pivotal to their strategy.

It is not surprising, therefore, that there has been some disagreement as to how influential experiences in America were on the main currents of European warfare. On the one hand von Ewald, who commanded the *Jäger* of the Hessians in British service in America, wrote *Abhandlung vom Dienst der leichten Truppen* (1790) in which he advocated that all the line infantry should be trained as light troops and that they should be dis-ciplined by encouragement rather than repression. In addition von Ochs, another Hessian, is held to have influenced Frederick in the formation of light infantry in Prussia. The American experience attracted attention primarily because it conformed to prevailing trends in European pol-itical thought. Self-sufficient individuals, maximising local conditions, appealed to intellects stirred by Rousseau, enamoured with the idea of the 'natural man', the noble savage of the New World. However, it has been argued that Frederick himself was unlikely to pay much attention to what seemed to be an inferior form of warfare. Not least was this the case because the employment of light troops was already well-established in European practice before the 1770s.

In 1757, a quarter of the Austrian army (34,000 infantry and 6,000 cavalry) consisted of light troops, irregulars from the Habsburg frontiers in south-east Europe, predominantly Croats, with a reputation – founded partly no doubt on their practice of living off the land – as unmitigated scoundrels. As effective as pillagers, and also occasionally useful in reconnoitring or in drawing fire, were the Russians' irregular army, the Cossacks, untamed herdsmen from their south-eastern frontier. The rela-tionship between backward, feudal societies and an adaptability to the demands of irregular war is buttressed by the British use of Highlanders as light troops in the War of the Austrian Succession and in the Seven Years' War. But both Croats and Highlanders were intended for the operations of petty war only. It was the Croats who harried Frederick's communications and convoys, while the main body refused battle, and so forced the Prussians to withdraw. In addition, they protected the Aust-rians' own line of march, thus forestalling the likelihood of an encounter battle. Occasionally they would mount independent raids, of which the thrust to Berlin in 1757 was one. The horsed component of this force of light troops, called Hussars, particularly caught the collective European imagination, and from the 1740s their styles of dress as well as fighting were aped throughout the continent.

Although the backward economies of Eastern Europe lent themselves to petty war and to the consequent development of light troops, such operations put a premium on loyalty. Peter the Great had spurned mercenaries and endeavoured (uniquely in the eighteenth century) to cultivate a spirit of nationalism within the Russian army. The Poltava campaign had elevated the status of petty war. In 1761 the Russians raised two battalions of light infantry from hunters and woodsmen. In 1765 sixty-five chasseurs were added to each regiment, and from 1770 they were organised in separate battalions, giving a total of forty-three such battalions by 1795. Contrast this with the experience of Prussia, which because of her reliance on mercenaries encountered peculiar difficulties in incorporating light troops into her service. The danger of desertion was such that the operations of petty war had to be curtailed and in 1745 Frederick put his patrols only 200 yards in front of the main body. Furthermore their lowly associations led Frederick to denigrate light troops, and in battle itself they were in consequence seen principally as a means to draw enemy fire or were used simply as conventional infantry. His *Jäger* were an élite but the slowness in loading rifles at the muzzle (caused by the difficulty of ramming the tight-fitting ball past the grooves in the barrel) meant that they were never anything other than a minor component of the Prussian army. In 1787 twenty fusilier battalions were formed and were trained to fight in two, not three, ranks. Some provision was therefore made for open order but it was a limited acceptance – a quarter of the battalion was to skirmish at a time, not the whole unit. Open order was socially and politically unacceptable in Prussia. Its emphasis on individual worth meant that a better class of recruit was required, and a new relationship between the officer and his men would have to be forged. This carried with it the revolutionary implications of the writings of Guibert.

In the employment of light troops in the main battle rather than in petty war, it was again France, of the continental powers, that was to lead the way. The war in Piedmont had proved instructive. As mountain men, the Piedmontese were better adapted to operations in broken ground, and in consequence at the battle of Campo Santo (1743) Charles Emmanuel had used light troops to engage the Spanish left while delivering the main attack on the right. The idea of skirmishers distracting the enemy's attention from the principal thrust was implicit in the use of columns. Large columns in particular dispensed with firepower in favour of shock, and light infantry were therefore to make up this deficiency.

Saxe proposed that skirmishers, armed with breech-loading fowling pieces, should form one or two hundred paces in front of the main body and maintain individual fire until the enemy was within fifty paces. At this distance they should retire through the intervals between the battalions. In theory, then, Saxe saw his skirmishers as the agents of disorganisation. In practice, he gave them a more direct role. At Fontenoy (1745), he dispersed Grassin's corps, irregular troops raised in France in 1744, along the edge of a wood, and its fire stopped the flank action of Ingoldsby's brigade.

Similarly, Lloyd suggested one light company in each battalion to cover gaps between the other companies. Its duties were therefore to lie in the main battle. Broglie in 1764 had a company of chasseurs in each battalion and employed them in screening battalion columns. The French troops serving in the American war therefore came back with such ideas confirmed by practice, and with several outstanding leaders – Lafayette, Berthier, Dumas and Jourdan – trained in the ways of revolutionary war. At home they found Guibert contending that armies should be more self-sufficient, their baggage less and their movements faster. Therefore the relative importance of petty war would decline. But in the set-piece attack, Guibert went further than Saxe, Lloyd or Broglie. In the name of flexibility, mobility and firepower all the foot should be trained in the skills of light infantry and the distinction between the two eradicated. The ordinance of 1791, by neglecting the specific use of light infantry, allowed the scope and the degree of improvisation which would encourage the French to do exactly this. The Revolution was to bring in the self-reliant, well-motivated men capable of it. But the Revolution notwithstanding, the ideas of using light troops as the precursors of shock action or of all infantry skirmishing in open order were most truly established in France.

Furthermore, it was in France too that the seeds of the third main tactical development of the Revolutionary and Napoleonic Wars had taken strongest root. At the beginning of the eighteenth century, the artillery played a minor role on the battlefield, its guns being distributed amongst the infantry. The shortage of wood in Western Europe starved the iron industry of charcoal for smelting. In consequence during the seventeenth century iron production shifted northwards, to the well-timbered Baltic States. Therefore, with demand rising, the costs of gun-founding had to be added to the other economic constraints on war. Such guns as there were required a large number of horses to draw them over the muddy roads – Guibert calculated that 400 guns and their accompanying 2,400 vehicles needed 9,600 horses – and their fodder compounded the supply problem. Guns were such a check on an army's mobility that Lloyd advocated thirty to forty 12-pounders (and the lighter battalion guns) as the maximum for an army of 50,000 men. Indeed so ponderous were the heavier pieces that he felt the enemy could easily manoeuvre to avoid their worst effects. These arguments for the neglect of artillery were reinforced by the fact that, as the artillery was a technical arm, its officers were more bourgeois than in the cavalry and infantry, and their advice despised in proportion.

An early exception to this neglect was Russia. Her abundance of timber allowed her pig- and cast-iron production to reach 15,000 tons per annum by 1725 and 160,000 tons by the end of the century. Peter the Great was thus able to compensate for deficiencies elsewhere in his army by the quality of his ordnance. James Bruce, a Scot, presided over the creation of an artillery regiment for Russia in 1712: he standardised the gun carriages and reduced the weight of the field guns, thus enhancing their mobility. During the course of the eighteenth century, Russia consolidated her advantage. Before the Seven Years' War Shuvalov introduced the 'unicorn', a piece combining the virtues of gun, howitzer and mortar, and in 1760 Russia's artillery park comprised a grand total of 603 guns, 280 unicorns, 169 howitzers and 117 mortars. In 1788 the weight of the 12-pounder gun was reduced by a quarter and that of the 6-pounder was almost halved.

Frederick developed his artillery in the wake of the Silesian War. In 1742 he mounted ammunition boxes on the gun-limbers, thus rendering the guns independent of their slower-moving ammunition carts. In 1747 the system of elevating the gun by a wedge was replaced by a screw, and greater precision could therefore be achieved in laying the piece. The Austrians followed suit in 1748, and five years later introduced a standardised range of lighter and more mobile pieces, of which the 12-pounder was the outstanding gun. At Leuthen, Frederick kept his cannon massed, moving them forward with his infantry, using them to break up the Austrian foot. Indeed at 1,000 yards, field artillery aiming at a company could reckon to inflict 40–70 per cent casualties. Herein, therefore, are grounds for Frederick's implicit neglect not only of his own infantry's firepower but also (in that he did not engage the Austrian artillery) of the effects of counter-battery fire. Frederick's contribution to the development of artillery tactics lay rather in an emphasis on mobility and concentration. This is best displayed by what was a state secret in its day, the establishment in 1759 of horse artillery. Its role was not so much to support the cavalry as to enable artillery to move rapidly to the decisive point. Indeed in 1768 Frederick recognised after the Seven Years' War (during which he had to import guns) that 'Artillery decides everything'. In the previous five years he had spent 1,450,000 thalers on his cannon, and had created a reserve of 100 field guns. By 1777, 868 additional field guns were cast, and between 1740 and 1784 a force of 789 gunners had been expanded to 8,600. This staggering growth in an unindustrialised country bears credit to Frederick's reform and control of Prussia's finances, his determination to create reserves meaning that he had 51 million thalers in the *Staatsschatz* by the end of his reign. Although Maria Theresa was virtually self-sufficient in iron, her experience provides a striking contrast. She increased her complement of field guns from 94 in 1745 to 1,060 in 1780, and of gunners from 800 in 1746 to 5,000 in 1769. But she was so weakened by war and military expenditure that noble resistance to taxation undid the best effects of her and her son's enlightened despotism.

The challenge thrown down by Frederick was taken up by a state far better equipped, in terms of centralised control and economic development, to accept it – France. In the 1730s Bélidor had demonstrated that the charge of powder could be reduced from half to a third of the weight of the projectile without reducing the range that would be thereby achieved. Because the effect of the concussion was therefore less, pieces could be rendered lighter and consequently more mobile. Gribeauval, who was attached to the Austrian army in the Seven Years' War, was in 1763 brought in to reform the French artillery and became its inspector-general in 1776. In a programme of major revision in gun construction, he standardised the calibres, carriages and equipment, and made the parts interchangeable. Above all, he applied Bélidor's principles, and a 4-pounder gun was thus reduced in weight from 1,300 pounds to 600. In consequence, he was able to carry through his tactical conception of artillery as the third arm on the battlefield by virtue of the mobility he had vouchsafed it. If guns could thus be combined and fired *en masse*, greater effect would be achieved by the same number. 'Rapidity and skill should make up for inferiority', he wrote. 'Make the perfection of the art to consist in firing a large part of a smaller number of pieces, to form the best possible artillery, rather than to procure the most numerous.'

Gribeauval was still averse to counter-battery fire and still saw the role of artillery as supporting the work of cavalry and infantry. His arguments were developed and expanded by du Teil in *De l'usage de l'artillerie nouvelle dans la guerre de campagne* (1778), a book which had a direct influence on a young artillery officer, Napoleon Bonaparte. Du Teil agreed with Gribeauval on the need for mobility above weight of metal, and on the value of oblique angles to obtain a crossfire. He, too, opposed counter-battery fire, since the main purpose should remain the destruction of the enemy's troops. But he departed from Gribeauval in arguing that massed artillery could in itself have decisive effects, if employed before the infantry assault, and he therefore called for more guns. France was reaching a position where such demands were not entirely fantastic: by 1789 her production of pig-iron was double that of Britain and in 1796 her total output of iron was 132,000 tons.

It is not only on the level of tactics that the antecedents of Napoleonic warfare are to be found, but also on that of grand tactics, or even strategy. That eighteenth-century war was limited by the size of armies and their immobility has been reiterated many times. If, however, an army could be divided into separate components for the purposes of movement, then the possibilities of forcing battle and of pressing the pursuit would be increased, and war thereby rendered more decisive. The divisions of the army could use separate routes, the encumbering effects of baggage columns would be reduced, and, by virtue of their being dispersed over a wider area, requisition simplified. In the advance, the enemy would be threatened at several points simultaneously and the commander could thereby retain several alternative objectives in his plan. His outlying divisions would threaten the enemy's flanks and communications, while protecting his own. Then the divisions would converge on the decisive point, to face an enemy perhaps weakened by attempting to meet every threat which this web of formations posed.

The fort in eighteenth-century warfare had fulfilled many of these functions. It had acted as a pivot around which the army manoeuvred. It was a shield against attack, protecting the flanks and the lines of communications, while allowing the field force itself to remain united. In addition, examples are to be found from the late seventeenth century of armies being divided on an *ad hoc* basis for similar reasons. Of Louis XIV's generals, Luxembourg detached a strong vanguard to control river crossings ahead of his main body, and Berwick in the Alps and Villars in Flanders split their armies into three closely linked groups, each strong enough to hold an enemy attack until the other two could concentrate on it. Saxe covered his communications and flanks with separate formations. The Russian army was encouraged by its supply problems to divide its armies and to use dispersed formations in battle. Peter the Great counselled his troops to march in separate but related bodies even when close to the enemy, and for independent tasks he suggested the formation of mixed bodies of cavalry, infantry and artillery, six to seven thousand men strong, which he dubbed 'flying corps'. Against the Turks in the war of 1768–74, Rumyantsev used divisional squares to hold the enemy from the front, while the remainder of the army fell on their flank or rear. But the divisional organisation adopted for the Russian army in 1763 was no more than a peacetime administrative arrangement. Therefore none of these examples had lasting effects.

The credit for initiating the use of divisions in European campaigning is usually bestowed on Pierre de Bourcet, an engineer, the author of a memorandum entitled *Principes de la guerre de montagnes* (1764–71) and an expert in Alpine warfare. Bourcet observed that 'A general who intends to take the offensive should assemble his army in three positions, distant not more than a march from one another, for in this way, while he will threaten all points accessible from any portion of the 25 or 30 miles thus held, he will be able suddenly to collect his whole army, either in the centre or on either wing'. These precepts were impressed on Bourcet as a result of his experience on the staff in the Franco-Spanish invasion of Piedmont. The Alps forced the army to disperse, as one pass could not contain the whole army and could in any case be easily blocked. In his plan for the campaign of 1744, Bourcet used a succession of passes through the mountains, all of them screened by Cuneo (see Map 4). He therefore needed to draw the Sardinian army way from Cuneo, and up one of the northern passes. Once it was caught there, it would face the fatigue of marching back down to the plain and up the passes employed in the main attack. The French by forming in division behind the Alpine screen could threaten to use every pass, and would concentrate on the least defended, particularly since their lateral communications were good. For the march itself, the army was organised into nine divisions, ranging from five to fourteen battalions each, over a frontage of seventy miles. In the event the Sardinians were not drawn to the north but that failure did not prevent the development of alternative branches of the plan in the south. As the advance progressed, the division in the Stura valley was checked by a strong position in the defile known as the Barricades. The French, using their knowledge of the mountains, turned the position by appearing from north and south at a point further down the pass. Thus did the 1744 campaign demonstrate the value of the division not merely in the organisation of marches but also in achieving decisive success on the battlefield. Pinning the enemy with one formation and then falling on his rear and communications with another was to be a classic feature of Napoleonic strategy.

In 1760 Broglie applied Bourcet's ideas to more normal country. He created four infantry divisions and two cavalry, with a staff to control each column, the logic being that his capacity for rapid deployment would cancel out the Prussians' superiority in drill. In his campaign of that year, Broglie scattered his formations, launched diversionary attacks, and then regrouped rapidly. The articulated components of his army spread without losing the ability for mutual support.

But the significance of Broglie's work was not apparent in 1760. There were too few roads to support a multiplying number of divisions, and agriculture still had not developed sufficiently to allow armies to reduce

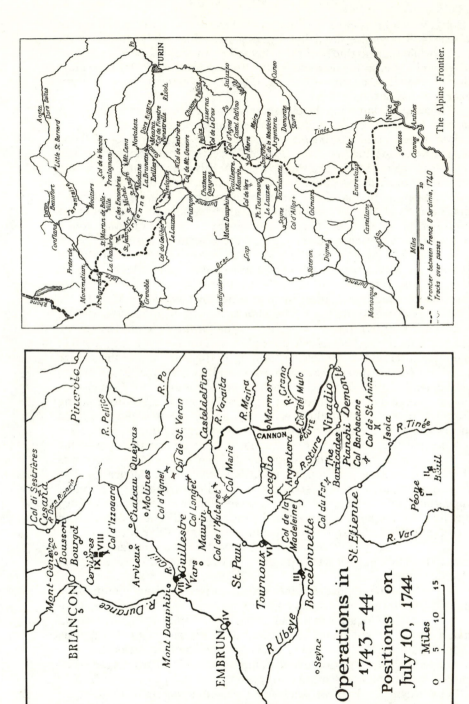

Map 4   Bourcet's plan of campaign, 1744

their baggage trains. In addition, in many European countries, the conduct of war had become divided from the job of supplying it. In France, the *intendants*, who were responsible for the organisation of supply, had the right of direct correspondence with Versailles and could also veto a proposed campaign. In Austria, the *General-Kriegs-Commissariat*, answerable for pay, rations and supply, secured its independence of the army's administrative body, the *Hofkriegsrath*, between 1746 and 1761. In Russia, the War College lost control of the *Kommissariat* during the reign of Elizabeth Petrovna (1741–62). Guibert argued that this allocation of supply to civilians should cease. In order to regain mobility, soldiers should feed themselves, 'war should nourish war', and strategy be freed from the constraints of subsistence. What he was saying was not new; it was simply impossible of fulfilment before the agricultural revolution. But with the improvement of farming techniques and the creation of a disposable surplus, armies could become less dependent on the attentions of the *intendant* – provided they continued to be mobile.

The work of the Enlightenment had its effects therefore on tactical thought. But many of the directions in which it had pointed were contingent on economic developments to enable their implementation. Perhaps the biggest stumbling block was the social transformation which they required of armies. The use of open order drill implied men of intelligence and initiative in the ranks. The growth of the artillery created a need for technologists. Professional training would also be necessary for the staffs to manage the divisions. And if, by virtue of all these changes, larger armies could take the field, the ranks would have to be filled by conscription.

The 1790s were to see a concurrent release of all these forces, but until Napoleon their application on the battlefield remained uncoordinated. The romantic in Guibert had even foreseen this eventuality. If his views on war were to be implemented, he argued, 'Let there arise – there cannot but arise – some vast genius. He will lay hands so to speak on the knowledge of all the community, will create or perfect the political system, put himself at the head of the machine and give the impulse of its movement.'

Guide to Further Reading

All the books mentioned at the end of chapter 2 remain relevant for this chapter. Quimby covers the main points as they relate to France. On the impact of Braddock's defeat and the appearance of light infantry, Houlding and Russell are more up to date than Fuller (1925), Pargellis and Robson. The American War of Independence is covered by Higginbotham (1971), and Weigley (1973) chapters 1 and 2. There are stimulating articles on the composition of the American army by Shy (chapter 9) and Nelson. Paret (1964) discusses the transfer of ideas from America to Europe in terms that may fit Prussia but seem less appropriate for Britain. Wilkinson (1915) has been supplanted (and is particularly suspect for chapters 6 and 7) but he summarises the work of Jean Colin painlessly. His book on Piedmont (1927) is more substantial.

Chapter 4

Napoleonic Warfare

The tactical debate in France before the Revolution was not an isolated phenomenon. A trio of reforming ministers of war – Choiseul (1761–70), St Germain (1775–7) and Puységur (1788–9) – modernised much of the organisational framework of the army. The progressive reduction of the purchase of commissions, the employment of fewer officers and the abolition of proprietary rights all enhanced the centralised authority of the king. But they also produced a counter-reaction, outstandingly embodied in the Ségur law of 1781, by which all candidates for commissions had to demonstrate four quarterings of nobility. This was a victory for the provincial, poorer aristocracy which wished to assert its rights as a military caste, and which saw itself challenged by the influx of recently ennobled and wealthy commoners. By 1789, of 10,000 active officers in the French army, barely 1,000 were commoners. A greater proportion of bourgeois officers were to be found in the technical arms, the artillery and the engineers, but even here the new professionalism of the nobility was making its inroads.

The conflicts among the officers of the royal army meant that its response to the events of 1788–9 was ambiguous. For many of them it was an opportunity to resolve their professional grievances. Furthermore, the lack of direction from above allowed the initiative to pass to the NCOs, men of a noticeably higher social class than the private soldiers, often artisans or shopkeepers and half of whom came from urban backgrounds. The length of the political debate and its demand that the army be involved in policing duties revolutionised arguments that might otherwise have remained professional. Thus by 1792 officers were criticised not because of their defects as leaders but because they were aristocrats.

The formation of the National Guard by the municipal authorities of Paris in July 1789 challenged the line army's monopoly of arms. The capital's example was followed throughout France. The National Guard's pay was more than double that of the line and its ranks were open to all. The inducements to forsake the line army were strong, particularly for ambitious NCOs searching for commissions. Between 1788 and 1790 the rate of desertion more than doubled. The progressive disgust among the officers with the indiscipline in the ranks was clinched by the king's abortive flight in June 1791. They had either to be for the Revolution or against it, and hopes for a moderate solution faded as Jacobin influence grew. The consequence was that by the end of 1791 6,000 officers had emigrated. Many of their replacements in the higher ranks were still noble, but lower down, in the battalions, the class composition reflected the attributes of the NCOs of 1789.

In 1793, 85 per cent of lieutenants in the line army had been sergeants fours years previously, and overall 70 per cent of regimental officers had experience in the ranks. It was therefore only their commissions, not their military expertise, that the officers owed to the Revolution. The same was true even of the formations created in the aftermath of 1789: in 1794, half the subalterns of the revolutionary armies, 73 per cent of the battalion commanders and 87 per cent of the generals had been already in service in 1789. The new officer corps was ambitious, professional and experienced.

The desire of the Assembly to have its own army, free of royal influence, meant that in the summer of 1791 volunteers were called for from the National Guard. They were administered and paid for by their local authorities, they elected their officers (the majority of whom came from the line) and they were committed to serve for only one campaign. The volunteers of 1791 were youthful, well-motivated and drawn disproportionately from among the bourgeois and artisans. Their social profile was therefore similar to that of the line army, and was rendered even closer by the boost given to the line army's recruiting in the following winter. By 1792, the majority of the line army had enlisted since 1789: therefore, they too were young and fired with Jacobin enthusiasms. In July 1792 the outbreak of war resulted in the declaration of *La patrie en danger*, and a further call for volunteers followed. But this intake was poorer: there were more peasants, the officers had less military experience and discipline proved lax. From over 400,000 troops in service in 1792, only 351,000 remained with the colours by early 1793.

In consequence, in February 1793 a levy of 300,000 men was instituted for which all single men aged 18—40 were liable, and for which each department had to provide its quota. But only half this number was obtained and the defeats and betrayals of the summer of 1793 demanded more dramatic solutions. On 23 August the Convention decreed that:

> From this moment until that when the enemy is driven from the territory of the republic, every Frenchman is permanently requisitioned for the needs of the armies. The young men will go to the front: the married men will forge arms, and carry food: the women will make tents and clothing and work hospitals: the children will turn old linen into bandages: the old men will be carried into the squares to rouse the courage of the combatants, and to teach hatred of kings, and the unity of the republic.

Estimates of the subsequent strength of the French forces vary. Certainly the initial response was excellent: 87 per cent of the levy was aged between 18 and 25; and one claim, albeit a high one, is that France had over 1 million men under arms by August 1794. The effective strength was put at 732,474. But disease and hunger took their toll. Peasants worried about the land and families they had abandoned. Desertion, which had fallen from 8 per cent of the army's strength in 1793 to 4 per cent in 1794, climbed back to its earlier figure by 1796. Fresh requisitions were paltry and did not make up the deficiencies: in 1797 the strength of the army stood at 381,909.

However, the soldiers of these years were welded into a homogeneous, hardy and experienced force. The propaganda of the Jacobins and of the *sans-culottes* proved an effective agent of politicisation. The Assembly's *commissaires aux armées* not only had administrative responsibilities but also kept a vigilant eye on the political reliability of the troops. They had powers to suspend and arrest officers. Seventeen generals were executed in 1793 and sixty-seven in 1794. Ideological conformity was further served by the creation of *demi-brigades*, a process begun in 1793, but not completed until 1796. Each *demi-brigade* consisted of two battalions of volunteers and one of the line. The elevation of NCOs to commissions meant that by 1793 the volunteers and the line possessed many similar features. Ninety-five per cent of the army had enrolled since 1789. The amalgamation not only recognised this but also simplified an otherwise multiplying administrative and staff problem. It allowed veterans to train recruits on their way to the front. Ideologically it confirmed the politicisation of the army, which was now fully identified with the Revolution.

In half a decade, therefore, the Revolution had transformed the ethos and size of the French army, and had based it spiritually and physically in the heart of the nation (or at least the revolutionaries' view of the nation). The outbreak of war meant that the army assumed simultaneously the defence both of France and of the new order, and that in consequence all three – army, nation and Revolution – were identified together. The *sans-culottes* saw themselves as the embodiments of these three elements. They brought the Terror of the French Revolution into warfare: the tyrants and aristocrats of Europe had to be destroyed as rapidly as possible in order to allow the people of France to return home to a peace dominated by reason and egalitarianism. The *arme blanche*, the bayonet and even the pike, was to be the agent of total victory. Carnot, a member of the Committee of Public Safety and, significantly, a former engineer officer, shaped the doctrine for the revolutionary armies. They should, he declared in February 1794, 'act in mass formation and take the offensive. Join action with the bayonet on every occasion. Give battle on a large scale and pursue the enemy till he is utterly destroyed.' The massive losses of the Revolutionary Wars were not inflicted by individual battles – the percentage of killed and wounded per action was much less than that of the Seven Years' War – but by the number of battles. Urged by Carnot to avoid geographical objectives, the soldiers of the Revolution aimed to destroy the enemy's field armies by continuous fighting. But it was also war on a new scale – a war for the survival of the Revolution and of the nation, in which losses were relatively less important. The *levée en masse* gave France a numerical superiority over her enemies, a seemingly inexhaustible reservoir of manpower which allowed her two or even three times as many losses as her opponents.

The political and social limitations on warfare were burst asunder by the enormous growth in the power of the state. Against a background of defeat and economic chaos, France opted for total war. At the beginning of the eighteenth century, her population and her commerce had made her economically the most powerful nation in Europe. During the course of the century, she declined relative to her neighbours, but in absolute terms the growth continued. The population increase was sustained (it rose by up to 40 per cent), her overseas trade expanded, in 1789 her output of pig-iron was twice that of Britain, and in 1785 at Le Creusot coke-blast iron was produced for the first time on the continent. The change of government allowed these resources to be exploited in a way that the administrative difficulties of the Bourbons had hitherto precluded. The declaration of August 1793 laid the basis. That same summer, the Committee of Public Safety set up a technical advisory committee, established daily supervision of the Ministry of War, and allowed its topographical department to begin to function as a true general staff. Prices and wages in the arms industry were controlled, and state weapons' factories multiplied. Scientific research was systematically put at the service of national defence, with another engineer, Monge, integrating arms and ammunition production.

Furthermore, during the course of the eighteenth century, some countries had undergone what has come to be called an agricultural revolution. Its leading feature was the move from subsistence farming to the creation of a sizeable surplus. This phenomenon was generated partly by the techniques developed in the Low Countries and fostered in Britain. The rotation of crops brought the introduction into the cycle of root vegetables, such as the potato and the turnip. In the last decades of the century, conditions of relative peace allowed the farmers of the campaigning areas of the 1790s – the Netherlands, the Rhineland and Northern Italy – to prosper. Elsewhere, the famines of the 1780s boosted the reputation of the potato, hitherto regarded as animal food. Germany in particular increased its cultivation: in 1765 the Prussian potato crop was a mere 5,200 tonnes, but by 1801 it stood at 103,000. France, which remained wedded to small-scale, subsistence farming, had the blows of the 1780s compounded by the war. On the eve of the Revolution, there were still only 50,000 acres planted with potatoes; between 1803 and 1812 765,000 acres were devoted to their production. For warfare the consequences were dramatic. The surplus enabled the mass army to be fed. The soldiers could take the potato from the ground, ready to eat. The transport of foodstuffs to the towns demanded improved roads and communications. Thus the role of requisition could expand, supply columns diminish, and mobility be maintained. From 1795 the French army subsisted mainly by plunder.

The tactical revolution of the eighteenth century could now be implemented in its entirety. But at first the French encountered problems of co-ordination. The nation in arms produced a less well-trained soldier, ill-adapted to close order formations, but arguably better educated and more literate. The vagueness of the 1791 ordinance allowed scope for individual initiative, and therefore, rather than use the disciplined drill of line or column, the troops of the revolutionary armies broke into swarms of skirmishers, using ground and firing independently. It was not a question of light infantry screening columns, but of company columns dissolving into looser groups, retreating when attacked, and allowing the fire-fight to predominate. However, such fighting was costly in ammunition and postponed the decision. The rapid expansion of the light infantry (it rose from being 4 per cent of the French infantry in 1789 to 23 per cent in 1795) reflected its low demands on training: whereas the British and Prussians were to regard the problem of light infantry training with special awe, the French gave it no particular attention. Closed formations were what required consideration. In the summer of 1793 a camp of instruction was held for the representatives of the *Armée du Nord*. By the following year, the *Armée du Nord* was already demonstrating the tactical flexibility that later came to characterise the other French armies. Exploiting the cult of the *arme blanche*, it attacked in shallow columns. The light infantry provided preparatory fire or undertook the traditional duties of petty war on the battlefield; but it did not usurp the decisive role of the main body of the infantry.

Gradually too, the divisional system was applied to the battlefield. The *ancien régime* had bequeathed an administrative divisional structure but not a tactical one. The size of the French armies rendered such an organisation indispensable, and furthermore the relatively enhanced position of artillery officers exerted pressure for it to be composed of all three arms. Carnot's *demi-brigades* were in theory to be grouped in divisions, but not until the end of 1795 was the concept of an all-arms division generally accepted. A typical division consisted of twelve battalions of infantry, a cavalry regiment and thirty-two guns. However, revolutionary generals still tended to employ their divisions separately, with little intercommunication and with considerable danger of defeat in detail. The divisions felt themselves to be entrusted with individual tasks rather than constituting a series of extended limbs which should suddenly close upon the enemy. Carnot saw clearly enough the application of the division – to separate for the approach-march but to mass for battle: 'Direct those independent fractions on a single point', he instructed. At Wattignies, fought on 15–16 October 1793, he and Jourdan gave a dramatic demonstration of how the division allowed manoeuvre to be fused with battle. They concentrated 50,000 men on a front of 140 miles, and then advanced to attack the Austrians who were covering the siege of Maubeuge. Although checked on the first day, the French brought troops from their left wing in order to extend their right and so overlap the Austrian left.

However, it needed a growth in the authority of the generals for their practice consistently to emulate this achievement. Although Carnot did his best to protect their professional qualities from the worst effects of the Terror, their performance in the field was bound to be uncertain while their loyalties were regarded as suspect. After the fall of the Committee of Public Safety, the generals gained increasing control of the administration of their forces and in December 1796 the *commissaires* were suppressed. Moreover, by 1797 the army held a commanding position in the balance of domestic politics. These were the circumstances in which an ambitious commander could engineer his rise to power.

The components, the technology and the techniques, of Napoleonic warfare were therefore all present before Bonaparte's first successful campaign in 1796. That this was so was obscured from the view of nineteenth-century commentators, even those as distinguished as Jomini and Clausewitz. Napoleon himself made the obligatory references to the influence of Alexander, Gustavus Adolphus, Turenne and Frederick, but so palpably different was his own conduct of war that his claims only served to point up his own achievements. It was not until the researches of Jean Colin and Hubert Camon at the beginning of the twentieth century that the roots of Bonaparte's thinking were laid bare. During his early career, and particularly at the artillery school of Auxonne in 1788–9, he fell under the influence of du Teil and his brother, and all the evidence conspires to argue that at this stage he read Bourcet and Guibert. Certainly his plans for the campaigns in the Alps in 1794–6 drew direct inspiration from the former's dispositions in the same area half a century before. His genius was that of drawing the threads together and his opportunity that of combining supreme political and military control.

In analysing Napoleon's conduct of war, a danger arises because he himself never formulated his views. His contribution was above all practical, and indeed much of it was carried through by force of will and by improvisation rather than by planning. But his principal message was unequivocal – the importance of the decisive battle. Requisition was his main means of supply and, with large armies, he had in consequence to move fast and to keep the campaign short. Furthermore the fall of a capital did not necessarily bring the enemy to terms – the Austrians fought on in 1809, the Russians in 1812 – and therefore the objective remained the army in the field.

Napoleon always fought offensively, even in 1813–14 when strategically on the defensive. The moral initiative was thus with him. His own growing reputation, the uncertainty as to his intentions created by the divisional system, and the speed of his movements, all conspired to ensure that the enemy conformed to the will of the French rather than think independently. His upbringing as an artillery officer meant that he had little understanding of what the poor infantrymen were capable, and thus he was forever setting targets beyond their marching capabilities. In driving them on he achieved concentration ahead of the enemy's expectation, and surprise was thus gained not least by his use of time. He held the loyalty of his *grognards* by his cultivation of the personal touch: emulation not repression was the key to the morale and discipline of the French, be it bestowed by an imperial tweek of the cheek or by the more enduring Légion d'honneur. It was, after all, Napoleon who declared that the morale is to the physical as three is to one.

In 1799, the French adopted the corps system, and in the *Grande Armée* there were seven corps. Each corps was composed of two to four infantry divisions, a brigade or division of light cavalry, and had its own artillery, engineers and train. A corps was thus able to conduct independent operations, to hold the enemy till the others had concentrated on it, or to fall on the flank or rear. But it was not to think of itself as an independent unit: rather it was part of an assembled army, with a day's march between each component, forming an interrelated but flexible whole. In 1805, at the outset of the Ulm campaign, the army was drawn up on a front of 200 kilometres and in 1812 on one of 400. The enemy had two equally disagreeable options: he also could spread out and be destroyed piecemeal, or he could mass and be enveloped. His uncertainty would be enhanced by the thick cavalry screen deployed in front of the French forces, which thus

ured their intentions while at the same time gathering intelligence.
essence of this organisation was that it fused manoeuvre with com-
its purpose was to enable masses of the French to move faster and to
concentrate more readily for battle.

Unity was imparted to the army's movements not least by its line of
operations. Its centre was the site for hospitals and magazines and in
retreat it was the focus – as was Smolensk in 1812 – for holding the army
together. 'The secret of war', Napoleon told Jomini, 'lies in the secret of
the lines of communication. . . . Strategy does not consist of making half-
hearted dashes at the enemy's rear areas; it consists in really mastering his
communications, and then proceeding to give battle.' His aim, therefore,
while masking his own line of operations, was to threaten that of the
enemy, ideally by turning the flank nearest to the enemy's base and thus
forcing him to come to battle to restore his communications.

The classic Napoleonic strategy was the so-called *manoeuvre sur les
derrières*. In its ideal form, one corps, having made contact with the
enemy, would pin him by a feint to his front, while the main force would fall
on his rear. The enemy could attack the pinning force, but even if he were
successful, he would lengthen his own communications and strengthen
the principal French position. He could turn on the French communications, but to do this he would have to split his force between the pinning
and main bodies, and might in any case reap only a dubious advantage
since the French were arguably more self-sufficient than he was. His third
option was to face the main French army and conform to Napoleon's
desire for battle. In all this terrain played a crucial role, as the 1796 campaign, culminating in the battle of Lodi, demonstrates (see Map 5). The
French lay to the south of the river Po, the Austrians under Beaulieu to
the north. Since the French held the crossing at Valenza, Beaulieu not unreasonably expected them to use it. Napoleon accordingly launched a
diversionary attack to Valenza, and then by forced marches took his main
body to Piacenza, and cut the Austrian communications by seizing the
bridge at Lodi. The switch of his centre of operations from Valenza to
Piacenza had altered the whole appearance of the campaign, the Po had
obscured his movements from the Austrians, and another river, the
Adda, forced them to fight at Lodi.

If Napoleon was faced by more than one enemy army or by a general
dispersing his troops as widely as Bonaparte himself did, he employed
what has come to be called the strategy of the central position. The principle was to bring the French masses against a part of the enemy, so that at
least local superiority might be assured. Napoleon would attack the hinge
or joint of the two armies. Particularly if dealing with a coalition, but
even with separate parts of the same army, a failure in the unity of command would encourage the divided elements to act independently. The
nearest wing of the French army would attack the nearest enemy army,
while the central reserve would support and go for the flank and rear, pinning the second enemy army. As soon as the nearest formation had been
dispatched Napoleon would embark on the third stage, against the second
army. This was the strategy used against the Austrian forces converging
from Bassano and Trent in 1796 in order to relieve Mantua. With his

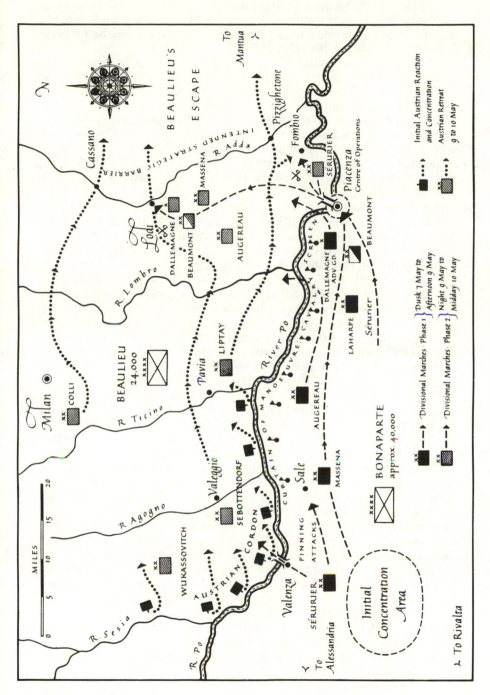

Map 5 *The Lodi campaign, 1796*

inferior forces, Napoleon employed it repeatedly between 1813 and 1815. But as these examples testify, it was essentially defensive, and certainly not decisive. The pursuit of either enemy force could never be properly carried through while the other remained in the offing.

The most striking feature of Napoleonic strategy to those reared on the limited possibilities of eighteenth-century warfare was the scale of his conception. His theatres of war were large chunks of Europe, and the necessity to disperse in order to feed enabled his massive armies to dominate rather than be submerged by the scale. In 1794, he suggested attacking the Austrians in Piedmont, thus forcing them to bring troops from the Rhine and weaken their position on a totally different front. This integrated approach was carried through in a similar context in 1800, when the Austrians were posted in Northern Italy and in the Black Forest (see Map 6). The French held Switzerland, thus being able to take both lines of communication in reverse, and Napoleon encouraged this ambiguity by concentrating his army at Dijon. The Austrians in Italy were tied by Massena, besieged in Genoa, and were anxiously looking along the Riviera, in expectation of the relief force. The Austrians in Germany were held by a diversionary attack by Moreau. Then Napoleon came through the Alps, using five passes, leaving – as Bourcet had argued – doubt as to which contained his main body. He had hoped to defeat the Austrians in detail as they turned back to recover their communications, but Genoa fell and he was instead faced by an enlarged Austrian army. Furthermore, he had weakened his forces by dispatching Desaix to Genoa for fear that the Austrians would reopen their communications by sea. Desaix, recalled in the nick of time, saved the day for Napoleon by returning to the field of Marengo when it seemed that the battle was already lost.

In 1805, the year of Napoleon's most spectacular successes, the Austrians were obligingly drawn in by a solitary corps, while Napoleon brought his six others across the Rhine, wheeled onto the Danube and cut their communications at Augsburg (see Map 7). Within twenty-six days, the Austrian army had been bottled up at Ulm and forced to surrender. After this virtuoso *manoeuvre sur les derrières*, Napoleon had to resort to his strategy of the central position. Substantial Austrian forces were intact in the Tyrol, to the north the Prussians were threatening, and from the east advanced the Russians. While the trusty Massena held the position in Italy, the emperor, on an inordinately long line of communications, drove straight on to Vienna and, before the others could become involved, had knocked the Russians out at Austerlitz.

The following year it was Prussia's turn (see Map 8). By concentrating in the area of Bamberg and Bayreuth, Napoleon threatened Leipzig or Dresden, and thence Berlin. The rivers Saale, Elster and Mulde were all available as strategic barriers – as the Adda had been in 1796 – when he decided to fall on the communications of the Prussian army, then at Erfurt. In case the Prussians should not conform to the emperor's seizure of the initiative, but instead aim for the French communications, forces were posted on the Rhine, from Mainz to Holland. The Prussians would thus have been caught between the hammer and its anvil. However, they attacked the French left as it advanced. Napoleon was therefore able to

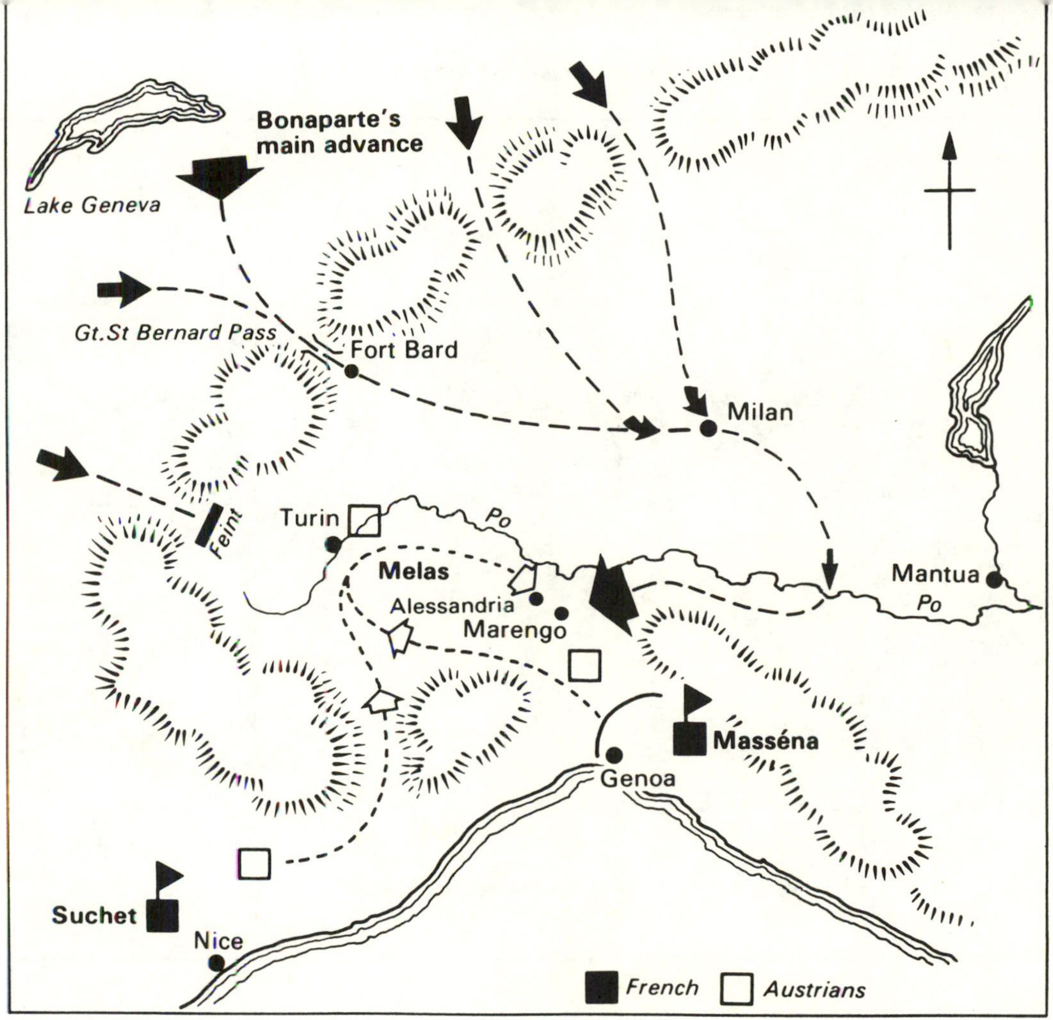

Map 6   *The Marengo campaign, 1800*

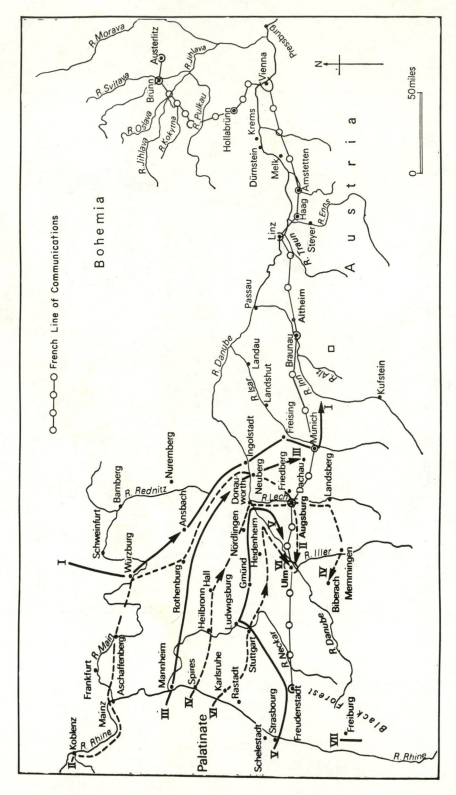

Map 7 *The Ulm and Austerlitz campaigns, 1805*

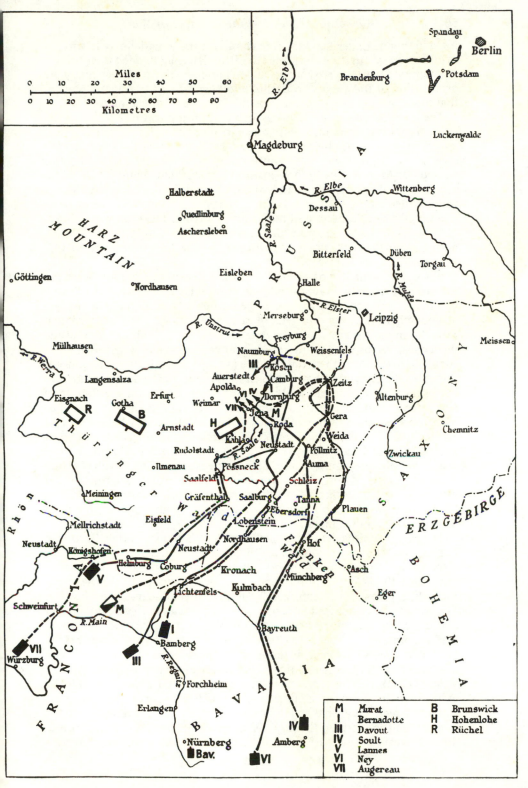

Map 8   *The Jena campaign, 1806*

leave his right, under Davout, free to fall on the Prussians' rear and cut off their retreat. In the event, since the Prussians had divided their forces, two separate battles were fought, at Jena and Auerstedt. It was really the prosecution of the pursuit to Berlin, and beyond, to Lübeck and Stettin, that made Jena so decisive and, for the Prussians, so traumatic.

The *manoeuvre sur les derrières* also had its application on the battlefield. Napoleon, in common with most great commanders before or since, aimed for victory on the flanks or rear. He could fight the Frederickian style of battle with extreme competence, as Austerlitz (1805) demonstrated (see Map 9). The French position was shielded behind a brook and a succession of ponds, on one of which its right flank rested, and its left was guarded by the Santon hill. The stronger left wing was covered to its front by the dead ground and the Pratzen heights. The right was deliberately weak in order to draw the Austro-Russian forces on to it, thus encouraging them to expose themselves to the devastation of Soult's advance from the left.

But whereas the use of ground and the extension of the line were the essence of Frederick's tactics, Napoleon preferred to envelop the enemy by the convergence of his corps on the battlefield. Admittedly at engagements such as Marengo and Jena there is more than a whiff of good luck rather than judgement about the practice. But even if this argues that the theory was retrospective, the results compel us to take it seriously. The enemy were drawn to the frontal battle as Napoleon's formations concentrated on the corps that had made first contact, until even their reserves were sucked in. Then part of the French army moved on the flank and rear, ideally that nearest the enemy line of retreat. As the foe turned to meet the fresh threat, he would upset the equilibrium of his front, and expose himself to the devastation of an attack on the hinge between front and flank. The attack itself, in the halcyon days of the *Grande Armée*, was a formidable combination of all three arms. The cavalry would threaten to charge, forcing the hostile infantry to form square. There it was more exposed to French artillery, and, firepower having wrecked its formations, the French columns would advance and the cavalry pour through the gap thus made.

The cavalry enjoyed an independence not granted it in other European armies. Formed in autonomous divisions, the light regiments were responsible for screening the approach march and then exploiting the pursuit, while the heavy were reserved for shock action in the battle itself. The artillery now finally emerged from its eighteenth-century backwater. The continuity among its bourgeois officers during the Revolution meant that it was the least disrupted of the arms: 55 per cent of the artillery in 1793 (as opposed to 5 per cent of the army as a whole) had enlisted before 1789, and over 80 per cent of the junior officers were regular officers of long standing. The artillery enjoyed the kudos of saving the Revolution at Valmy (1792). Furthermore Napoleon himself was a gunner. In 1800 he militarised the corps of civilian artillery drivers. Three years later he abolished regimental artillery in order to speed the movements of the infantry and to increase the number of guns allocated to higher formations. Increased weight of metal (4- and 6-pounders were replaced by 8

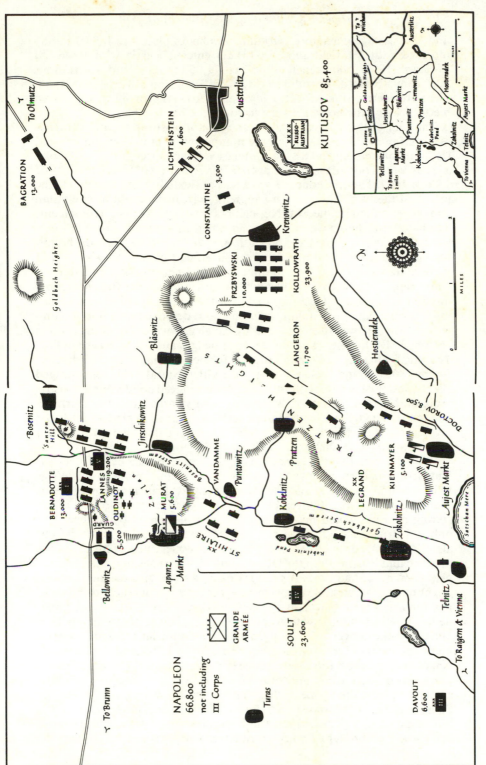

Map 9   *The battle of Austerlitz, 1805*

and 12) was augmented by a spiralling number of pieces. In 1805 the army marched with 286 field guns; in 1812 it entered Russia with 1,146. At Wagram (1809), 500 French guns fired 71,000 rounds, and it was in his later campaigns – at Borodino (1812) and Waterloo (1815) – that Bonaparte concentrated his artillery into larger batteries of up to a hundred pieces, leaving the horse artillery to roam the battlefield.

The spur to this tactical innovation was not least the declining quality of his infantry, his demands on the manpower of France giving less and less time for training and his leavening of veterans succumbing to the ravages of war. Four-fifths of the army after Eylau (1807) were recruits of 1806 or 1807. The consequence was a loss of flexibility and mobility in the tactics of the foot. The *ordre mixte*, with, say, two battalions in column and one battalion in line, was Napoleon's favourite form of deployment. The battalion column was not the solid wedge of myth but a formation 25 yards deep (twelve ranks) and 50 yards across. Indeed by 1809, the battalion was formed in six not eight companies, and in column was now 75 yards across and 15 yards deep (nine ranks). Using Guibert's method, it could rapidly form column to advance and line to give fire. Morand's division at Auerstedt (1806) approached the action in column of battalions, formed line in battalion columns, and deployed into line to commence firing. It was then attacked by cavalry, and part of it drew up in square, while the rest, using the cover of hedges and walls, stayed in line. The cavalry having been repulsed, it reformed columns for the advance. But by 1809 training could not keep pace with the intake. This encouraged the formation of massive columns, which were indeed ponderous battering-rams: at Wagram Macdonald's corps of twenty-three battalions formed a column of 8,000 men, and Marcognet's division at Waterloo arranged seven battalions, each three ranks deep, one behind the other, producing a body of 4,200 men, 200 yards across and 52 yards deep.

With the benefit of Clausewitzian hindsight, it can be argued that Napoleon was eventually vanquished because of his failure to relate war to its economic, political and even global context. British seapower meant that the Berlin decrees (November 1806), designed to starve Britain of her European trade, could never be properly implemented by France. Not only did Britain have the rest of the world available for commerce, but also Napoleon's desire to enforce the decrees was a cause of his invasions of Spain and Russia. Both the latter countries had space to trade for time: Napoleon never had time. A greater grasp of some of these implications might have prompted the emperor to accept the innumerable opportunities for negotiated peace. In the eighteenth-century manner, his opponents preferred to settle with Napoleon rather than undergo the political and economic dangers of prolonged war. Up until Ulm and Jena, Austria and Prussia managed to avoid major catastrophe. Thereafter, however, Napoleon gave them the choice between the reform of their states, and in particular of their armies, or total defeat. They had no choice but reluctantly to opt for the former. Their determination was reinforced by the Spanish victory over somewhat inferior French forces at Baylen in 1808. For Napoleon, Baylen marked the beginning of protracted war: rapid conquests had brought France considerable profits, but henceforth the

emperor's campaigns would no longer pay for themselves. For hi
nents, Baylen signalled the awakening of national resistance. In
year, the Archduke Charles of Austria tried to raise the Bavarian
the French. He was unsuccessful, but the performance of his
Aspern-Essling provided a fresh rallying point. Popular risings rone
in Tyrol and Westphalia. More importantly the Russians and Prussians
had found in Austria a viable ally. Relatively speaking, the populations
and economies of these powers had, during the course of the eighteenth
century, begun to catch up with those of France. In conjunction they
could overwhelm her. At Leipzig (October 1813), the three allies put
365,000 men into the field: Napoleon, with 195,000, was massively outnumbered. Moreover, France herself had been so drained by the imposi-
tions of prolonged war that, whatever the glories of the empire, no
flickers of the popular support that had aided the Spaniards and the Russians were evoked when finally the allies crossed the frontiers in 1814. The
people of France had ceased to fight for a revolution and had become the
tool of one man's ambitions. The irony in the political explanation for
Bonaparte's downfall is that it was the very fact of his combining political
and military control that enabled him to get as far as he did.

Furthermore, the irony is a double one. For, however flawed Napoleon's grasp of political, economic and even maritime realities, it was on
the battlefield that the defeat was inflicted. Part of the cause was indubit-
ably the very unity of command that ensured his power. At Lodi he was
manoeuvring an army of 20,000 men. Using the same principles scaled up,
he attempted to control 600,000 troops over a 500-mile area. Until 1812,
he directed operations in Spain himself, although he had not been in the
Peninsula since 1809. The increased size of his armies worked havoc with
his tight schedules. The problems of communication between scattered
formations were compounded by the lack of a proper staff. Napoleon's
reluctance to delegate meant that Berthier, his chief of staff, remained a
glorified head clerk and that his marshals – with the exception of men like
Massena and Davout – lacked initiative. In particular this was true of
Ney, who increasingly during 1813–15 held semi-independent commands.
The problems of concentration on the battlefield might be overcome with
outstanding generals, but at Bautzen (1813) Ney never understood his role
and at Dresden (1813) he took the pressure off Blücher rather than drive
him back. At Ligny (1815), Napoleon planned for Ney to fall on Blücher's
flank and rear, but as he marched he ran into the British at Quatre Bras.
The emperor tended to blame his subordinates on such occasions, but his
own neglect of the control of the actual battle little accords with an attitude which paid such scant attention to the development of his staff. On
the latter occasion, d'Erlon's corps hovered between the two actions and
failed to intervene decisively in either. Similarly at Eylau (1807), Ney did
not receive his orders until 2 p.m., and Bernadotte got none at all. The
need to be able to concentrate rapidly was the essence of the corps or divisional system, but Bonaparte had not necessarily developed the mechanics
for doing so.

The arguments for dispersal were not merely tactical; they were also logistic. Napoleon had not escaped the constraints of his eighteenth-century

predecesors as completely as he might have wished. Agricultural development could never remove the major supply problem of ammunition consumption, particularly as firepower developed. Requisition could dominate only if the army remained in fertile territory. Like Prussia's in the eighteenth century, France's army went abroad because it could not be fed at home. Food was Napoleon's avowed reason for leading his soldiers to the productive plains of Italy in 1796. In the Cisalpine, 4 million inhabitants paid 33 million francs to the French army and furnished supplies in kind whose total value was put at 160 million francs. In 1806 the *Grande Armée* stayed in Germany after Jena so that it could feed at the expense of France's new allies and not at that of France herself. On campaign, mobility was crucial. On the occasions when forts barred Napoleon's path, breakdown was imminent. He had to bypass and mask Fort Bard to enable the Marengo campaign to continue. The resistance of Mantua in 1796 and Acre in 1799 effectively wrecked his plans in both those years. Furthermore the plunder of the local population's reserves could provoke guerrilla war in his rear areas. The French armies in Spain were emasculated by the need to patrol the entire countryside, with the result that in 1810 Massena could only put 70,000 men out of the 300,000 Frenchmen in the Peninsula into the advance on Lisbon. Spain and Russia had not undergone their agricultural revolutions. Therefore in both countries armies proceeded with supply trains and depots. Wellington's thorough organisation of his supply lines, fed from the sea and supplemented by carefully regulated requisition, gives an eighteenth-century aura, which is enhanced by the dominance of sieges in his conduct of the Peninsular War. Russia was simply incapable of supporting an army the size of Napoleon's, and even lacked the roads for its supply train. The emperor's strategy was conceived in the economic conditions of the Mediterranean, not those of north-eastern Europe. Although he organised transport battalions for the invasion, the French lack of experience in their management and the impossibility of procurement, let alone distribution, meant that they were totally inadequate for the task. He marched with sufficient for 400,000 troops for twenty to twenty-five days. The Russians, wary of Napoleon, withdrew. After two months Napoleon had still not fought his early, decisive battle. He had already lost 150,00 men, and desertion and sickness were carrying off five to six thousand a day. The crucial engagement was not Borodino (7 September), the defensive action before Moscow, but Maloyaroslavets (24 October). It forced Napoleon to use the same route back to Smolensk as that along which he had come and whose resources he had already plundered.

But it was above all tactics that Napoleon neglected, and it was with tactics that he was defeated. Training by means of the *amalgame* could no longer cope with the flow of recruits. The decline of the French infantry was evident by 1809. The loss of horses on the 1812 campaign so crippled the cavalry that it never recovered. It failed in screening and reconnaissance in 1813, and it failed in shock action at Waterloo. Furthermore as the *Grande Armée* passed its peak, its opponents began to assimilate some of the lessons of the Revolutionary Wars, and to incorporate them into their eighteenth-century dynastic armies.

Neither Wellington nor the Archduke Charles, two of the more success-ful opponents of the French, departed dramatically from Frederickian principles. The duke's remarks about his men and his faith in corporal punishment to discipline them reflect not the nation in arms but the small, professional bodies of the Age of Reason. Strategically, he was a past master in the organisation of marches and supplies. He took pains to feed his army and to clear its communications not simply because the poverty of Iberia compelled it but because that was his view of generalship. But he remained incapable of the flash of Napoleonic or Malburian insight. His greatest assets in Portugal were the brevity of his supply line (only to the sea-coast, whereas that of the French ran all the way back through Spain and the Pyrenees) and the guerrillas of Spain, who compelled the French to scatter to hold the country. And yet in 1809 he advanced directly on Madrid, via Talavera, thus facilitating the French army's concentration and extending his own line. After a defensive battle, he was forced to retreat. In 1815, when Napoleon had put himself in the central position between the British and the Prussian armies, Wellington's immediate con-cern was for the safety of the Channel ports and the sea, whence he had been maintained in the Peninsula. Thus he widened the gap between him-self and Blücher, rather than closed it.

Similarly Wellington's tactics were defensive; he understood and exploited to the full the use of terrain and the firepower of the Brown Bess musket. The line, normally only two ranks deep, was the essence. The ground was normally of his own choosing, so that it protected his flanks, and ideally so that he could place his infantry behind a crest, out of expo-sure to direct fire. The other arms, the cavalry and artillery, were not as fully integrated into the pattern as in France, and both complained of their neglect to Wellington. The French columns of manoeuvre would advance, not certain when to deploy into company columns or line, because they could not see the main line and in fact on occasion confused it with Wellington's thick skirmishing line. As the French topped the crest, the British would fire a volley. Although inaccurate at much beyond 150 yards, at a third of that distance the massive 0·7 inch ball of the Brown Bess inflicted frightful casualties. Immediately the British would confirm their advantage by charging with fixed bayonets. Thus they com-bined fire and movement to devastating effect: the musket was the agent of disorganisation, the charge its confirmation.

The influences that bound the morale and training of the armies of Europe broadly speaking derived from the period before the Revolution. The *esprit* of the British soldier, although fostered by successive victories in the Peninsula, originated with the experience of the American War of Independence and with the subsequent rebuilding of the army. A perma-nent commander-in-chief was appointed in 1792, and from 1795 that officer was the reforming Duke of York. The Royal Military College was opened in 1799 and regimental schools established in 1812; appointments and promotions were controlled so that the worst features of purchase were eradicated; regulations for the cavalry (1795 and 1797) followed Dundas's for the infantry (1792) and thus tactical uniformity was estab-lished. Sir John Moore followed on the work of Howe and Gage at the camp of exercise set up for the light infantry and the experimental rifle corps (formed in 1800) at Shorncliffe in 1803. The emphasis on initiative and individual responsibility meant that discipline rested on emulation rather than repression. The Light Division was to regard itself as the élite unit in the Peninsula, and Wellington's faith in fire meant that he could never have enough battalions so trained.

Russia also grafted on some of the new tactical thought. The veteran Suvorov, who was dismissed in disgrace on the death of Catherine the Great, was recalled in 1799 and inflicted a succession of defeats on the French in Italy. A great trainer of troops, he emphasised speed and shock, spurning rigid linear formations in favour of units entering the fray as they arrived on the battlefield. He is often cited as an advocate of the bayonet, but he was no denigrator of firepower. He used lines against regular armies, while favouring shallow regimental squares for their flexibility. He covered his advance with skirmishers, and kept his artillery well forward to ensure close co-operation with the infantry. Although retrospectively seen as a father figure in Russian military thought, Suvorov's immediate impact was eclipsed with his death in 1800. Paul I (1796–1801) spurned the emerging independent Russian military tradition, which traced itself from Suvorov through Rumyantsev back to Peter the Great, and instead embraced the sterile formalism of Prussian drill. He reduced the *Jäger* and the light cavalry and ran down the general staff. But he did reassert central control of the army, curbing the independence of regimental colonels, inculcating new standards of professionalism and giving attention to the soldier's welfare. The last theme was developed by a fresh reformer, Barclay de Tolly, appointed minister of war in 1810. Barclay drew up regulations for the handling of higher formations. The divisional organisation, suppressed by Paul, was revived, and in the spring of 1812 the armies of the West were organised in twelve infantry and five cavalry corps. The artillery, upholding its relatively greater importance in the Russian army, received a new manual in 1812, instructing it to fight *en masse* and to co-operate with the other arms. The conception of the 1812 campaign, which is also attributed to Barclay, was Petrine. The withdrawal into Russia mirrored that of 1709, and, like Peter, Tsar Alexander aroused in his people a sense of nationalism and a determination to drive out the enemy.

In Austria, the consequence of the defeats of 1805 was the restoration of the emperor's brother, the Archduke Charles. As President of the Supreme War Council from 1801 to 1805, Charles had imparted unity and direction to Austria's military effort, but had fallen from favour in the latter year partly because he considered the Austrian army not yet ready for renewed fighting with the French. The 1796 regulations had stated, 'Regular, well-drilled and steady infantry cannot be impeded by skirmishers. All the shooting and skirmishing decides nothing': but in 1800 the third rank of the line was ordered to skirmish and in 1806 columns of attack were introduced. Conditions of service were improved, and Charles tried, with only partial success, to limit the period of enlistment. He massed his artillery and cavalry, reduced his baggage trains, introduced requisitioning, established a rudimentary staff and adopted the corps and divisional system. But he remained a true dynast, opposing a popular national militia in 1807, reluctantly agreeing to it in 1809 and allowing it to wither thereafter. As a union of such diverse ethnic groups, Austria could ill afford to find military expression in the revolutionary implications of the nation in arms. But this updated and yet fundamentally unaltered army fought Napoleon to a tactical standstill at Aspern in 1809. Like the British, its virtues lay in the defensive virtues of firepower, delivered in line. Schwarzenberg and his brilliant chief of staff, Radetzky, were to apply this instrument to the attack with excellent results in 1813.

None of the major powers whose progress we have so far reviewed felt sufficiently radical or sufficiently desperate to adopt universal conscription. The principle of obligatory service was well-established in the eighteenth century. However, rather than reflect the duties of citizenship, conscription was based on civic inequality. Peter the Great introduced compulsory military service in Russia, and the luckless recruit served for life. By adopting the canton system in 1727–35, Prussia produced an army half the size of France's when its population was only a ninth. The canton linked the regiment to a specific area, and so embraced every male in the country's defence. The desire to have the peasant productively engaged on the land meant that in peace for about ten months of the year the native troops could leave the regiment for their localities. Between 1770 and 1781 Joseph II grafted cantonal conscription on to the existing Austrian systems of recruiting, requiring the conscript to serve six weeks in the year. A second form of conscription known before the Revolution was that established for the militia. In the seventeenth century the emergent towns of Western Europe had set up part-time militias, thus establishing their exemption from conscription for regular service. In 1688 Louis XIV adopted conscription for the French militia and one calculation has reckoned that in the ensuing War of the Spanish Succession probably one out of every six Frenchmen was called to arms. In 1757 the English militia was ordered to be raised by ballot. During the eighteenth century, however, the militia became increasingly a reserve for a regular and professional army, and not an alternative. Compulsory service in the militia does not therefore indicate a progression towards a true citizen army, particularly as the obligation was hedged round by exemptions and could be ducked by the procurement of a substitute. This was just as true of states with compulsory regular service, such as Russia or Prussia. Until 1776, conscription in Russia was confined to Great Russia alone, and merchants, manufacturers, freeholders and priests were all exempt. In 1805 in Prussia, of 2,320,122 liable for military service, 1,170,000 were exempt on the basis of territorial privilege, and 530,000 because of their estate, profession, religion or property. In consequence the implication that citizens' duties also involved citizens' rights was confined to revolutionary France.

But in 1806 Prussia was defeated at Jena. The impact first of the Enlightenment and then of the French Revolution meant that reform of the Frederickian state, and in particular of the army, had long been posited. The effect of the defeat was to remove the more ancient officers, promote the brilliant and admit the bourgeois. By 1818, almost half the officer corps was not noble. The humanisation of the disciplinary code was – as elsewhere – the concomitant of higher standards of literacy and of their corollary, looser infantry formations. In 1807 the third rank became light infantry, in 1808 all infantry were to be trained as marksmen and in 1812 new regulations drew together much of this tactical innovation, introducing an element of free will to the battlefield and trying to amalgamate light infantry and the line. The authors of much of this were Scharnhorst, a Hanoverian by birth and significantly a gunner by education, and Gneisenau, who had served fleetingly in America. As friends of Clausewitz and important moulders in the development of the general staff, their influence permeated far. But the most radical step – the declaration of the nation in arms – was to be made in 1813 by Yorck. A combination of French limitations and conservative opposition to Scharnhorst's desire for conscription meant that between 1807 and 1812 Prussia built up her strength by rotating troops rapidly through the ranks, the so-called *Krümper* system, thus creating a reserve. But the impact of this in terms of disposable manpower was not great. In 1813, Yorck, in command of the Prussian troops serving under the French in Russia, arrived in East Prussia, together with another paladin of the reformers, Stein. The two declared a national revolt against France, and founded a *Landwehr*, or popular militia, to carry through the revolt. They had given vent to the feelings of a widespread group of reformers in the Prussian army. The king was forced to act, and conscription, without exemption, followed for the duration of the war. The step was revolutionary in its implications for citizenship and in its elevation of nationalism above loyalty to the monarch.

Prussia alone therefore went all the way in adopting French systems to beat Napoleon. She, like Spain and Russia produced a truly national response to the challenge of the Revolution, but Spain and Russia never transformed the structure and ethos of their armies as fundamentally as did Prussia. However, even here the effect was transitory: Prussia was to devote much of the postwar period to undoing the effects of the 1813 *Landwehr*. Furthermore, broadly speaking, as Scharnhorst realised, it was tactical competence that brought success in 1813. Light infantry, massed artillery and the division had all arrived as features of the battlefield. But neither strategic insight on a Napoleonic scale nor the concept of the nation in arms had found their true imitators. Europe as a whole was to take at least fifty, and arguably a hundred, years to exorcise and analyse the effect of Napoleon and his armies on the conduct of war.

Guide to Further Reading

The social transformation of the French army under the impact of the Revolution is admirably covered by Scott and Bertaud. On the tactical aspects, read Lynn on the infantry, Lauerma on the artillery, and Ross (1965–6) on the division. Colin, although some of his work on the Revolutionary Wars has now been overtaken, has much of moment to say on the whole subject of the history of modern warfare.

Standard works on Napoleon, such as Lefebvre, tend to cover the military aspects only indirectly. However, Tulard is suggestive. Rothenberg

(1977) provides a good general guide to European warfare in the age of Napoleon. On France, Chandler (1967) is comprehensive. Esposito and Elting have some beautiful maps. The British army is covered by Glover for the period before the Peninsular War, and by Oman and Ward for the period during it. Griffith (1981), chapter 3, has some interesting observations on the hoary question of line versus column. Rothenberg (1973 and 1982) gives the Austrian army a comprehensive re-examination. Russia can be pieced together from Duffy (1981), chapter 9, and Josselson. On Prussia, Paret (1966) is an object lesson in how tactical history can become total history; he also has some sharp criticisms of Shanahan, without totally replacing him.

Chapter 5

Jomini and the Napoleonic Tradition

Napoleon had appalled and terrified his contemporaries as much as he had dazzled them by his successes on the battlefield. His armies represented the naked fury of Revolution and yet they had accomplished military feats hitherto undreamt of. The outright rejection of the Revolution, the restoration of the old order, could be attempted at the governmental level. But was it possible on the military? True, armies were the apotheosis of state centralisation in the eighteenth century. Their organs could conform to dynastic precedent. The conduct of war, however, had been elevated to a new and more awful plane, whence it seemed there was no turning back.

The desire to assimilate Napoleonic precept within the existing framework was rendered easier to fulfil by the fact that the emperor was a pragmatist not a theorist. He therefore left to others the analysis of his conduct of war. In the twentieth century, the best known of these interpreters is Carl von Clausewitz, who will be discussed in chapter 7, but in the fifty years after Waterloo the position was held unassailably by Antoine Henri Jomini. Jomini was a Swiss bank clerk, who in 1805 managed to attach himself to Ney's staff, while at the same time producing his *Traité des grandes opérations militaires* (1804–11). The *Traité* covered the campaigns of Frederick and of Napoleon in Italy: based on Tempelhoff, significantly it related the revolutionary way in warfare to its eighteenth-century predecessor. Jomini's future reputation was assured after Austerlitz. The emperor himself read the *Traité* and concluded: 'Here is a young *chef de bataillon*, and of all men a Swiss, who teaches us things which my professors never told me and which few Generals understand. How could Fouché allow such a book to be printed! This is giving away to the enemy my whole system of war!' In consequence it was on Bonaparte's staff that Jomini served in the Jena and Eylau campaigns. Spain, where he was Ney's chief of staff, was to prove a major determinant in the formation of his views: not only did he see the triumph of an old-fashioned professional army, but also he simultaneously witnessed the horrors wrought by an impassioned people fighting a guerrilla campaign. A man prone to resignation – he resigned from various posts fifteen times in his life – he felt his full worth was never reflected in the appointments he held. His vainglory, perhaps even incompetence, as a staff officer, gave rise to constant clashes with Berthier. Finally, in 1813, he left the French service and threw in his lot with the Russians. His output in the many years still remaining to him (he died in 1869) was prolific, but the most influential of all his books was the single volume, *Précis de l'art de la guerre* (1838).

Jomini's vocabulary was derived on the one hand from Lloyd, who had taken the line of operations as central to strategy, and on the other from Bülow, whose *Geist des neuren Kriegssystems* (1799) had stressed the objective of the army and the base of its operations. The Swiss's contribution lay, therefore, in strategy, in the planning of war according to mathematical and geographical formulae. He did not address himself to the 'spirit' of war; he professed in consequence to find Clausewitz's logic faulty. But there is danger in over-stressing the distinctions between the two. After all, Jomini wrote, 'War, far from being an exact science, is a terrible and impassioned drama, regulated, it is true, by three or four general principles, but also dependent for its results upon a number of moral and physical complications'.

From this premiss, he none the less wished to introduce order and precision, for thus might the worst excesses be eliminated. 'As a soldier', he stated, 'preferring loyal and chivalrous warfare to organized assassination, if it be necessary to make a choice, I acknowledge that my prejudices are in favour of the good old times when the French and English Guards courteously invited each other to fire first, – as at Fontenoy – preferring them to the frightful epoch when priests, women and children throughout Spain plotted the murder of isolated soldiers.' The nation in arms was not totally rejected: a disciplined militia to supplement the regular troops was acceptable, but an armed and angry population was undesirable, both on humanitarian grounds and in terms of simple military effectiveness.

Jomini's critics often neglect his discussion of the relationship between war and politics. Thus can the contrast with Clausewitz be once again highlighted. In fact, Jomini was quite categorical that the conduct of operations should be subordinate to the war's objective. Indeed, how else could he contrive to bring its horrors under effective control? Thus the 1812 campaign earned his censure because Napoleon failed to assign a proper limit to the enterprise. Wistfully, Jomini looked to a day when nations would forget the experience of 1792–1815, would fight once again for the adjustment of frontiers and the balance of power rather than for their survival. Then perhaps a mean would have been struck between the decorum of a war of positions and the speed and violence of Napoleonic campaigning. Armies could be smaller and the effect of war more circumscribed.

Jomini reflected Napoleon in agreeing that the object of strategy was the destruction of the enemy army. But by his choice of the lines of operation, a general could command the theatre of war and force the enemy to leave the zone rather than give battle. Thus for Jomini the political aim needed to be limited to the acquisition of a province and the means to its implementation could become manoeuvre rather than combat.

The strategy to achieve all this was based on principles. 'All my works', he wrote, 'go to show the eternal influence of principles, and to demonstrate that operations to be successful must be applications of principles'. On these terms, the normal course of a campaign proceeded as follows. The general would choose his base of operations within the theatre of war. He would then settle on his first objective and the line of operations towards it. As he approached his target, the enemy would either be attacked or would be forced to retreat by manoeuvre. With the first objective gained, a supply line would be established back to base, and either the army would press on to its second objective or, if it had been weakened by battle or by the rigours of the campaign, it would simply cover the first. Then it would go into winter quarters. 'Such is the ordinary course of a war.'

Strategy therefore consisted in making a number of important choices – the theatre of war, the combinations which the terrain of the theatre would allow, the decisive points in those combinations, the direction of the operations, the site for their base and, of course, the objective of the operations. In getting the right mix, in co-ordinating marches and establishing depots, in mounting diversions and committing reserves, the commander had to bear constantly in mind Jomini's fundamental principle of war. This was expressed in four ways. First, strategic movements must aim to throw the mass of the army successively upon decisive points and also on the enemy's communications without compromising his own. Secondly, the army should manoeuvre so as to engage fractions of the foe with the bulk of its forces. Thirdly, on the battlefield, the general must throw masses on the decisive point, and fourthly, he must do it so that they engage at the proper time.

As the art therefore consists of putting the greatest number on the decisive point, it becomes clear why the choice of the correct base and line of operations was so crucial to Jomini. Bases of operations wisely selected could give such direction to the campaign as to enable the enemy's communications to be seized without forfeiting one's own. What Jomini meant can best be illustrated by the diagram he himself used (see Figure 2). In the case of the Jena campaign CD was the river Main, and AC the Rhine (both held by the French), AB was the North Sea and BD the Saale. The French army, by moving from its base CD to a fresh line FGH, theatened the communications of the Prussian army, then on the line I. Jomini maintained that the same principles lay at the base of the Marengo and Ulm campaigns.

Jomini saw the line of operations as being so strongly linked with the base and the marching capabilities of the army as to have direct strategic implications. The unity between line and base ensured the safety of the general's own communications while he threatened the enemy's. Thus did the French advance from the line FGH, swinging towards that of AB, derive its unity, direction and authority from its base. Furthermore, whereas Lloyd and Bülow had taken the line of operations as a simple link with the depots, Jomini distinguished between exterior and interior lines. Interior lines implied the concentration of the army rather than its dispersal. He took as his example the defence of the Belgian frontiers in 1792, where by forming a cordon the Austrians made themselves weak on all points. They should have placed themselves well back, ready to exploit the unity of their base of operations to meet separately the converging thrusts of the attackers. 'Simple and interior lines', Jomini wrote, 'enable a general to bring into action, by strategic movements, upon the important point, a stronger force than the enemy . . . . An undue number of lines divides the forces, and permits fractions to be overwhelmed by the enemy.'

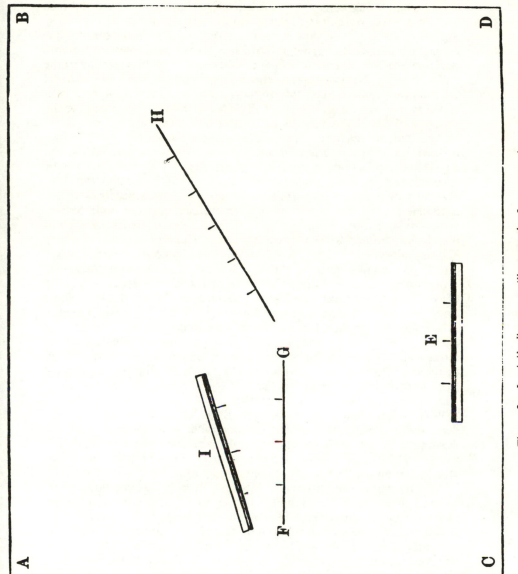

Figure 2   *Jomini's diagram to illustrate the Jena campaign*

Even if the terrain forced a general to advance on double lines of operation, they should still be interior to enable faster concentration.

Jomini took the advance on interior lines as Napoleon's main manoeuvre – 'the strategy of the central position' of the previous chapter. Thus he had brought his theories full circle. A large army could not feed and move while concentrated. Furthermore, if it was opposed by converging enemy forces, it was slow in turning from one to meet the other. Thus from the 'fundamental principle' of mass on the decisive point, Jomini was able to advocate smaller armies and hence support his rejection of the nation in arms. The examples he chose suggested that, since they allowed an army to assume the tactical offensive, interior lines were indeed well-suited to an army on the defensive. But he did not address himself to the problem of the commander faced by a united enemy army, nor – apart from acknowledging its existence – did he tackle the danger from envelopment to an army operating on interior lines. Even more seriously, the aggressive implications of the corps system were totally lost. The web of formations threatening a number of objectives and concealing the commander's intentions were forfeit to the principles of concentration and mass. He argued that, if left too late, the forces' junction could be prevented by an enemy on interior lines. Converging on the battlefield was thereby condemned, and so the execution of a *manoeuvre sur les derrières* in its full glory rendered less likely. Napoleon had indeed operated to good effect on interior lines – in 1813 and in meeting with Austrians endeavouring to relieve Mantua in 1796 – and so had Frederick in fending off France, Austria and Russia in the Seven Years' War. But in all these cases the exponents were on the defensive and in all they were limited in the exploitation of their victories by the threatened approach of another enemy army. Jomini's principle could thus also make war less decisive. Its attractions for a would-be conqueror were thereby diminished. But all this assumed a commander who thought as Jomini did. Having started from limited political objectives, he had ended by evolving a conduct of war that had its own in-built constraints.

What Jomini had to say about grand tactics confirms the drift. He defined grand tactics as the art of making good combinations before and during battles, and their guiding principle once again was the direction of masses on the decisive point. He enumerated a dozen possible orders of attack, but all of them involved connected formations rather than divisions converging from different directions. Even in turning movements, he warned against over-extension. Similarly he advocated the nomination of a separate reserve, whereas Napoleon used the division most conveniently situated in relation to the others at any one moment. Surprise did not enter the equation. The timing in the co-ordination of Napoleon's attacks and the emphasis on distraction and flexibility on the battlefield were thus forfeit.

Whatever Jomini's defects in his interpretation of Napoleon, his contribution to the development of the military profession was immense. He had defined the terms of strategy and in the *Précis* presented them in a comprehensible and assimilable whole. The implication of his advocacy of small armies was that they should make up in quality what they lacked in size. They should be kept well-prepared even in peacetime, with an effective organisation for the reserves, a firm but humane system of discipline and rewards, a good administration for the hospitals and commissariat, and, above all, adequate training for officers and men. In particular he required a 'general staff capable of applying these elements, and having an organisation calculated to advance the theoretical and practical education of its officers'. Both Napoleon and Wellington had emphasised personal command, but Jomini elevated the chief of staff to a position where he relieved the commander not merely of the tedium of organising marches but also of much of the direction of strategy as well. He defined the staff's duties and in the *Précis* gave it a manual by which to learn them. At this level war was teachable. 'War in its *ensemble* is not a science, but an art', he wrote. 'Strategy, particularly, may be regulated by fixed laws resembling those of the positive sciences, but this is not true if war is viewed as a whole.' Combat itself then, because morale lay at its centre, and because the right choice of combinations was a matter of individual circumstances and particular skills, was independent of science. But at the staff level the conduct of war was more precise. 'Correct theories, founded upon right principles, sustained by actual events of wars, and added to accurate military history, will form a true school of instruction for generals.' Therefore, however inflexible Jomini's teaching may have been, it provided the basis for a self-regard among the officers of Europe.

These officers – at best the victims of slow peacetime promotion after 1815, and many of them unemployed and on half-pay – generated a prodigious literature on the Napoleonic wars. Their writings were the basis of a professionalism that was confirmed by the staff and officer training schools that had also emerged from the wars. The military academies founded in the first half of the eighteenth century were predominantly for the instruction of the technical arms, the engineers and the gunners. Artillery schools were set up in France in 1679, in Russia in 1701 and in Britain in 1741. But later in the century, the aristocracy's need to justify its hold on the military profession led to the establishment of cadet schools for the other arms – the Noble Land Cadet Corps in Russia in 1731, Wiener Neustadt in Austria in 1752 and St Germain's Ecole Militaire in France in 1776. Under the impact of the Napoleonic wars, this education became more strictly professional. Britain's Royal Military College, established in 1799, was not therefore unique: Russia remodelled the Noble Cadet Corps in 1800; in France St Cyr dates from 1803 and Saumur (the cavalry school) from 1814; the United States Military Academy at West Point was founded in 1802; Scharnhorst's reform of Prussia's military schools culminated with the establishment of the *Kriegsakademie* in 1810; and the pattern was confirmed in the peace, with Holland setting up a military academy in 1828, Russia in 1829 and Belgium in 1834.

The impact of Jomini and his ilk, either direct or indirect, was in these circumstances immense. Russia, his country of adoption, appointed him chairman of a commission to formulate the syllabus of its new academy. He accompanied Tsar Nicholas I in the 1828 Balkan campaign, and in 1854 advised him to be wary of the threat to Russia from Austria, thus neglecting the more pressing dangers in the Crimea. France, with the monarchy restored, stressed that limited war was the dominant historical pattern, and consequently her soldiers (at least until 1848) analysed not so much the Napoleonic experience as the writings of Frederick and Guibert. But the emergence of a fresh Bonaparte prompted a revival of imperial fashion in military as in other matters: Napoleon III asked Jomini for his views on the impact of the new rifle on tactics in 1851 and in 1859 consulted him on the strategy to follow in his Italian campaign.

In Austria, Jomini's influence was muted by the fact that the Archduke Charles had prefaced an account of the 1796 campaign in Germany with a preliminary discourse on strategy. But Charles's success at Aspern had been a tactical not a strategic victory, and his preconceptions varied little from those of the essentially eighteenth-century army that he led. Not unreasonably he stated that war was 'the greatest evil a state or a nation can experience', and then proceeded – *à la* Jomini – to sketch out a mode of conducting it that was essentially defensive. The best guarantee of success was to control a country's resources and the routes by which they could be delivered to the theatre of war. The safety of the base of operation he regarded as such a fundamental precondition that flanking or turning movements were deemed very risky and the specification of reserves to guard it more important than mass on the decisive point. He practised what he preached. A third of the Austrian troops at Aspern were never committed to the battle, and nor was the reserve at Wagram. In 1806, he instructed his generals to direct their offensives against strategic points, not against the enemy's army. The archduke's influence was therefore to compound rather than to mitigate the more defensive and limiting qualities of Jomini.

The stage in Prussia was initially held by Willisen, a Hegelian, a self-confessed disciple of Jomini, and professor of military history at the *Kriegsakademie* in the 1820s. He wrote commentaries on many of the principal campaigns of his time – 1831, 1848, 1859 and 1866 – and included a course of theory in his series of lectures, which he published in 1840. Much of what he said reflected the Jominian throwback to the eighteenth century. His contribution in the attempt to see Napoleon in the context of Frederick was to argue that, if the latter had rid himself of the fetters of his magazines, he would have achieved as much. But, although he repeated the traditional emphasis in averring that strategy is 'the theory of communications', he did make some original contributions. He added to the conceptual framework which Jomini had provided by distinguishing between the strategic offensive or defensive and the tactical. A general fighting offensively in strategic terms needs only to invade and then hold territory to enable him to adopt the tactical defensive. Similarly Napoleon in 1813, on the strategic defensive, fought offensively the whole time. This was perhaps an obvious point but not one thereto made so coherently. But more than this, Willisen moved nearer to accepting the element of risk in Napoleon's conduct of war. 'Strength against weakness,' he wrote, 'front against flank, superior force against inferior force, masses against the decisive point.' Despite the Jominian imagery, there is here a fuller acceptance that a turning move against one flank was the great fundamental in every attack. Alone of the Jomini school, Willisen stressed surprise, the use of feints, the value of night-marches and the importance of a vigorous pursuit. Willisen perhaps deserves to be better remembered, but his reputation was eclipsed by his defeat while in the service of Schleswig-Holstein at the battle of Idstedt in 1850.

Britain was an unconscionably long time in breeding a home-grown strategist – partly for reasons that will become clear in the next chapter. It seemed unlikely that she would have to manoeuvre large armies in a continental war. Partly too it was attributable to the nature of Wellington's victory – tactical, eighteenth-century precepts had prevailed, and so scant pressure existed to analyse Napoleonic warfare in its wider sense. Strategy became little more than a scaling-up of the principles of Frederickian tactics. Prussian drill formations still predominated, and the texts cited were Tempelhoff, Lloyd and Saxe. Sir Charles Napier, whose reputation perhaps rested not so much on his conquest of Scinde in 1843 as on his eccentricities, trenchant prose style and penchant for controversy, simply stated 'Fred's the man'. His brother William's *History of the War in the Peninsula* established for its author a position as Britain's pre-eminent military thinker, but he refused to write a general work of theory. He praised and accepted Jomini. However, nobody translated the *Précis* or the *Traité* into English: instead they were known and pirated by a number of lesser writers, and thus did Jominian phraseology enter English usage.

In 1856, Patrick MacDougall, to become the first commandant of the Staff College and already William Napier's son-in-law, published *The Theory of War*. It was drawn straight from Jomini. He took the campaigns of Marlborough and Frederick, and of Napoleon in 1796 – but not later – as 'an infallible test by which to judge of every military plan; for no combination can be well conceived, no maxim founded in truth, which is at variance with them'. The concentration of forces must be performed at a good distance from the enemy to avoid the danger of defeat in detail, and independent formations should not attack when a short delay would permit them to do so with masses.

MacDougall's book was superseded by that of the first professor of military history at the Staff College, E. B. Hamley. *The Operations of War* (1866) was also derived from Jomini. This presented the perceptive and highly literate Hamley with some problems of logic. He attacked the prevailing tendency to discuss war in a mathematical and geometrical fashion: works 'treat their subject in too abstract a form, and become obscure in attempting to be scientific'. He acknowledged that his study was based on the Napoleonic system but, as in the end Bonaparte had been defeated, clearly that system could not be embraced in its entirety. 'The Napoleonic system is more successful in single campaigns than in protracted wars'; the cumulative losses after 1809 had robbed the *Grande Armée* of the power of manoeuvre. Therefore, Hamley contended, the object of a war must be limited to that achievable in a short campaign. But he had already acknowledged by implication the importance of economic factors in the ability to sustain war, and in his own day the American Civil War provided as dramatic example as did the eventual defeat of France. 'Lee, like Napoleon,' Hamley wrote, 'wins campaigns by making skill compensate for numbers; but like Napoleon, he yields at last to the super-ior resources of enemies who continue to press him to exhaustion'. Hav-ing got so far in an analysis that came close to accepting the principal lesson of the Union's victory, Hamley went sharply into reverse. Limited war was his aim and citizen armies were condemned, for 'the moral of this book is not that numbers and wealth must prevail'.

Thus, in the end Hamley's strategic precepts revert to the eighteenth-century tone. The object of strategy was not to seek battles, which were 'merely incidents in the campaign'. As the axiom was to bring strength against the enemy's weakest point, it followed that that point might well not prove decisive. In any case the very act of concentrating masses on one sector weakened another part of the line and exposed it to the dangers of counter-attack. It therefore followed that 'Modern battles are for the most part partial attacks, where the assailant puts forth his foot no further than he can be sure of drawing it back again'. And so manoeuvre dominated Hamley's conception of war. 'It is the object of strategy so to direct the movements of an army, that when decisive collisions occur it shall encounter the enemy with increased relative advantage'. But although marches against enemy communications concerned Hamley, he did not then proceed to countenance a *manoeuvre sur les derrières*, since it endan-gered the attacking army's own lines. What was truly central to Hamley was the question of supplies: 'Two armies are not like two fencers in an arena, who may shift their ground to all points of the compass; but rather resemble the swordsman on a narrow plank which overhangs an abyss, where each has to think not only of giving and parrying thrusts, but of keeping his footing under the penalty of destruction'. Thus, once again, although Hamley penned a plea for war to be limited by its political objec-tives, he actually so hedged about its conduct as to argue that its limita-tions were inbuilt.

As with so many other theorists, doubts were cast over Hamley by his performance in the field – in this case in Egypt in 1882. None the less *The Operations of War* was adopted as the official volume at the Staff Col-lege, was also approved for use at West Point, and was still the principal book at the Quetta staff college in India immediately before the First World War. Although in 1894 it ceased to be the sole text in military his-tory at the Staff College, its seventh and last edition was not published until 1922 and it even attempted to embrace the First World War in its framework. Sir John French referred to Hamley as having prompted his decisions on the retreat from Mons in 1914.

In sum then the strategy enunciated by Jomini and his disciples had a pronounced eighteenth-century feel about it. By stressing masses on the decisive point, they rejected the division of troops and so made armies small if they were not to be unwieldy. By massing too, they were commit-ted to operating on internal lines, although this was the least decisive of Napoleon's manoeuvres. In a cyclical process, a united force operating on internal lines was slow in manoeuvre and therefore encouraged the need to keep it small. In trying to fit Napoleonic strategy into the eighteenth-century framework, Jomini and his disciples had to divorce it from its econ-omic, social and political context. They thus managed to produce a form of war which – although the perceptive saw could only be restrained by its political objectives – could all too easily be seen as limited in itself.

The success of the Jominian school is attributable to the fact that it had enunciated a strategy adapted to professional, long-service armies fighting for limited objectives. In other words, it had produced a doctrine that suited the political context of Europe in its own day. The re-establishment of the *ancien régime* which Metternich fought so hard to achieve at the Congress of Vienna was likely to be most evident in the armies of Europe. In the main they had made no more concession to nationalism and revolutionary fervour than they had to. Dynastic control had never really been forfeited, and thus was relatively easily maintained. The British army was commanded by a member of the royal family, the Duke of Cambridge, as late as 1895. The German, Colmar von der Goltz, writing in 1883, said 'That nation will be most secure whose rulers are also its military commanders, and whose royal house knows how to maintain the will and the vocation for the arduous duties of supreme command'. In Austria, much of the Archduke Charles's emphasis on preserving the army intact in the field derived from its identification with the Habsburg dynasty. His son, the Archduke Albrecht, was inspector-general of the army until 1895, and in December 1916 the Emperor Charles followed the example set by the tsar in Russia the previous year and assumed supreme command of the army. Even if the manifestations elsewhere were not as overt as these, the links between ruling houses and their armies did – and even do – remain close. The dialogue between monarch and army endeavoured to exclude Parliament: the senior officer normally had the right of direct access to the king, and was thus on a par with, or even stronger than, the war minister. Continuing the eighteenth-century role of the *intendant*, civilian and parliamentary control remained purely financial, and was distinct from the executive and military authority. Parliaments found it hard to do more than refuse to vote supply.

The triumph of the monarchs was epitomised in the reversion to long-service professional armies. The idea of the citizen army had been bestowed with revolutionary and nationalist overtones, and service in it implied at least the right to vote. In Prussia, Prince Wittgenstein went further: 'to arm a nation means merely to organise and facilitate opposition and disaffection'. Although short service (two years from 1833) remained the rule in Prussia, a reversal from the position of 1813–15 was achieved. The *Landwehr*'s independence of the regular army was compromised in 1819 and lost completely in 1860, and a contraction of the officer corps left it more aristocratic and dominated by a professional ethos. Elsewhere in Europe long service was the norm. France settled first (in 1818) on a six-year enlistment period, and then in 1832 on seven years. The soldier became too attuned to military life by the end of his time to be prepared to quit it, and in 1861, for example, there were 28,894 re-enlistments. Piedmont in 1832 opted for eight years. In Britain service was limited to eleven years in 1847, and Cardwell's so-called short service act of 1870 still stipulated six years. The Austrian law of 1845 set an eight-year period. The *Landwehr* was completely shelved in 1831. The results were manifest in 1848: armies remained loyal to their monarchs, and in Paris, Berlin and Vienna they crushed the revolutions.

Paradoxically, some liberals, particularly those of Britain, found themselves supporting this pattern of military organisation. Their reasoning was economic. Adam Smith had favoured a regular standing army rather than a citizen militia on the grounds of military effectiveness. But his theories on the division of labour suggested too that a popular force would be harmful to industrial productivity. Much of the radical opposition to the reintroduction of the militia in Britain in 1852 was rooted in the damage that its training requirements would have on output, and indeed the force remained worst recruited in the manufacturing counties with full employment. Two years later, Britain opted to meet the crisis of the Crimean War by forming units of German and Swiss mercenaries rather than conscript at home. Even France was prepared to shelve the principle of national homogeneity: in 1831 she formed the Foreign Legion for service in North Africa. Thus liberals could on economic grounds oppose the military organisation with the most revolutionary implications. Forfeiting an effective counterweight to professionalism, they therefore reckoned it important to keep the army small. Its monarchical and aristocratic associations and its monopoly of arms meant that even in Britain as late as 1844 the size of the army could be viewed (in the words of a motion in the House of Commons) as 'contrary to the principles of constitutional liberty and dangerous to the rights of the people'. The army in that year was a mere 138,000 strong, of whom only 30,000 were at home. On this level, moreover, economic argument could buttress the political. The principles of *laissez faire* suggested that the taxes designed to pay for defence curbed the very trade the forces were intended to protect. Furthermore liberal energies were channelled into commerce or the professions of law and teaching, and were content to acquiesce in the archetypal army of rural recruits officered by noble landowners. The latter resented the disruption of urban, educated and possibly nationalist influences, and the former on the whole were quite happy to leave the army to its own devices. In Britain in particular many of the features of the eighteenth-century professional army remained long after they had disappeared in the rest of Europe. The purchase of commissions was not abolished until 1871 (even Austria had ended the practice in 1848); the officer's pay remained constant from 1806 to 1914 despite inflation; and, although only 12 per cent of the British labour force in 1912 was employed in agriculture, 65 per cent of senior officers in 1914 came from rural backgrounds. Significantly, Russia had the largest army in Europe, but its industrial development was slow, and the rise of representative government or a vociferous middle class consequently checked. The majority of officers were noble. Conscripted for a period of fifteen to twenty-five years, the Russian soldier was not on a par with his French counterpart of the 1790s: in 1848 a fifth of the families of European Russia were exempt and the emphasis on long rather than short service was impelled by the fact that more men through the ranks would have freed more serfs and so undermined the social fabric of the country. Russia was not an exception but an eighteenth-century army writ large.

Economic and social arguments therefore shaped armies for which Jominian strategy was well adapted. Over these domestic pressures was cloaked a panoply of increasingly sophisticated international relations. This too had its roots in the previous century. War was the product of revolution: a stable world in political terms would – as Kant's *Perpetual Peace* (1795) had argued – also become a more pacific one. Metternich's 'Concert of Europe' revived the aspects of harmony fostered by the Enlightenment. As late as 1884–5 the great powers in the conference at Berlin were reverting to the same ideals, albeit as members of a continent where neither Russia nor Austria any longer held sway, and where agriculture and aristocrat were being ousted by industry and entrepreneur. Much of their military and expansionist effort was directed towards the colonies, away from Europe itself. In France, Thiers, a minister under Louis Philippe and to become the first president of the Third Republic in 1871, held that *grande guerre* was a phenomenon that would only occur every fifty or a hundred years, and indeed French experience confirmed his hypothesis. In 1823, 1828, 1831, 1832, 1848, 1849, 1854 and 1859, the French army fought in Europe without incurring dramatic consequences for its parent state. Britain, the premier industrial country of the world – at least until 1870 – elected to support its diplomacy with its navy. Therefore, although the economic effects of blockade could be far-reaching, the impact of violence itself was self-contained, confined to the high seas.

So effective was the settlement of 1815, and so strong were governments' fears of revolution at home, that for over thirty years no major wars occurred. Even those that followed the revolutions of 1848, and spanned the period to 1866, continued to confirm the pattern of a strategy of limited war. The Piedmontese attempt to oust the Austrians from Italy in 1848–9 was ably countered by Radetzky. Now 83, the veteran of Napoleon's wars had, significantly, entered the service before the French Revolution. Nor was he alone: the same was true of Wellington, commander-in-chief in Britain from 1842 to 1852. Forts dominated Radetzky's initial strategy. He had to set aside twenty-two of his forty-seven battalions as garrisons. He opened the campaign by retreating to the Quadrilateral of fortified towns between the rivers Mincio and Adige. Thus on the defensive he could employ interior lines against the Piedmontese while awaiting reinforcements. When he turned to the offensive he pierced the Piedmontese front at Custozza by concentrating masses against a solitary sector. The Piedmontese army remained intact but domestic divisions and a reluctance to engage in a truly revolutionary war caused it to suspend hostilities. Fighting was renewed again in 1849, and was distinguished by each side endeavouring to fall on the other's flanks. Radetzky eschewed the opportunity to master the Piedmontese communications and his second major victory, at Novara, although a model of mid-nineteenth-century manoeuvre, was not fully exploited in military terms. None the less the Piedmontese sued for peace. The Austrians had conducted an ideal campaign in Jominian terms: the strategy was the correct one because its restraint in the use of violence minimised the legacy of bitterness and prolonged Habsburg hopes of maintaining their Italian possessions.

Prior strategic planning in the British and French invasion of the Crimea in 1854 was rudimentary. Indeed the armies had gone to Turkey to defend the Dardanelles against seizure by the Russians, and the British at any rate were envisaging a replay of the Peninsular War, with their fleet feeding them from the sea and their foe exhausted on the end of a long line of communications. When the Russians pulled back out of Turkey, Sebastopol was attacked because it was the main Russian port in the Black Sea. The destruction of its naval installations would remove the latent threat to British naval hegemony in the eastern Mediterranean. The war was therefore limited in two distinct but interrelated ways. The principal if unstated concerns were maritime, and the incidence of naval actions all round the periphery of the Russian empire reflects this. As a by-product, land operations were confined to one area, remote from mainland Europe. The fighting in the Crimea was marked by no decisive battle but was instead dogged by the problems of communications and supply. The allies had a fleeting chance of a major victory in the field at the river Alma. But their concern to remain close to the sea and thus to their communications meant that their attack was delivered from that direction, and left open the Russians' line of retreat back to the town of Sebastopol. Even at this stage a vigorous pursuit might have brought the allies to their goal. However, they elected to move round the town, to the south, in order to secure the harbours of Kamiesch and Balaclava. A formal siege, dominated by the traditional technicalities of sapping and bombarding, then ensued. Troops had to protect the besiegers from the Russian army still in the field, and a large influx of stationary men in an underdeveloped area posed constant provisioning problems. In the end it was indeed the Russians – although on their own territory – who found it harder to feed an army on the end of a long land line than did the allies from the sea. Exhausted though undefeated in battle, they abandoned Sebastopol and its naval installations. The war was finally concluded at Paris in 1856, by a treaty which aimed to reassert international controls and in particular to define the terms of naval blockade.

The peace conference helped bring about a pact between France and Piedmont, designed to secure the expulsion of the Austrians from Italy. Again the war, when it came in 1859, was limited geographically. Napoleon III tackled the Habsburg empire in Lombardy alone. Once successful, the emperor was too fearful of other powers intervening (especially Prussia) to continue his support of Piedmont. Again inadequate supply arrangements lay at the heart of operations. Despite their commitment the French had made few preparations. Although entering a land of rivers and forts, they had no bridging equipment and no siege train. Their artillery was short of 25,000 horses on 1 January 1859. On 23 April Canrobert was ordered to cross the frontier: he still needed blankets, tents, water-bottles, ammunition and hay. The Austrians were as badly off, and even lacked maps of an area already familiar to them. Also short of horses, they were reluctant to requisition for fear of fomenting popular resistance. Caught in the thrall of the Archduke Charles, they preferred to echelon their reserves rather than concentrate at Montebello, the decisive point. Defeated by inferior forces at Magenta, they withdrew to the safety of the Quadrilateral. The Emperor Francis Joseph himself took command, and the two sides clashed at Solferino. With their fronts parallel to each other, their line of communications were safe, and the withdrawal of the defeated side (the Austrians) guaranteed. Francis Joseph caught the spirit of the *ancien régime* exactly: he concluded, 'I have lost a battle. I pay with a province.'

Solferino was a slogging, bloody battle. The indecisive, cautious nature of strategy, the limited theatres and the small-scale objectives of war, gave tactics a proportionately greater importance. But in the American Civil War (1861–5), the theatres were large, and the objectives were ideological and therefore open-ended. American military thought had, even more than in Europe, fallen under the influence of Jomini. Deprived of direct confrontation with Napoleon, Americans studied him all the more assiduously. Halleck, the commander of the Union armies from 1862 to 1864, continued working on his translation of Jomini while in the field. For the South, Robert E. Lee had also immersed himself in Jomini. Throughout the war, Lee showed himself a brilliant exponent of the strategic defensive on interior lines. When, in 1863, the Confederates decided that they must do more than fight for their survival and took the offensive, they were checked at Gettysburg.

For the Union, McClellan too had imbibed the Jominian orthodoxy. He tried to manoeuvre but at the same time to concentrate masses on the decisive point. In consequence he was confounded by logistics. In July 1862, he protested to Lincoln about the subjugation of the rebels, about the confiscation of property and about its corollary, the forcible abolition of slavery. 'Woe to the general', he intoned, 'who trusts in modern inventions, and neglects the principles of strategy.' But modern inventions, the railroad and the rifle, had conspired with mass citizen armies, themselves reflecting the ideologies of democratic society, to undermine the principles he espoused. The conduct of the war was not limited in itself, and nor were its objectives.

In the month before McClellan penned his appeal to Lincoln, the president was writing: 'I state my general ideas of this war to be that we have the *greater* numbers, and the enemy has the *greater* facility of concentrating forces upon points of collision; that we must fail, unless we can find some way of making *our* advantage an over-match for *his*; and that this can only be done by menacing him with superior forces at different points, at the *same* time'. Masses on many points, directed in independent, convergent assaults, would allow the North to bring its industrial and economic strength to bear. In Grant, who took supreme command of the Union forces in 1864, Lincoln found a general to implement such a strategy. Grant had never read Jomini and denied the existence of general principles: 'There are no fixed laws of war which are not subject to the conditions of the country, the climate and the habits of the people. The laws of successful war in one generation would ensure defeat in another.'

While Grant waged a war of attrition in the east, Sherman unleashed the new thinking in the west. In his advance from Chattanooga into Georgia in May 1864, he four times held the Confederates to their front and executed a turning movement to their flank (see Map 10). A frontal attack would only have driven the Southern forces back on their communications and hence on their strength. But for Hamley – brought up in the Jominian persuasion – Sherman was taking unjustifiable risks. He had

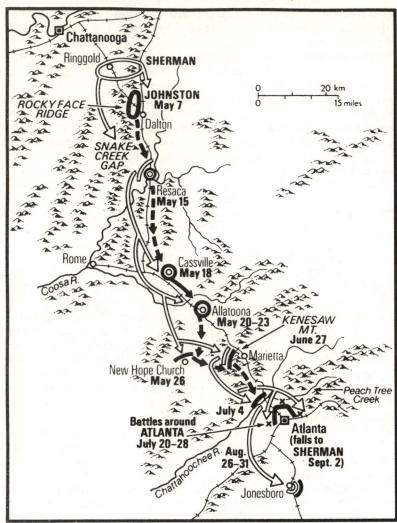

Map 10   *Sherman's Georgia campaign, 1864*

divided his forces, not massed them. He had risked his own supply lines. Far more shocking, however, was the campaign Sherman then waged from Atlanta to the sea. The army in the field could not be the only target in a peoples' war. Grant told Sherman to lay waste the Shenandoah valley: his concern was to limit the South's economic ability to fight on another year. But Sherman aimed further: he wanted to crush the will to fight. 'We are not only fighting hostile armies,' he wrote, 'but a hostile people, and we must make old and young, rich and poor, feel the hard hand of war.'

Europeans were slow to realise what had happened. Either the American war was an irrelevance fought out between amateurs, or alternatively

the generalship of Lee and Stonewall Jackson showed that Jomini's interpretation of Napoleon should still guide strategic thought. In truth, however, the dicta of Sherman – 'war is cruelty, and you cannot refine it,' and
'war is simply power unrestricted by constitution or compact' – were the
more accurate pointers to the future.

Guide to Further Reading

The best approach to Jomini and the other strategic theorists is to sample
their works. Howard's essay on Jomini is to be found in his books of 1965
and 1970. Elting is also helpful on Jomini. Von Caemmerer discusses the
Archduke Charles, Willisen and much else. Luvaas (1970) covers the British writers.

The organisation of the Prussian army in this period is dealt with by
Ritter (1970–3) and Craig (1955), the British by Strachan (1977 and 1980)
and Spiers (1980), the French by Griffith (1975) and Holmes, the Austrian
by Rothenberg (1968 and 1976) and Sked, and the Russian by Curtiss. For
a brief discussion of armies and economic thought, see Neimanis: Silberner is more theoretical.

The operational aspects of the campaigns of 1848–9 and 1859 both
need fresh treatments. The strategy of the Crimean War is approached
from the French perspective by Brison D. Gooch and from the British by
Strachan (1978).

The American acceptance of Jomini was most strongly stated by
Donald and Williams (1962), was revised by Jones, and reassessed by Williams (1975). Parish provides an up-to-date and comprehensive history of
the Civil War.

Chapter 6

Colonial Warfare, and its Contribution to the Art of War in Europe

The ways in which European armies conducted their colonial operations have received little attention. The great period of imperialism, the 'scramble for Africa' of the 1880s and 1890s, and the simultaneous realisation that many of the wars of the nineteenth century had been fought outside Europe, all coincided with the emergence of German military hegemony. The study of strategy and military history was therefore centred on the writings of the Germans, but the Germans themselves had precious little experience of colonial fighting. It was as a continental power that Germany founded her claim to attention. This in itself is an indicator of where the priorities of the more truly colonial powers – pre-eminently Britain and France – lay. Orthodox war was European war. Theory and staff work were derived from Frederick and Napoleon. Between 1815 and 1914 the British army fought a European opponent only once, in the Crimea: outside Europe it barely ever stopped fighting. And yet a search in the Staff College texts of Hamley or Clery for a discussion of such operations proves vain.

The enormous variety of colonial campaigns was itself a powerful disincentive to rationalisation. It was very hard to generalise when there were so many variables. However in 1896 C. E. Callwell made just such an attempt in his book, *Small Wars. Their principles and practice* (third edition, 1906). *Small Wars* is a minor classic of compression and sophistication, and much that it says antedates the precepts of counter-insurgency operations, relearnt in the withdrawal from empire since the Second World War. Much too of what follows in this chapter relies heavily on it.

Overseas, even more than in Europe, the truism that an army is a product of its parent society held true. Military service still often remained a feudal obligation, the conduct of war the vital test of manly virtues. The adoption of the tactics and technology of their professional European opponents might undermine the very fabric of the society which its members were protecting. In 1844 Britain exported 83,721 muskets to Africa, and in the 1860s and 1870s, with the adoption by European armies of breech-loading rifles with metallic cartridges, antiquated firearms flooded the African market. There were technical problems in the use of firearms. Repair and replacement were difficult; ammunition supply was slender and the poor powder used increased the fouling and damage to the weapon. But the slowness with which muskets replaced sword and shield reflected more than this. Tribes with little formal military structure, accustomed to taking the defensive against the raids of neighbours, more readily adapted their methods of fighting to the new weapons. Thus the Pedi in 1876 successfully resisted the Boers, whereas their near-neighbours the Zulus, facing the British in 1879, used firearms only as secondary weapons, relying on the assegai and shield, the arms round which their existing regimental structure and tested tactical doctrine were built.

Callwell's categorisation of potential foes in colonial operations carried an implicit recognition of these social determinants. There were armies with a regular organisation, and often trained by Europeans. The Sikhs (finally conquered in 1849), the sepoys of the Indian Mutiny (1857) and the Egyptian nationalists crushed by Garnet Wolseley at Tel-el-Kebir in 1882 were all in this group. Often their arms were comparable to those of the Europeans: the weight and disposition of the Sikh guns was a powerful incentive in British reform of her own artillery. The same was true of Callwell's second group, semi-organised troops, the products of a reasonably structured society. He cited the Algerians, whose armament in 1830, partly thanks to British imports, included about 8,000 muskets, enough to deprive their French invaders of any technological advantage. Thirdly Callwell listed organised troops with primitive weapons – such as the Zulus. Fourth, and a little lower down the order in military sophistication, came fanatics, by which Callwell meant in particular Muslims fighting a holy war, the Hadendowa of the Red Sea coast, the Pathans of Afghanistan. His fifth category was exceptional, because racially they were European. The Boers too believed they had God on their side. They also had, by 1899, a considerable stock of experience in native wars, a state artillery armed with 155 mm Creusots, and large numbers of Mauser rifles. Administratively weak and not really capable of a major offensive in either war against the British (1880–1 and 1899–1902), they were none the less individually very hardy, expert shots and fine horsemen. Kitchener contemptuously described their tactics: 'The Boers are not like the Sudanese who stood up to a fair fight. They are always running away on their little ponies.' These were the techniques of guerrilla war, which Callwell, with examples as diverse as the Montenegrins, the Bosnians, the Maoris and the Kaffirs, put in his sixth category. The true guerrilla shuns decisive action, and therefore races such as the Ashanti, who on occasion massed to fight, formed a separate group. Last he listed irregular cavalry, men who provided their own mounts, such as the Marathas of India and the Arabs and Moors of North Africa.

Clearly many of these opponents had overlapping characteristics, but much more striking were their variations. In three successive years (1878, 1879 and 1880) in one theatre, South Africa, British troops were called on to fight Kaffirs, Zulus and Boers. Sir Neville Lyttleton cited the contrast between the battles of Omdurman (1898) and Colenso (1899): 'In the first, 50,000 fanatics streamed across the open regardless of cover to certain death, while at Colenso I never saw a Boer all day till the battle was over and it was our men who were the victims'.

Therefore the first problem of colonial warfare was not how much influence it had on European armies, but how quickly and how effectively European armies adapted to local circumstances. The disasters the British suffered at the hands of the Zulus at Isandlwhana in 1879 and of the Boers at Majuba in 1881 can be ascribed to ignorance of the likely tactics of their enemy. Most field experience in South Africa had been gained fighting Kaffirs. The gathering of intelligence was therefore the first task. But often the land in which the army was to fight was unmapped and even unexplored. In 1873 the Dutch mounted an expedition against the Sultan of Achin's stronghold at Kota Raja, on the northernmost tip of Sumatra. With part of their force they undertook an attack on a village, found the resistance stronger than expected and then withdrew. They never realised that they had actually entered Kota Raja itself. In 1864 the British dispatched a punitive expedition into Bhutan, on the borders of Tibet; 2,000 men and 150 elephants were sent 40 miles over difficult and mountainous country to capture the hill fort said to be at Bishensing. On arrival, they found a stone house inhabited by a solitary lama priest. In default of good intelligence, the tendency was to underestimate or to exaggerate the capabilities of the enemy or the problems of the terrain.

Not surprisingly, the identification of the objective was just as important as in the conduct of European war. The most successful colonial campaigns were those with specific aims and full preparations to match. Sir Robert Napier's expedition to Abyssinia in 1867–8 and Sir Garnet Wolseley's against the Ashanti in 1874 are examples. Callwell identified three types of objective. First came straight conquest or annexation: the early British campaigns in India (up until 1849) were of this type. Secondly, insurrection might follow the acquisition of territory, as the Mutiny did in India. And finally, campaigns might be needed to avenge an insult or to pacify a border. Napier's and Wolseley's wars, mentioned above, both involved penetration and then withdrawal, as did the host of punitive expeditions on the North-west Frontier. The continued wear and cost of these campaigns could eventually persuade the European power that it was cheaper to annex and settle the area. Thus the process would come full circle.

Finding a strategy to meet the end in view remained remarkably problematic. Napoleon had concentrated on bringing the enemy army to battle not least because the army was the greatest manifestation of a state's wealth, its centre of gravity. In a modern state the focus may lie in its commercial centres or its cities. But the opponents of the colonial powers rarely had a capital. Often they had no army as such, were not identifiable by uniforms and, if defeated, melted back into the bush or were reabsorbed in the civilian population. Even if they did have an army, it might still refuse battle. Therefore an alternative objective should be found: 'Your first object', Wolseley advised, 'should be the capture of whatever they prize most, and the destruction or deprivation of which will probably bring the war most rapidly to a conclusion'. Destroying their means to livelihood might thus absorb as much energy as actual combat — rounding up cattle to bring the Kaffirs to terms, eliminating the buffalo herds to press the Red Indian to settle. Burning villages on punitive raids was unlikely to be as grievous a blow as it might seem. They were so simple and the materials so ready to hand as to be easily rebuilt. The point was that, although there were inherent in these sort of strategies tendencies to total war, political sense counselled restraint. There needed to be enough violence to bring the tribesmen to terms, not so much as to drive them to unquenchable fury. 'The overawing and not the exasperation of the enemy is the end to keep in view', wrote Callwell.

The emergence of a strategy of conquest and settlement can be followed in the case of French North Africa. After their initial success in Algeria in 1830, the French found themselves embroiled in a decade of desultory war. Applying the tactics of the *Grande Armée*, they continually lashed out at thin air as the Arabs abandoned positions of no strategic significance. In 1840 Marshal Bugeaud was appointed governor-general and commander-in-chief in Algeria. Bugeaud had served in the Peninsula and therefore had some experience in the handling of guerrillas. He recognised that war in Europe and war in Algeria were different undertakings, not least because in the former the objective was an army and in the latter it was the population as a whole. He gave the French a mobility to rival that of the Arabs: columns of 6,000 men and 1,200 horses, their baggage reduced to a minimum and carried on pack animals rather than wagons, mounted rapid raids over short distances. He thus caught the enemy before they had time to disperse. At the same time, he stressed the longer term, political aim: 'The object is not the present war; victory will be sterile without colonisation. I will therefore be a fervent coloniser, for I attach less importance, less glory to victory in battle than to the establishment of something valuable and useful for France.' He built roads and bridges. He established colonies of soldier–settlers so as to provide an indigenous militia and to form the nucleus of a white population. In 1847, the British launched a similar scheme for New Zealand and South Africa, but both nations found them relatively unsuccessful.

Bugeaud's ideas were refined and developed by Galliéni (whom we will encounter later) and by the greatest of French colonial soldiers, Lyautey, commander-in-chief in Morocco from 1912 to 1925. Galliéni realised that a colonial opponent tended to retreat before advancing troops and then to return when the troops withdrew. The troops should therefore stay. In Tonkin he established posts at 25-mile intervals, and in 1893 he accompanied his military measures with the resuscitation of village economies and with the establishment of an equitable taxation system. Galliéni's practice found theoretical expression in an article written by Lyautey for the *Revue des Deux Mondes* in 1900 and entitled 'The colonial role of the army'. Lyautey put colonial operations firmly in their political context, and stressed that the two responsibilities – military command and political administration – should be united in one man. (The British in India had generated strong animosities by dividing them.) The military column, he argued, was but the first thrust. It should be followed by a well-organised occupation aimed at permanent settlement. The trappings of colonisation must therefore march with the army – 'a road is no longer simply a line of operations . . . but also the route for the commercial penetration of tomorrow'. Villages will be stormed one day and become garrisons and trading centres the next. The soldier's conduct of the war must be moderated accordingly, or bitterness will generate fresh insurgency. Lyautey saw the French soldier as teacher and craftsman, and hoped that he would eventually take his discharge and make his home in the colony he had helped establish.

Morocco provided Lyautey with an opportunity to implement his theories. In the unsettled areas, he employed mobile columns *à la* Bugeaud (although now supplemented by aircraft), but elsewhere he established towns and trading centres to draw the Arabs in and so undermine the hostile chief's authority. He likened the influence of this commercial activity to a patch of oil, gradually oozing over the countryside.

The general principles of war against guerrillas, aided and abetted by a sympathetic population, had thus become clear. First was the need to co-ordinate political control and military command, supplementing it with accurate and full intelligence. The territory had then to be divided into sections, and each section have its forces allocated to it. Thus they could get to know the area, establish local sources of information, and respond quickly to any crisis. The land had to be systematically cleared of anything on which the guerrilla could subsist. It might be flocks or herds, it might prove necessary to move the population. Flying columns needed to be poised, ready to catch the guerrillas whenever they showed themselves and before they had time to disperse again.

Many examples, with countless variations, could be cited of the application of these principles by a colonial power. In the Caucasus, the Russians tried to foster commerce, built bases and roads, and at the same time cleared the woodlands which protected the guerrillas. In the second half of the Boer War, the British drove the women and children into concentration camps, established lines of block houses and barbed wire, and formed mobile columns for great sweeps between the lines. The Field Intelligence Department grew ten times between 1900 and 1902. From late in 1901 areas were systematically cleared and then declared protected zones. Half a century later, in countering the communists in Malaya, the British army established a similar pattern. In 1952 Sir Gerald Templer was given both political and military control, whole villages were moved from the edge of the jungle and re-established elsewhere, the civilian population's security was guaranteed and bit by bit areas declared free of insurgents. The mobility of flying columns was greatly aided by the use of the helicopter.

It was the economic and political battle which really proved the foundation for military success. In Malaya Britain offered independence as soon as the communists were checked, and thus took from them their best claim to popular support. In the United States's battle with the Red Indian, it was the economic instrument which eventually broke the tribes.

Between 1840 and the end of the American Civil War in 1865, the US army did little more than patrol the frontier – and this it did inadequately. Once outside the protection of their forts, the patrols were too few and too hampered by their baggage to police the country effectively. After 1865, the wastefulness of the operation and the renewed drive westwards, headed by the railway, prompted a fresh initiative. Sherman, reflecting the axioms he had applied in Georgia, declared total war against the Sioux in 1866. The policy of putting the Indians on reservations (adopted in 1867–8) gave the army a specific target and allowed it to move over to the offensive. Sherman told General Phil Sheridan that all Indians were to be treated as enemies: 'The more we can kill this year, the less will have to be killed the next war, for the more I see of these Indians the more convinced I am that they will all have to be killed or maintained as a species of paupers'. Sheridan took the war to the Indians in the winter, when their camps were stationary and shortage of fodder rendered their ponies weak. In 1868 three columns converged on the tribes in Oklahoma and North Texas. In 1874–5, Sheridan mounted a similar campaign in North Texas and in 1876 against the Sioux in Dakota. He destroyed the buffalo herds, on which the Indians' economy was centred. Towns were established in his wake to draw the Indians into commerce. Their nomadic way of life punctured, the Indians did indeed become 'a species of paupers'. But perhaps politically the battle was never won, because the brutality with which it was conducted has left its own legacy of myth and resentment.

Improvements in cartography and mounting technological superiority helped swing the balance in favour of the colonial power. But it remained true, as Callwell observed, that 'It is perhaps the distinguishing characteristic of small wars . . . that they are in the main campaigns against nature'. The lack of intelligence, the vagaries of the climate and the ruggedness of the terrain were all major determinants in the conduct of operations. Both Napier in Abyssinia and Wolseley in the Ashanti had to time their expeditions in order to avoid the rains. Not until 1898 was the mosquito identified as the bearer of malaria, although from the 1850s quinine was in regular use as a preventive. Disease not battle was the major killer. Of 11,021 deaths in the Indian Mutiny, 8,987 were from sunstroke and sickness. In the South African war, 7,792 men were killed in action or died of wounds but 13,250 died of disease.

It is a tribute to Napier and Wolseley that in both the Abyssinian and Ashanti campaigns deaths from disease totalled only 35 and 55 respectively. This was due above all to their organisation of supply. Supply in particular depended on the geographical factors; it lay at the root of most operational difficulties and to a large degree determined the pattern of a campaign. Battles were fought to secure water. Lines of wells dictated lines of march: Wolseley's expedition to relieve Khartoum in 1884 was directed down the Nile valley, rather than by the shorter but waterless route across the desert from Suakin to Berber. Realising the mounting urgency of the situation, Wolseley detached a force ahead of the main body, which clashed with the Dervishes in a fight for the wells of Abu Klea. Although victorious, they were too late: Gordon was already dead. Not only did the men need to drink, so also did the transport animals. Animals draw more than they can carry and therefore, if the terrain was too mountainous to permit wagons, the number of beasts increased enormously. Furthermore they must bear their own feed as well as that of the troops. In Abyssinia, 13,000 combat troops required a train of 36,000 animals and 7,000 followers to tend them. The Russian force that marched from Tashkent to Khiva in 1874 had 5,500 men with 8,800 camels. In the Second Afghan War (1878) it was reckoned that to maintain an expeditionary force 36,000 strong for fifteen days 70,000 mules were required. Convoy protection therefore drew in a large proportion of the fighting force. The bigger the convoy, the slower the movement and the more difficult it proved to bring the enemy to battle. Thus supply problems kept armies small. On the North-west Frontier, where pack transport was obligatory, a column of 5,000 mules on a narrow track was about ten miles long, and it was therefore reckoned that no force should be more than four or five battalions strong. At the same time communications back to base had to be kept open. In 1898 Kitchener, in his reconquest of the Sudan, built 230 miles of railway line to effect this, but the pace of the campaign could in consequence be no faster than the rate of construction. The protection of the line of communications and the intermediate depots took men away from the striking force. In 1879, in Russia's operations against the Turkomans, only 1,400 of the original force of 16,000 were left for battle. In the Second Afghan War, the line from Kabul to Peshawar was guarded by 15,000 men, leaving only 12,000 for the field force. By the time Kitchener had allowed for the protection of garrisons and railways in the Boer republics in March 1901, only 22,000 of his original force of 200,000 remained available for offensive operations.

The enemy, however, being native to the land, were less circumscribed by problems of supply and were inured to local climatic conditions. Therefore in terms of strategy and grand tactics they at first normally possessed the advantage. But, by the beginning of the twentieth century, the progress of technology had whittled away much of their lead. Medicine had made the health of the white man more resilient. The railway had eased the supply and transport problem; it had aided the process of pacification by economic development and had broken the particularisms of tribal loyalties; and it had speeded the concentration of occupying forces to meet insurrection and disturbance. Communications were improved by the adoption of the heliograph (first used in the Second Afghan War) and then of the field telegraph. The advent of the aeroplane gave the colonial powers not only a flexible and speedy means of response but also an agent of terror.

None the less, these technological advantages were cumulative and gradual in their application to strategy. For the Europeans, the benefits of technology and also of organised discipline were much more immediate at a tactical level. The introduction of the breech-loading rifle, of the machine gun and of the pack howitzer reinforced an existing superiority in firepower. Therefore, in contrast to the emphasis of Jomini and his ilk, the object in colonial warfare was to fight, not to manoeuvre. The careful preparations and initial strategic caution that were the hallmarks of successful colonial operations were replaced by decisiveness and even rashness at the prospect of battle. A rapid victory would prevent the dissolution of the regular army through sickness or lack of supplies. Moreover, if the opportunity to do battle was not taken, the enemy might disappear again, or his confidence might soar and the Europeans' moral superiority be lost. 'That is the way to deal with Asiatics – ', Callwell wrote, 'to go for them and to cow them by sheer force of will'. In consequence Clive took 3,000 into battle against 50,000 at Plassey (1757), and Sir Charles Napier led 2,200 men against five to ten times as many Baluchis at Miani (1843). In 1865, 2,000 Russians wrested the fortified town of Tashkent from

30,000, and the following year Romanovski with 3,000 troops defeated 40,000 Bokharans at Yedshar. Vigour was made to compensate for numbers, the courage of the European was to overawe 'the lower races'. Implicit in all this was a sense of racial superiority, which admired a fine opponent as it might a fox that had provided a good day's hunting.

The importance of battle condoned various operational gambits which were not acceptable according to the Jominian canon of *grande guerre*. Forces often had to be divided into separate columns owing to the difficulties of supply and movement. It could be assumed that tribal chiefs did not know of the virtues of fighting on interior lines. In the Ashanti War, Wolseley advanced in four columns, of which two were barely worth attention but still tied down a large force. In order to give the commander a greater chance of forcing a decisive battle, it was even considered legitimate for him to abandon his communications and form flying columns. In his epic march from Kabul to Kandahar (1880), Roberts and 9,987 men, 7,000 non-combatants and 8,419 animals broke their communications through the Khyber pass, marched 300 miles in 23 days, and then reopened contacts with India through the Bolan pass in the south-east. Small forces operating in this way over a short period were essential to catch guerrillas – as Bugeaud showed in Algeria, or Kitchener in South Africa. But it could not be prolonged without damage to men and horses. If the whole army forfeited its communications, it would have to take so much baggage that its gain in mobility would be minimal. Weighed by heavy loads, the soldier's tactical alertness would be sacrificed and defeat would turn to disaster.

Once the enemy had been committed to engage, it was therefore essential for logistic and psychological reasons that a decisive victory be secured. In an economically underdeveloped country, few positions were worth strenuous defence. A frontal attack would consequently do little more than cause the enemy to fall back, whereas envelopment would cut off his line of retreat. A holding operation to the enemy's front would therefore be supplemented by an attack from the flank. Often native troops were too ill-disciplined to hold their ground, and the Afghans at Peiwar Kotal (1878) were drawn to meet the threat from the flank, thus opening their position to the front. So in colonial warfare attacks by independent but converging forces could be condoned more readily than in European war. But there remained the danger of defeat in detail. The massacre of Custer's 7th Cavalry at Little Big Horn in 1876 demonstrates this twice over: Custer had divided his force, so that one squadron was not engaged at all, and he himself led only one of three converging but separate columns. The British invasion of Zululand three years later is even more instructive. The force commander, Lord Chelmsford, appreciated that his baggage would preclude a war of manoeuvre. Instead he directed three converging columns on the Zulus' capital at Ulundi, in order to force them to give battle. He timed his invasion to precede the gathering of the harvest, so as effectively to equalise the supply problem. One of his columns was defeated at Isandlwhana, but the other two met at Ulundi, formed a massive square and broke the Zulus on its fire. The cavalry completed the action. The strategic concept with its threat of famine hovering over all Zulus – not just the warriors – collapsed at Isandlwhana, but eventually allowed the exploitation of European tactical superiority at Ulundi.

In some respects, therefore, colonial warfare undermined the precepts of *grande guerre* orthodoxy. The division of forces, the abandonment of lines of communication, the push to total war, all were pointers to the future. Other aspects were retrogressive. The tactics of each arm pick out even more clearly this two-edged effect.

The most grievous consequence of prolonged colonial campaigning was the derogation of artillery. Its relative immobility, and its compounding of the supply and transport problems, encouraged its dispensation. But, more than that, artillery preparation could actually have an adverse effect. It might drive the enemy from the field before the other arms had an opportunity to close. If guns were used, they were dispersed and kept well forward. Their role, by firing on the retreating enemy, was to complete – not commence – the battle.

Cavalry retained an importance in colonial war long after it had been lost in European war. The lack of cavalry for reconnaissance was a grievous loss to the British at the outset of both Boer Wars. But in addition, the shock action of cavalry was deemed to have a disproportionate moral effect on natives. Its mobility aided the development of flank attacks and allowed the full prosecution of pursuit, turning defeat into rout. Probably the biggest problem it faced was the procurement of adequate forage. Poorly fed horses rapidly became broken and unfit. The British lost 66 per cent of the 500,000 horses they used in the Second Boer War. Cavalry so stricken had to limit its scouting activities and at Poplar Grove in 1900 Sir John French's division could not even charge. The next constraint on the cavalry's effectiveness was not the enemy's fire (which was unlikely to be very disciplined) but the looseness of his formations. As Callwell put it, 'In regular warfare the main object of the charge is to throw the adversary into just such confusion as constitutes the normal battle order of Pathans, Sudanese, Somalis and their like'. The cavalry might therefore pass through without great effect. The Sudanese in particular lay on the ground, out of reach of the sword. Consequently the lance retained a relevance that it had lost in European war. Many of the famous charges with the lance belong to colonial, not European, history – the 16th Lancers against the Sikhs at Aliwal (1846), the 21st Lancers at Omdurman (1898). But in both casualties were disproportionately heavy, and in both the value of the arm questioned. In was useless in mêlée, since a lancer had to keep his opponent to his front and right (and at a distance) if he was to deliver the blow. None the less in 1914 the lance had the widest distribution it had ever enjoyed in the cavalries of Europe. Observers had failed fully to appreciate that the shock effect of a cavalry charge derived not from weaponry but from the impact of galloping horses.

If colonial warfare had an unfortunate influence in its encouragement of the lance, a reverse case – of colonial practice running ahead of continental precept – can be found in the development of mounted infantry. The difficulties of supply, quite apart from the reluctance to spend money on colonial operations, meant that small bodies of men had to fulfil several roles. Furthermore the strategic value of mounted troops, in their ability to mount flying columns or patrol great areas, meant that cavalry needed to be able to operate on foot as much as on horseback. European orthodoxy tended to argue – whatever the tactical flexibility – that dismounted cavalry could never match true infantry and mounted infantry would be but bastard cavalry. However, at the Cape from the 1840s the British found a pressing need for more mounted infantry; cavalry were given long rifles, not carbines, and infantrymen found themselves astride ponies. Each war in South Africa only re-emphasised the need for horsemen. In North Africa, the *Chasseurs d'Afrique* rapidly established themselves as a *corps d'élite*, and it was their dismounted fire which covered the withdrawal of the Light Brigade after its notorious charge at Balaclava. At Little Big Horn too, the 7th Cavalry dismounted to fire. Their performance might seem to confirm all the suspicions about hybrids: they discharged over 40,000 rounds for 60 Indians killed and 100 wounded. But the development of firepower in Europe deprived the cavalry of its shock effect in the charge, while leaving the strategic importance of the horse in raiding, reconnoitring and reinforcement unimpaired. Pointers from colonial warfare were not in this case irrelevant.

A similar process – of getting as much for as little money as possible – blurred distinctions in the infantry. The separation into light infantry and infantry was a specialisation no longer relevant in most colonial theatres. It was not so much the enemy's weapons and tactics as the nature of the terrain that dictated formations. The accurate musketry of the hillmen of the North-west Frontier compelled dispersion. All infantry had to be adept as skirmishers and sharpshooters. In the bush or the jungle, ranges were short and close-quarter fighting the norm. The problems of fire control and communications meant small sections with control delegated to junior officers and NCOs. At these levels, the tactics of colonial warfare were abetting the drift in Europe.

However, in open ground, especially in the desert, the battle harked back to the practices of the previous century. The shock of a massed native charge could break a loose skirmishing line. What was needed was close order. At Tel-el-Kebir (1882), Wolseley's men attacked in two continuous lines, and at Atbara, in Kitchener's Nile campaign of 1898, the front was formed in line and the rear in company columns. In the offensive, there was a consequent tendency to rate the firmness of the onset over the effect of firepower. Skobelev, the brilliant Russian commander, told his men in their operations against the Turkomans in 1880: 'We shall conquer by means of close mobile and pliable formations, by careful, well-aimed volley firing, and by the bayonet which is in the hands of men who by discipline and soldier-like feeling have been made into a united body – the column is always terrifying'. The deliberate onset of a disciplined body intimidated the enemy, avoided over-heating the men, and allowed them to be sufficiently steady to pour in volleys on the fleeing foe. It all assumed that the fire of the enemy was itself poor.

In defence, the virtues of solidity and discipline were again pre-eminent. With breech-loading rifles, line might be sufficient, but for real security the square was preferred. Tribesmen tended to push to the flanks and rear in enveloping movements. A square countered these tactics, while at the same time protecting the non-combatants and allowing efficient fire-control. It had disappeared in European warfare because it provided a good target for hostile fire, especially artillery, and also because its own fire in any one direction was only a quarter of the musketry available to it. Movement across ground was very slow and easily disrupted the formation. At Abu Klea, a square was broken by the camels within it causing it to bulge and by the simultaneous withdrawal of skirmishers back into the square, who thus masked the fire of their colleagues. Once the enemy was inside the square, the break in cohesion could be disastrous. Therefore reserves were kept within, particularly near the corners, where the fire was less and where the enemy attack tended to be directed. Cavalry outside the square could screen it. They could dismount to fire from the flanks to help it restore its order. Similarly two squares, not one, could support each other with flanking fire. After the British disaster at the hands of the Zulus at Isandlwhana (1879) the volley-firing square became an increasingly important response to the exigencies of colonial war. But the fire-swept battlefields of Europe demanded open order formations, and a degree of individual initiative and self-imposed fire control which the square actively discouraged.

The fundamental tactical debate in Europe between 1870 and 1914 concerned the response to the development of firepower. How was the offensive to be maintained? What role remained for shock action? These questions will be discussed in chapter 8, but they had their colonial parallels. The British army, fighting in the clear air and open country of South Africa, with smokeless powder, against an opponent skilled in marksmanship and reluctant to engage in a conventional offensive, found itself faced by this dilemma. As early as the battle of Elandslaagte (October 1899), Ian Hamilton got one battalion to deploy on a front of 1,000 yards, in a formation almost a mile deep. Furthermore its attack was held up until that from the flank had developed. Rather than achieve the early decisive victory of colonial war, the British had to accept a prolonged campaign. The Boers on the Tugela river dug deep entrenchments, and had their artillery in prepared and concealed positions. Gradually the British learnt how to respond: the artillery must not only prepare the assault, it must also continue to fire ahead of the infantry; the infantry should advance in dispersed order and in rushes; the cavalry must rely as much on the rifle as on the sword and lance. But, the war over, the problem of analysis began. How far were the experiences of South Africa unique, and how far were they pointers to future trends? British tactical doctrine was thoroughly reworked before the First World War, and South African experience was crucial in that analysis. Lord Roberts was the dynamic force. He had the ability to integrate his experience: South Africa confirmed the views his Indian service had already fostered. He had used cavalry as mounted infantry in Afghanistan in 1879, he had urged the adoption of quick-firing artillery in 1893. And he then related the South African to European war: speaking of artillery, he said, 'Our experiences in South Africa have shown us, that . . . we were considerably behind the European nations at the commencement of the late war'. Between 1902 and 1905 the training manuals of all three arms were revised, with the emphasis on defensive firepower. But then the doubts set in. European practice still stressed the cavalry charge: the extreme ranges of South Africa would not be repeated in the confined terrain of Europe. In 1909 the *arme blanche* was restored and the 1904 cavalry training manuals' emphasis on dismounted duties was offset by continued talk of the moral effect of the charge.

Clearly some colonial experience was irrelevant in other theatres. Frederick in the eighteenth century failed to see the application of American irregular warfare to Prussia. But it still affected British thinking. At the very least, the handling of mounted infantry, the resort to dispersed infantry formations, even if seen as confined to colonial warfare immediately, made their eventual adoption easier when their need in European war was established. Officers' attitudes had been subliminally undermined, the men's training at least half-effected. The failure was one of analysis. The difficulty of deciding which experiences in colonial warfare had long-term value might not be appreciated until comparable trends were evident in *grande guerre*.

The problem was also one of personnel and personalities. In Britain, the thinking officers tended to fall into two camps: those around Roberts were schooled in India and saw the subcontinent as the heart of British strategy; Wolseley's ring increasingly looked to Europe and to the imagined invasion of Britain, not least in order to undermine the influence of Roberts. In consequence, the tactical lessons of South Africa and India might be underplayed. In the United States, the war in the West had a similarly divisive effect. The Indian wars made the soldiers fighting them professional but isolated. Those less cut off, and they were always more than half the officer corps, were to be found in the East. What they said could be heard, what the Indian fighters said could not. Wendell Phillips declared in 1870: 'I only know the names of three savages upon the plains – Colonel Baker, General Custer, and at the head of all, General Sheridan'.

In France, the integration of colonial and continental thinking was fuller than elsewhere. Between 1830 and 1854, 67 of 100 French infantry regiments served in Algeria for an average of six years. Up to 1870, four to six cavalry regiments were in North Africa at any one time. Although specialist colonial corps were formed, they were in a minority, constituted an élite and were used elsewhere – in the Crimea, in Italy, in Mexico, and ultimately in France itself. When Napoleon III came to power in 1851, he elevated young generals who had made their names in Algeria – Bosquet, Bourbaki, Trochu, MacMahon, Canrobert, Pelissier and St Arnaud. These were the commanders who led the French army in the subsequent European wars. The successful generals of the later stages of the Franco-Prussian War, Faidherbe and Chanzy, and the commanders of the Marne in 1914, Joffre and Galliéni, all boasted a colonial heritage. The colonial army was given a separate constitution in 1900. It came to see itself as breathing life and spirit into a metropolitan force that was otherwise vulnerable to the decadence and bureaucratisation of home service.

The effects of this colonial experience could – without rigorous analysis – be highly damaging. Bugeaud's strength had lain in his realisation that

Algeria was different from European war. His successors admired him but failed to apply the distinction. Regiments arrived from North Africa to defend France in 1870 with completely self-sufficient baggage trains suitable only for the desert. In his retreat to Metz, Bazaine followed Bugeaud's principles for desert war – they stressed the need to keep contact with the rearguard and to care for the wounded. Troops closed up at night, and thus the rear battalions set off late and arrived late, often under arms continuously for twenty-four hours. In this way Bazaine limited his column's movement to 1 kilometre an hour. In other respects, however, and particularly with reference to tactics, the effects were more beneficial. It was the African troops who performed best in 1854 and in 1870; their reconnaissance, their skirmishing, their use of ground, and their construction of field fortifications struck a note of independence which was exemplified above all in their self-sufficiency in the field. In the Crimea, British commentators again and again observed the Zouave carrying all his own equipment and foraging successfully for food, which he then prepared with the skill for which his nation is renowned.

In the final analysis then, small wars imparted readiness in the field, the military habits of resilience and instinctive behaviour under fire. But because the forces engaged were small, the staffs remained underdeveloped and the emphasis still rested on personal leadership. The impact of technology on war between civilised armies might also be obscured. The professional qualities of courage and initiative still seemed more important than the administrative ability to handle mass armies.

In general terms therefore colonial warfare confirmed the trend already implicit in Jomini back to an eighteenth-century conception of war. War was pushed to Europe's peripheries. If the great powers clashed in the colonies – as Britain and France did at Fashoda in 1898 – then they were at pains to confine the clash to that area. And war itself had eighteenth-century features. Armies were small because of the problems of supply – no agricultural revolutions here to allow large-scale requisitioning. The organisation of marches therefore became central to strategy, and made it difficult to achieve battle. A limited conception of strategy was compounded by the relative importance of tactics. The European armies' preeminence resided in discipline and in technology: tactics not strategy were the means to apply this superiority. And so the professional arcana dominated. The difficulties of slow transport and long acclimatisation, the need to have a readily disposable force rather than a large reserve, meant that long-service professional armies were as well-adapted to the needs of empire as they were to the thinking of liberal economists. Thus, the values of the army, or even the regiment, rather than society as a whole, lay at the heart of military thought. Particularism made for high morale, even arrogance, but it was ill-adapted to rapid expansion in the event of European war. However, Prussia, free of colonial experience, beset by the most acute of all strategic problems in the defence of her frontiers and with a radically different military heritage, developed in a quite distinct and independent fashion.

Guide to Further Reading

The gaps in the literature are considerable. There are insufficient general treatments, insufficient analyses of specific operations, and insufficient accounts of individual colonial armies. Kiernan (1982) gives a breezy and somewhat cynical chronological résumé, but his brief is too great and his compass too short for a sophisticated treatment. Callwell, as the major work of theory, remains essential: it has recently been reprinted. For the impact of technology outside Europe and for some bibliographical suggestions, see Headrick. The *Journal of African History* (Vol. 12, 1971) has two special issues devoted to the subject of firearms in Africa.

The ideas of Bugeaud are discussed by Bourgin, and those of Bugeaud, Galliéni and Lyautey in Earle, chapter 10. Munholland gives a case study. The French colonial army still awaits a major book, but its impact on the metropolitan army is considered by Regnault and Porch (1981), chapter 8.

For the Americans, Weigley (1973), chapter 8, gives a brief introduction, and this can be supplemented by R. M. Utley's 'The contribution of the frontier to the American military tradition', in Tate. Utley's two volumes, *Frontiersmen in Blue* (New York, 1967) and *Frontier Regulars* (New York, 1973), deal with the US army's war against the Indian.

Bond (1967) provides a general introduction to Britain's problems, and goes on to cover some of the nineteenth-century campaigns. The outstanding exception, the Boer War, is dealt with in lively and controversial fashion by Pakenham. Donald C. Gordon has a bibliographical essay in Robin Higham (ed.), *A guide to the sources of British military history* (London, 1972), chapter 11. Bailes (1980) looks at technology and the British army in Africa. On Wolseley and Roberts, see A. W. Preston (1978).

Chapter 7

Clausewitz and the Rise of Prussian Military Hegemony

In the English-speaking world, Clausewitz has for long laboured under the accusations of obscurity and complexity. Typecast as a verbose Teuton, he has been often quoted but rarely read. The encapsulations of Cyril Falls, who dubbed Clausewitz 'the high priest in the Temple of Mars', and of Liddell Hart, for whom he was 'the Mahdi of the Mass', demonstrate how even normally perceptive observers have succumbed to the attractions of pernicious phraseology. But by endowing Clausewitz with the aura of semi-mystical prophet, they do at least reveal a common thread in the military response to the outstanding European writer on war.

Clausewitz's principal work, *Vom Kriege*, was left unfinished, and the main themes of its books one and eight were never fully incorporated into the rest of the text. Inconsistencies do therefore arise and, to the military mind especially, these inconsistencies appear far more damaging than in fact they are. Searching for principles, for system, soldiers have been confused to find instead a philosophical and historical discourse. However, approaching *Vom Kriege* as Clausewitz himself approached the problem of war – with an open mind – its thrust is clear. It says much for a work concerned with a *métier* so prey to technological change that, although written in the 1820s, it continues to stimulate strategists in the nuclear age. Thanks not least to Peter Paret's and Michael Howard's admirable new translation, *Vom Kriege* is rid of the worst accretions and accreditations of Prussian militarism. The inspiration of its author can now be put more clearly in the context of his times.

Carl von Clausewitz was born in 1780. Shortly before his twelfth birthday, he entered the Prussian army and in 1793 came under fire for the first time. He saw the clash of the old order of Prussian absolutism and the new of revolutionary France, he was present at the eclipse of the former by the latter at Jena in 1806, and then, infuriated by his nation's complaisant attitude to the French, in 1812 threw in his lot with the Russians. The year 1815 found him restored to the Prussian army and serving at Ligny. All these were experiences crucial to the writing of *Vom Kriege*. In 1818, he was appointed Director of the *Kriegsakademie*. It was a post he owed to Gneisenau, the intemperate advocate of a Prussian nation in arms, and it was again Gneisenau who asked that Clausewitz serve as his chief of staff in the Polish campaign of 1831. Both contracted cholera and died.

Suffering and sadness were important themes in Clausewitz's understanding of his own life. Blessed with a wife, Marie von Brühl, whose devotion ensured the posthumous publication – albeit unrevised and unfinished – of *Vom Kriege*, he none the less had to undergo an eight-year courtship and the prolonged separations military service imposed. He coveted noble status and yet did not have it confirmed until 1827. On his own terms his career was a failure. Like the other Prussian reformers, he was caught between his respect for the Crown and his admiration for some of the ideas of the French Revolution. His decision in 1812, to turn against his king, represented a personal crisis as much as a set-back to his hopes of advancement. Although, relatively speaking, still professionally successful, he remained in the second rank of Prussian reformers. He was no Gneisenau himself. He never commanded an army in the field, he never won the plaudits due a conquering hero. And yet his thirst for military glory, coupled perhaps with its destructive aspects (especially his hatred for the French), revealed the inner tension in a man whose forte was as a student and thinker. Much of Clausewitz's brilliance lies in this personal torment, in his embodiment of seemingly irreconcilable poles – the military virtues, with their drift to brutality and their suppression of self, and the academic refinement of individual judgement, where the right questions are more important than pat answers.

An influence comparable to Gneisenau in Clausewitz's life was another paladin of the Prussian reformers, Scharnhorst. In the years before Jena, through the Berlin Institute for Young Officers and the *Militärische Gesellschaft*, Scharnhorst restored the confidence of the youthful Clausewitz who in turn saw his mentor as a second father. It was at this stage of his life that Clausewitz began to form the leading ideas of *Vom Kriege*. Scharnhorst was contemptuous of theories of war. The important thing was to see war as it really is, and for this history – not logic – must be the guide. Intellectually, Behrenhorst, with his emphasis on the contradictions and imponderables of war, was the military writer who most clearly foreshadowed this approach. Furthermore Behrenhorst had recognised that total military change could not be achieved without political reform. It was this emphasis on the primacy of politics, of which military force was simply one expression, that made the writings of Machiavelli so attractive to Clausewitz.

On the other side, *Vom Kriege* is the fruit of philosophy. Clausewitz himself said he took Montesquieu as a model. The short chapters and apparent lack of system give *Vom Kriege* a resemblance to *L'Esprit des Lois*. At the Berlin Institute, Clausewitz was influenced by Kiesewetter, a populariser of Kant. Kant's distinction between things as they really are (noumena) and things as they may appear (phenomena) is a tension reflected throughout *Vom Kriege*. Like the products of the *Sturm und Drang* movement, Clausewitz's work builds on the Enlightenment but recognises that not everything is susceptible to reason; it is a flower of German Romanticism. War is depicted as above all uncertain, an area in which the individual is always striving to rationalise the inchoate forces he encounters. This he does by understanding the essence of war itself. Success in the struggle means that the conquering general is a hero. Kant's influence can clearly not be pushed too far: the *Perpetual Peace* is hardly compatible with *Vom Kriege*. Clausewitz's style, the combative approach of question and answer, is more suggestive of Hegel. His hatred for the French and his view of the nation as an individual organism coincide with a Hegelian interpretation of the relations between nation states. However, in the last analysis, Clausewitz is himself. Hegel's dialectic aims at the establishment of principles, Clausewitz's at the acknowledgement of a genuine and insoluble tension. *Vom Kriege* sustains a balance: on the one hand it incorporates emotional and unknowable factors and on the other it relates them to personal observation, historical interpretation and speculative reasoning. Military history was the key to the development of a soldier's judgement. It must of course be accurate military history, that goes remorselessly back to prime causes, that does not discard facts which fail to fit the pattern.

Such a study confirmed Scharnhorst's tenet, that the factors at the heart of war were unquantifiable. This led Clausewitz to outright dismissal of the strategic theorists searching for the general principles of war and for the establishment of systems of universal validity. The Napoleonic Wars had not proved conclusively the worth of the system of the *ancien régime* or of that of the Revolution. Jomini and Bülow, with their emphasis on geometry and their synthesis of only those factors susceptible to calculation, were Clausewitz's main butts. He did not deny the value of their precepts, provided only that their limitations be fully acknowledged. The axiom of numerical superiority on the decisive point had become oversimplified. Supply, because it was a reckonable factor, had assumed excessive importance. 'If war is to be waged in accordance with its essential spirit', Clausewitz wrote, ' – with the unbridled violence at its core, the craving and need for battle and decision – then feeding the troops, though important, is a secondary matter.' Armies had become more self-sufficient in the field, and a disruption to their lines of communication was not necessarily, in the short term, significant. A general with the will to battle, such as Napoleon, would not be put off. Bülow's emphasis on the base of operations was helpful but obscured the fact that the base was an expression of physical geography not of geometry, and that the use of local resources and depots spread it over such a wide area that it could no longer be treated as an entity. Jomini's interior lines were valid but through exaggeration had become distorted: the commander in a central position could, by driving one of the opposing forces back with vigour, force the other to conform rather than have to turn to fight it separately. Jomini and Bülow had aimed 'at fixed values; but in war everything is uncertain, and calculations have to be made with variable quantities'. Anything that could not be assimilated within their framework was beyond scientific control and ascribed to genius.

Therefore, Clausewitz argued, genius and intellect were chief among the uncertain factors that lay at the heart of the understanding of war. The routine and method of tactical precepts gave junior commanders rapid reactions in critical situations: the solidity they imparted ensured confidence in the troops and bought time for their leader to consider his next move. But, as the smashing of Frederick's army at Jena had so vividly demonstrated, routine in strategy destroyed the flexibility essential to genuine awareness. A general had to be able to respond positively to the unexpected.

The romantic in Clausewitz called for 'an intellect that, even in the darkest hour, retains some glimmerings of the inner light which leads to truth; and second, the courage to follow this faint light wherever it may lead'. So much of war passed in a fog that genius, coupled with strength of will, presence of mind, ambition and imagination, was essential if fleeting opportunities were to be seized. And for this, above all, was required courage. 'Boldness can lend wings to intellect and insight.'

The preparation of the individual for this supreme moment was the task of theory. Its role was not utilitarian, but it should teach by way of conceptions; it should facilitate understanding and provide standards of evaluation. Rather than dogma, criticism should come to the aid of sound judgement. The relationship between history and theory was close. For the former enabled the student to see how things occur, while the latter provided a tool to clarify its most important points. The education of the officer should not therefore prescribe formulae but should sharpen the individual's critical faculties. Reflecting the influence of Pestalozzi, who had defined education as more a process of drawing men out than driving information in, Clausewitz liked to see the *Kriegsakademie* not as an institution for professional training but as a small university.

This Socratic approach allowed Clausewitz to consider the study of war as a *tabula rasa*. The reason for his greatness is that he alone of military writers assumed nothing. Shibboleths came crashing down behind him. First of these was that war could never be limited of itself. 'War is an act of force', he wrote, 'and there is no logical limit to the application of that force.' Violence is at its core: killing and maiming are absolutes. International law and custom exercise little practical restraint. For his own generation, Napoleon had given fresh and horrific meaning to what in previous generations might have been only concept. But even if fought for limited aims, the belligerents could not justify the employment of limited effort. The other side might use all the means at its disposal, and therefore the most direct and immediate way to victory was best. Absolute war was therefore a unified concept which could embrace the interpretation of all wars, whatever their aims. It resolved (or perhaps skirted) the problem of whether the wars of Napoleon were normal or abnormal, whether the style of eighteenth-century warfare would be revived.

In practice, Clausewitz argued, the ideal of absolute war was unattainable. The first and most pervasive limitation on war's conduct was its subordination to politics. Political circumstances gave rise to war, political consequences accrue from it, and therefore politics should determine the direction and course of its strategy. The insight was not new. The absolutism of eighteenth-century monarchs gave them control of both the military and political spheres, and their conduct of strategy represented the interplay of the two. Reflecting this inheritance, Scharnhorst, as well as many lesser figures, had dilated on the need to integrate politics and the art of war. Clausewitz's contribution was to give it priority, and to show its relationship to 'absolute' war. It is the contribution to strategic thought for which Clausewitz is justly most celebrated, and, if he had lived, it would have become the main theme throughout *Vom Kriege*. However, the fact that he had started but not completed this revision has left inconsistencies which confuse the argument. At one stage Clausewitz writes: 'War is not a mere act of policy but a true political instrument, a continuation of political activity by other means'. He seems here to be equating the two, even to be condoning the dominance of war over politics, but elsewhere the drift is firmly to emphasise the subordination of war to politics. War is incomplete and self-contradictory, and therefore inherently unable to follow its own laws. Consequently it must be treated as a part of a greater whole. War may have its own grammar but not its own logic: the logic is determined by politics. 'Policy is the guiding intelligence and war only the instrument.' Therefore politics moderate the conduct of war. If war becomes an untrammelled act of violence, it can usurp policy for its own ends. Thus, in the context of the previous chapter, a vicious suppression of a tribal uprising could leave a legacy of animosity which would undermine the subsequent peace and might even lead to fresh insurrection. The crucial point was the need always to remember that war springs from a political purpose, and to allow the prime cause 'to remain the supreme consideration in conducting it'.

Initially Clausewitz engaged in little discussion about what the political aims might be. He simply envisaged either the complete defeat of the enemy or the achievement of something more restricted, such as the acquisition of a province. In his last book, book eight, he expanded (although not to great length) his ideas on wars of limited aims. Assuming the defeat of the enemy was impossible, a power might either fight defensively in the hope of the situation improving or alternatively it might wage an offensive war but with a limited aim. It could seize territory in order to weaken the enemy's resources and equip itself with a bargaining counter, it could launch a pre-emptive or preventive war before the enemy's strength increased, or – if the future remained indecisive – it could go to war while it had the political initiative. In all this Clausewitz still tended to talk in operational terms, and therefore to offset what he said by stressing the primacy of the rapid and decisive offensive. Policy may have been the overarching consideration but *its* nature was not discussed. He therefore treated war as an integral part of the world order: the liberal optimists of the Anglo-Saxon world could hardly receive a more realistic (or pessimistic) corrective to their view of international affairs. War was regarded as inevitable, not impossible. Its outbreak was treated as a question of timing – not 'never' but 'when?'

The aims to be achieved in war would limit the means employed. Particularly in a pre-industrial society, all the resources of a country could not be deployed instantaneously or simultaneously. However, Clausewitz defined these resources in much wider terms than simple manpower: he spoke of possible allies, of the strength of the government, of the innate qualities of the peoples. He saw fresh heights in mobilisation as the product of 'the peoples' new share in these great affairs of state'. The other shares, in Raymond Aron's analysis of Clausewitz, were taken by the general and by the government. These three constitute a 'trinity', an idea which Aron sees as a fruit of Clausewitz's later revisions. The 'trinity' occupies a spectrum where emotion gradually gives place to reason: the people are guided by violent feelings, the general submits to the dictates of his own genius, while the government provides political direction. It is striking that this analysis of war's own nature owes more to the French Revolution than to the Industrial Revolution. Clausewitz did not envisage technological developments in themselves raising the means employed, and nor – a much more striking omission – did he really talk about economic mobilisation. The determinants remained social and political. The danger in defeat leads each side to increase its effort, but the brake on this interaction is the threat of domestic problems should the means cease to be commensurate with the ends.

Clausewitz argued that the ideal of 'absolute' war was limited in a second, much more immediate way, which he dubbed 'friction'. 'Four elements make up the climate of war,' he wrote, 'danger, exertion, uncertainty and chance.' These inbuilt characteristics thwart the achievement of great conceptions in war. He likened war to walking on water: the problems of the individual, sickness, exhaustion, human error and poor morale, are multiplied many times over in an army of thousands. And in such large bodies of men irrational forces can play a disproportionate part. Rumour before the battle can undermine confidence; the battle itself bears little resemblance to that which peacetime manoeuvres have led the soldier to expect, and in the course of it subjective impressions predominate over mature reflection. The general himself is prey to 'friction' in innumerable forms – his army is never as strong in the field as it is on paper, his intelligence is never as detailed as he might wish it to be, his supply arrangements are perpetually threatened with breakdown. But his skill as a commander lies not in dismissing these matters as aberrations, imagining that great captains before him have by luck or good judgement been free of them. Rather, it lies in his acceptance of them: by understanding 'friction' and its constraints, the general is better able to master it.

Consideration of friction led Clausewitz to discussion of war itself. Here too the ideal of 'absolute' war, the acknowledgement of violence, led to a sharp distinction between him and the Jominian school. The destruction of the enemy's forces is the implicit object of war, and battle is the only means by which to achieve that. 'Since the essence of war is fighting, and since the battle is the fight of the main force, the battle must always be considered as the true centre of gravity of the war.' Furthermore that battle must be conceived as potentially decisive – 'a struggle for real victory, waged with all available strength'. The purpose of manoeuvre, therefore, is not to threaten lines of communication but to come to grips with the enemy. Strategy Clausewitz defined as 'the use of the engagement for the purpose of the war'. The number and scale of engagements were therefore far more important than 'the pattern of the major lines connecting them'. The divisional or corps system was not so much an order of march, designed to simplify logistic problems, as a potential order of battle, each formation being ready to support the other.

The true commander should put aside procrastination, should not let fears generated by the nature of the terrain or the lack of intelligence deter him from seeking battle at the earliest possible opportunity. The awareness of the significance of a major battle, the suspense generated in the two camps the previous night, ensures that victory or defeat can perhaps have a moral effect far greater than their intrinsic worth. But it was not simply psychological effect that Clausewitz sought in battle: 'We are not interested in generals who win victories without bloodshed. The fact that slaughter is a horrifying spectacle must make us take war more seriously, but not provide an excuse for gradually blunting our swords in the name of humanity. Sooner or later someone will come along with a sharp sword and hack off our arms.' It is this sort of passage, the emphasis on the direct annihilation of the enemy, that has encouraged the portrayal of Clausewitz as a butcher. Furthermore, he argued, the trend towards major battles in the Napoleonic Wars, the growing size of armies, the availability of reserves and the rapidity of their deployment, meant that there was a much greater reluctance to concede victory. Battles were tending towards attrition: victory was gained through the exhaustion of one or other side. Therefore numerical superiority was central, and the winners must take the opportunity of success to guarantee a favourable balance of forces. The memory of Jena pressed on Clausewitz's mind as he pointed out that pursuit of the retreating army was the true opportunity to inflict really crippling loss.

In talking about battle, therefore, Clausewitz found himself in one respect at least in accord with Jomini. The most common element in victory was superiority of numbers on the decisive point. It was important in strategic terms to be able to concentrate all available forces on the day of battle, even if in tactical terms they might be committed gradually according to the enemy's position and strength. Although – like Jomini – Clausewitz preferred to advance with his army massed, he had grasped sufficiently the essence of Napoleonic success to see that terrain and transport might make a converging attack alone possible. A successful envelopment battle, which cut off the enemy's line of retreat, was indeed the most decisive form of battle. In implementing it, as the difficulties of communication would render full co-ordination impossible, each column should act independently, with only the general outline of the plan specified.

Clausewitz said that the destruction of the enemy forces was the path to victory, but he none the less acknowledged that the main pivot of their power might in fact lie elsewhere – not with their army but in a major city or with an ally. This distinction is more meaningful today than it was then. It was essential to identify this focus, and then attack it with speed and mass, forcing all subsidiary concerns and objectives to conform to the importance of the major one. By decisive action, using surprise and relegating Jominian concerns about lines and bases, the attacker wrests the moral initiative from the enemy.

Eventually, however, the drive of the attack exhausts itself. Victory no longer seems imminent. Clausewitz dubbed this phase 'the culminating point of victory'. If success has not yet been secured, a period of defence must now follow. Every attack which does not lead to peace must necessarily give way to defence.

Clausewitz, alone of his contemporaries, and almost alone among military theorists of any generation, saw defence as the stronger means. The moral importance of the attack, which Clausewitz himself embraced, has led soldiers to regard it as necessarily the first stage in a war. Clausewitz, however, saw that the first stage might be to wait. Allow the enemy to exhaust himself and his men: he advances, his communications lengthen, his fear of counter-attack increases. The defender falls back on prepared positions, his communications become shorter and more direct. In the short term he seems to be losing; in the long term the balance is swinging to him. Historically Frederick's conduct of the Seven Years' War hallowed this advice for Prussians. More immediate examples for Clausewitz were the Peninsular War and, above all, Napoleon's 1812 campaign. As the defender gives ground, so he can denude his country of crops and livestock: partisans fall on the flanks and rear of the invader. Eventually the attack passes the 'culminating point of victory', and the defender, his strength concentrated and husbanded, counter-attacks. Clausewitz is here talking of the value of the defence in strategic terms. However, in the second half of the nineteenth century, technology gave it also the tactical advantage, and his acknowledgement of the strength of the defence endowed Clausewitz with a continuing relevance not vouchsafed to his contemporaries.

Clausewitz's assertion that defence is the stronger means sets up a tension with his earlier emphasis on the will to battle. The contradiction is more apparent than real. There is no logical flaw, but to soldiers looking for distinct guidelines this sort of complexity encouraged a tendency either to regard *Vom Kriege* as useless or to use it selectively. It is Clausewitz's very honesty which has led to cynicism in his interpretation. But we must not be led into hero-worship. Some omissions in *Vom Kriege* have already been cited. The value of surprise received little attention. Clausewitz's use of history was more selective than he liked to admit: a specific event was used to illustrate an idea or to develop a conception, while 'friction' could cover evidence that might prove discordant. Liddell Hart castigated his neglect of seapower. Much of his specifically military thinking was no more than the orthodoxy of his day – massing on the decisive point, and so on. Many examples and ideas were naturally enough derived from the eighteenth century. Even his central concept of the relationship between war and politics testifies to this, but there are other examples. In his portrayal of war, reason and deliberation are threatened by chance and uncertainty, but in the end rationality is assumed to dominate in political counsel. War does not develop its own momentum through the arousal of popular passions, but is guided by enlightened and far-seeing statesmen. On the other hand some eighteenth-century concepts were too readily jettisoned. Morality may play a greater part in restraining the push to absolute war than Clausewitz was prepared to admit: war is a state activity, not an individual's resort to violence, and armies employ force with deliberation. Their members are themselves educated in the values of their own societies: in Clausewitz's Europe the Christian respected the life of a fellow Christian. At the more mundane level of operations, Clausewitz glossed over the problems of supply. His anxiety to combat the prescriptions of Jomini and his predecessors added to his topicality but undermined the comprehensiveness of his analysis. In the long term his neglect of the economic factors and of the impact of technological advance was an outstanding weakness. Absolute war was to become progressively less conceptual and more real. The time taken to mobilise its resources no longer impedes the nuclear state's ability to fight total war.

In recent years Clausewitz's reputation has waxed ever stronger, but for his own generation *Vom Kriege* had minimal impact. Willisen was read at home, Jomini abroad. The first edition of 1,500 copies was still not sold out twenty years after its publication in 1832. His brother-in-law then revised *Vom Kriege* for a second edition, simplifying the text and in certain cases laying the foundation for subsequent misinterpretation. Clausewitz had argued that the commander-in-chief be a member of the Cabinet, so that the latter could be fully informed on military matters. The second edition of his book suggested that the purpose of the commander-in-chief's membership was to allow him to take a part in the Cabinet's ordering of civil affairs. Rather than guarantee political control of the conduct of war, the emphasis was being swung towards war's equality with politics. It was an interpretation which had its roots in the incompleteness of the book, but it was one which gained progressively in weight.

The European discovery of Clausewitz is closely related to the emergence of Helmuth von Moltke, chief of the Prussian general staff from 1857 to 1888. Although Moltke was a widely read man, *Vom Kriege* was the only military work that influenced him decisively. Like Clausewitz (and indeed many other luminaries of the Prussian army), he was an outsider. In the former's case the distinction was social, in Moltke's national – he was born and brought up a Dane. Like Clausewitz too, his command of troops in the field was very limited. Moreover, although seen as the harbinger of a new order in warfare, Moltke possessed many of the characteristics of an eighteenth-century rationalist. He viewed his defeat of Austria in 1866 – with its limited aims, and with an army that was more truly royalist than it was popular – as a Cabinet war. Indeed, after 1848 statesmen such as Bismarck, Prussia's minister-president in 1866, had come to see war as a possible means with which to implement policy. However, Moltke departed from Clausewitz in his attitude to morality. The discipline of the troops, the cultivation of universal values and the humanity of one individual for another were seen by Moltke as genuine restraints on the conduct of war. But in his belief in the rivalry between Germany and France, part of a Hegelian interpretation of the struggle for national survival, he inherited a formative influence on Clausewitz himself.

His general views on strategy owed much to Clausewitz in their flexibility and adaptiveness. Rigid systems were anathema. Nothing in war was certain, and the role of the commander was to use every opportunity, adjusting his plan accordingly. 'Strategy is a system of expedients', Moltke wrote, and he went on, in his *Instructions for Superior Commanders of Troops* (1869): 'The doctrines of strategy do not go much beyond the rudimentary propositions of common sense; they can hardly be called a science; their value lies almost entirely in their application to the particular case. We must with proper tact understand a situation which at every moment assumes a different aspect, and then do the simplest and most natural thing with firmness and circumspection.' Moltke's practice was to give his field commanders no more than the general outlines. Relying on the uniform doctrine of the general staff, he could leave the detail to the individual. Therefore the difficulty of co-ordinating detached bodies of troops, be they corps or divisions, was overcome. Jomini had seen security in massing, but so limited the flexibility and mobility of armies. For Moltke, 'the normal state of an army is its separation into corps'. Thus could an army be supplied and billeted, and then march and operate. The corps would not mass before battle, but converge on the field itself. 'Incomparably more favourably', wrote Moltke, 'will things shape themselves if on the day of battle all the forces can be concentrated from different points towards the field of battle itself – in other words, if the operations have been conducted in such a manner that a final short march from different points leads all available forces simultaneously upon the front and flanks of the adversary.' Clausewitz himself, as we have seen, had recognised the decisiveness of a converging attack. Clausewitz had also argued that the purpose of manoeuvre was the seeking of battle. The close reciprocal action of movement and combat was a hallmark of Moltke's wars. An army not only marched to fight, but also fought to continue its advance. The consequent battles of envelopment aimed not simply at a first victory in a prolonged campaign but at the immediate and outright destruction of the enemy's forces.

What Moltke was advocating was of course a revised version of the Napoleonic *manoeuvre sur les derrières*. In some senses, however, it was new: technical advances made its implementation more perfectible than it had been for Napoleon. The railway allowed large forces to converge by different routes. The growth of military academies and the creation of a true general staff fostered the common doctrine that could be more genuinely ubiquitous than Napoleon had managed to be. The telegraph allowed at least some communication between units in the field. And technological development itself forced flank attacks, since the growth in firepower precluded frontal assaults. Envelopment caught the enemy in a crossfire. Thus the operational and tactical requirements fused. Although directed towards battle, strategy was still concerned with the regulation of marches, with determining the distances between corps to enable rapid and timely concentration.

All this appeared not only novel, but also – to a generation convinced of the importance of interior lines and of the need to mass in advance of combat – wrong. When, in 1866, war broke out between Austria and Prussia, the aged Jomini proposed that the Prussian forces should concentrate in Silesia and advance on a single line to Vienna. The Austrian forces were scattered over the empire, and the Prussians would thus operate on interior lines. However, the Prussians were anxious not to seem the aggressors: they were keen to leave the initiative in concentration and mobilisation to Austria. Moltke could reckon to mobilise twice as quickly as Austria and had five railway lines available to dispatch his armies south to Bohemia. The Austrian commander, Benedek, reflected the tradition of Archduke Charles: his reserves in battle were to comprise 47,313 infantry, 11,435 cavalry and 320 guns. With only one railway line available, he massed his armies, and proposed to defend his bases and lines of communication. Moltke's Elbe and 1st Armies united in the mountain passes of northern Bohemia (see Map 11), and then struck south-east towards the Austrians on the upper Elbe. The 2nd Army approached from

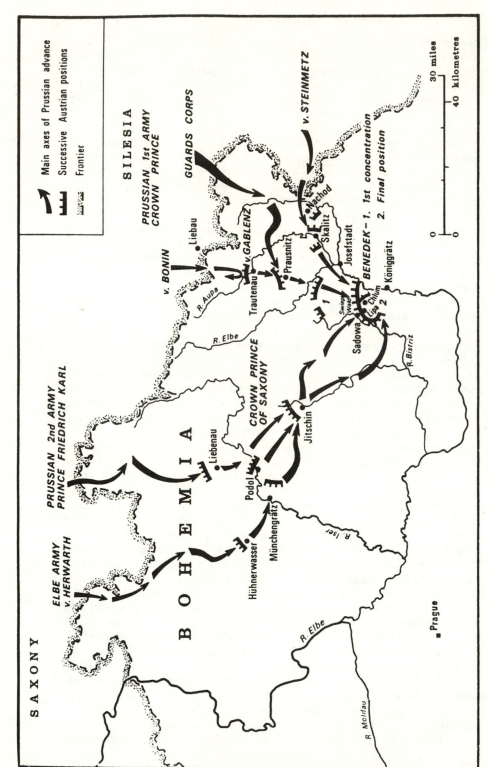

Map 11   *The campaign of 1866*

the north-east. As they converged so the Austrians' advantage of interior lines vanished, because a blow in one direction would expose their flank in another. Near Königgrätz (the battle is also known as Sadowa), on 3 July, the Elbe and 1st Armies attacked – albeit earlier than Moltke wished, and with the Elbe Army not sufficiently far south and thus not threatening the Austrian left flank. Their assault became a frontal one against strong defensive positions. The Prussians were now desperately dependent on the aid of the 2nd Army, marching south with all dispatch. At about mid-day, the 2nd Army entered the battle from the north against the Austrian right flank. Its arrival was decisive. But despite the magnitude of Moltke's success – the allegedly inferior Prussians had vanquished the white-coated Austrians in seven weeks – critics of his strategy were not wanting. Willisen condemned the division of forces which might have brought disaster. Of the battle itself, Rüstow, another distinguished German military writer, expected a Prussian frontal attack with a reinforced wing. The Austrian artillery superiority would have precluded this. Neither commentator saw the division of forces as the essential preliminary to success. Prussia's victory at Königgrätz was attributed less to Moltke than to the breech-loading rifles of her infantry. Thus tactical analysis dominated over strategic.

However, four years later, when the Prussians achieved similarly decisive success in virtually as short order, tactical superiority could no longer be seen as the principal cause. For their invasion of France in late July 1870, the Prussians launched three armies from the region west of the Rhine, deployed between Trier in the north and Landau in the south (see Map 12). A number of encounter battles on the frontier were hallmarked by the rapidity with which the Prussians supported their dispersed formations, marching to the sound of the guns. The French troops under Bazaine were sluggish in their abandonment of the great fortress of Metz, but Moltke, not fully aware of French movements, imagined they were rapidly retreating west. He crossed the Moselle to discover that he had now put himself to the flank and rear of the French, who were concentrating only a few miles west of Metz. A series of actions, culminating in the battles of Gravelotte-St Privat (18 August), bottled up Bazaine's forces. A new French army under MacMahon was pressed to the relief of Bazaine. He advanced on a northerly line, along the Belgian frontier. The Prussian 3rd Army had remained detached from the battles round Metz. Moving westwards, it was aided by part of the original 2nd Army, and together they pinned MacMahon's force against the frontier at Sedan. The French surrendered at Sedan on 1 September, and at Metz on 27 October. The fall of Napoleon meant that in the event the war continued for another six months. However, again a strategy of envelopment had brought decisive and rapid success in the field.

The second stage of the Franco-Prussian War highlighted Moltke's interpretation of the relationship between war and politics. Bismarck, although Prussia's minister-president, was excluded from operational discussions. When the Prussians laid siege to Paris, he was anxious to bombard the city and secure a rapid peace before the other European powers could intervene. However, Moltke considered the matter from a

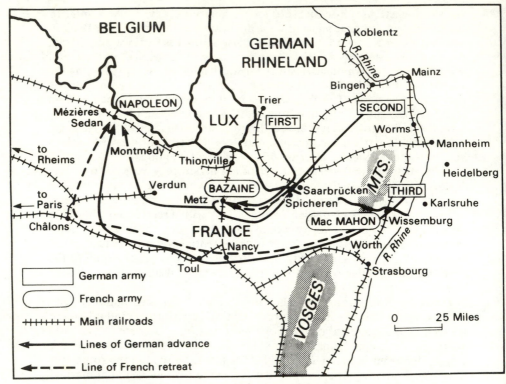

Map 12   *The campaign of 1870*

military perspective alone. Premature attack at Sebastopol sixteen years earlier had given the Russians the opportunity to strengthen their defences and in 1870 an attempt to bombard Strasbourg into surrender had merely stiffened resistance. Starving Paris into submission therefore seemed preferable. Failing that, Moltke argued, bombardment could not begin until there were sufficient guns to carry it through. He told the king that, 'The question when the artillery attack on Paris should or can begin, can only be decided on the basis of military views. Political motives can only find consideration in so far as they do not demand anything militarily inadmissible or impossible.' Bismarck was regarded as an interloper at Prussian headquarters, justifying his desire to be informed of plans by the overall political perspective, but in reality anxious to acquire influence in military affairs.

The discord continued into the peace settlement. In 1866 the blows after Königgrätz had been deliberately softened: too exhausted to pursue, the Prussians had instead concentrated on minimising the sting of defeat in order to lay the foundations for a lasting peace between the German-speaking nations. Potential differences between Moltke and Bismarck were thus not brought into view. Prussian attitudes to France were different, and were still coloured by the wars with Napoleon. The French were seen as an inveterate and adventurist foe. Moltke was therefore anxious to make a lasting impression of German military might. The memory of a campaign of destruction, coupled with annexations in Alsace-Lorraine to form a strategic glacis between the two countries, would be the only future guarantees of German security. In the event a more moderate, Bismarckian approach triumphed. Bismarck argued that 'The object of an army command is to destroy the enemy forces. The object of a war is to achieve peace under conditions that are in accord with the country's policies.'

Moltke would have agreed with both sentiments. But in the Franco-Prussian War the conflict between himself and Bismarck was really generated by their differing interpretations of the first not the second. The army was trying to establish unfettered control in wartime. Moltke accepted that diplomacy was crucial in the outbreak and settlement of wars, and would adjust its demands in the course of the war. But, within that framework, 'Strategy has no choice but to strive for the highest goal attainable with the means given. The best way in which strategy can cooperate with diplomacy is by working solely for political ends but doing so with complete independence of action.' In the conduct of operations, 'political elements merit consideration only to the extent that they do not make demands that are militarily improper or impossible'. In other words, Moltke had departed dramatically from Clausewitz's position. He had accepted the push towards absolute war, and had started a train of thought which logically concludes that a totally defeated enemy is the best basis for negotiation. War once begun therefore ceases to be a political instrument, and becomes a means with its own end – complete victory. Since absolute war sets its own ceilings of achievement, political control in the course of war is unacceptable.

Moltke was sufficiently realistic to appreciate that the search for total defeat of the enemy would provoke prolonged resistance. A nation would not be able to afford defeat, and would go on feeding the fight until utterly broken. Short campaigns marked by decisive battles, of the 1866 and 1870 variety, would therefore give place to wars of attrition. Moltke's successors failed to comprehend this corollary of the division of the political and military spheres. The tragedy for Germany was that, although the Franco-Prussian War revealed the drift in her military thinking, the boil was never lanced. Its immediate influence was limited by the countervailing strength of Bismarck, and by the maturity of Wilhelm I. With the former's fall and the latter's death, Germany's military excellence could not be guided into more sophisticated political channels.

The irony for Clausewitz was that, although the Prussian victories had won him posthumous fame, he was now being recast and misinterpreted throughout Europe. So axiomatic was Clausewitz's superiority as a military theorist that Colmar von der Goltz's *The Nation in Arms* (1883) likened his influence to that of Shakespeare and Goethe. But, following Moltke's interpretation, von der Goltz rendered the concept of absolute war a reality, which then becomes its own means and ends. 'War', he wrote, 'aids policy in the attainment of its objects; yet, if only for the sake of subordinate interest it must aim at the complete subjection of the enemy. This necessarily entails the decisive use of all means, intellectual and material alike, tending to subdue the foe.' He felt that, by seeking the complete defeat of the enemy, 'the greatest freedom [is] assured to politics ... [and] ... the widest scope is allowed in the employment of the fighting forces'. At an operational level, the importance of dispersion, the art of timing the concentration for battle, now constituted the essential principles of command. But von der Goltz took issue with Clausewitz's analysis of the defence. He felt that Clausewitz might well have revised this section of *Vom Kriege*. Logically it was flawed. Even Clausewitz had accepted that eventually the defenders would counter-attack. Indeed they could not guarantee that they would be attacked in the positions they had chosen. The moral advantage lay with the offensive. The object of war could only be achieved by attack, and the purpose of manoeuvre (here he was at one with Clausewitz) was to seek battle. Since he felt that only the tactical offensive was compatible with the strategic offensive, he had to conclude that 'to make war means to attack'.

Here we encounter a fresh departure from the spirit of Clausewitz's intentions. By 1914, not only did many general staffs feel that war possessed its own logic as well as its own grammar, they also argued that the offensive was the stronger means. Their case for doing so was still indebted to Clausewitz, for it was his emphasis on moral factors that provided the grounding, and, since the precepts were applied at a tactical level, Clausewitz had little to say as he had been discussing the defensive in strategic terms. The wars of 1866 and 1870 had both been won by the army on the offensive. But instead of treating the problem as technical, it became confused with the imagery of social Darwinism and the vocabulary of Romanticism. The most extreme example was to be found in France.

The French were understandably confused by what had happened in 1870. They had fought defensively, in accord with the tactical wisdom imposed by the development of firepower. None the less they had been comprehensively defeated. Their faith in the Napoleonic legend had also taken a knock. And yet Gambetta had resurrected an older and earlier spirit, that of the Revolution and the defence of France in 1792. Civilians were called in to the military administration; *francs-tireurs* conducted a guerrilla war on the Prussian rear; in short, the nation in arms found new – if not totally justified – adherents.

Curiosity about Prussian doctrine prompted France's discovery of Clausewitz. It was argued that, since the inspiration for Clausewitz's writing had been the campaigns of Napoleon, French national pride would not be compromised by the study of a German writer. In 1885, Major Cardot lectured on Clausewitz at the Ecole de Guerre. Clausewitz was presented as advocating the destruction of enemy forces by battle, and that the means to achieve this was through moral force expressed in a direct attack. This amazingly simplistic treatment continued. In 1890 Captain Gilbert reduced Clausewitz to three laws: to operate simultaneously with all troops concentrated, to operate quickly and most often with a direct attack, to operate continuously and without a pause.

At least the emphasis on moral factors had some genuine grounding in what Clausewitz had written. The discovery of the work of a French officer killed in 1870, Ardant du Picq, confirmed the drift. His *Etudes sur le combat*, published posthumously in 1880, stressed moral force above all other things. A charge succeeds because the defence falls back before the attackers make contact, or fails because it stands firm. The control of fear is the crucial element. Since this is achieved by discipline, du Picq's book constituted an argument for professional, not conscript armies.

A pupil at the Ecole under Cardot, and an instructor from 1894, was Ferdinand Foch. Will played a crucial part in Foch's analysis of war. The will to battle must be obeyed, and victory is no more than the will to conquer: 'A battle won', he wrote, 'is a battle in which one will not confess oneself beaten'. The offensive was therefore the path to ultimate success. Like his contemporaries he accepted the realisation of the ideal of absolute war.

However, Clausewitz pushed other Frenchmen back to a rediscovery of Napoleon. Soldier–scholars like Hubert Camon and, above all, Jean Colin established that converging movements were not a Moltkean but a Napoleonic invention. They held that Clausewitz's own experience, particularly in 1812, had coloured his entire analysis of the nature of Bonaparte's system of war, and in particular neglected the earlier triumphs of manoeuvre. Colin therefore attacked the emphasis on shock and the neglect of firepower that had arisen through the worship of moral forces. Reflecting an approach that was truly Clausewitzian in its rationality, he wrote that the proper study of military history would avoid 'the pretentious metaphysical vocabulary that had been so much abused for the last twenty years'.

None the less, the spirit of the offensive found its way into official French military thought. Its outstanding embodiment was to be the plan with which France went to war in 1914, but it was incorporated in field service regulations by 1895: 'Combat . . . has for its end to break by force the will of the enemy and to impose on him our own. Only the offensive permits the obtaining of decisive results. The passive defence is doomed to certain defeat; it is to be rejected absolutely.'

To Republicans in France, anxious to avoid the pitfalls of professionalism and seeing in the nation in arms an embodiment of the revolutionary spirit, the offensive offered a durable tactical law. Conscripts, lacking in training and discipline, and drawn from an economy that might not long survive their absence, seemed to have to force a rapid decision and therefore to attack. Motivated by the worth of their cause, they would surely prevail. The French general staff failed to resolve these debates in a clear doctrine, and left scope for improvisation within the general framework of the offensive spirit. Thus historical interpretation was brought to bear: the tradition of the French penchant for the attack was tied in with the release of individual genius for patriotic and revolutionary ends.

None the less, the spirit of the offensive was not confined to those to whom it seemed politically well-adapted. In Russia, Miliutin, minister of war from 1861 to 1881, and Dragomirov, who commanded at the Staff College from 1878 to 1889, reached it through the renewed study of Suvorov. Skobelev, the most dashing commander of the 1870s and 1880s, preached a similar doctrine. The morale of the soldier was the key to success. Conrad von Hotzendorf, Austria's chief of the general staff from 1906, followed the Hegelian near-orthodoxy of the day, that nations were in a permanent state of latent conflict, and that war was therefore endemic in the international system. Conrad felt that, as chief of the general staff, he had responsibility for decisions regarding the making of war and peace. 'Clausewitz', he said, 'is quoted out of context here. Politics consist precisely of applying war as a method.' More immediately he emphasised the offensive, even to the extent of believing that infantry, unsupported and inferior in numbers, could gain victory (in the words of the 1911 Austrian field service regulations) 'as long as it is tough and brave'.

Britain between 1870 and 1914 spawned its own share of works on military theory, many of them translations from German and French writers, and including in 1874 a rendering of Clausewitz. But Clausewitz remained impenetrable. Colonel G. F. R. Henderson, the outstanding lecturer at the Staff College and the author of an enormously influential book on Stonewall Jackson, opposed the abstraction of principles and argued that detailed military history should speak for itself. He praised Clausewitz for his emphasis on moral factors, 'But', he nevertheless went on, 'Clausewitz was a genius and geniuses and clever men have a distressing habit of assuming that everyone understands what is perfectly clear to themselves.' Spenser Wilkinson, the first professor of the history of war at Oxford, found *Vom Kriege* bulky and obscure. For him too moral forces were the message: 'It seems to me that war is essentially a conflict between two wills, and that a distorted view must be the consequence of putting mere machinery – the weapons – in the forefront. For this reason discipline – the training of the will – is always, and will always be, the foundation-stone of an army.'

Therefore, by 1914, Clausewitz's thinking on the relationship between war and politics had been wrenched from the guidelines he had set. The full consequences of this failure to comprehend the desirability of a close bonding between the two were as yet obscure. What was much more evident was the way in which his stress on the individual's motivations and on the need for decisive and destructive battle had been distilled into a new set of principles. Clausewitz was taken to be pressing for an offensive with maximum effort on the decisive point, and it was assumed that the side with the stronger will would prevail. But at the same time technological and industrial development meant that European society was increasingly able to fight an 'absolute' war. Could the offensive prevail in such circumstances? Would the will? And what would happen when both sides rested their wills on the assumption that they had the monopoly of wisdom and on the knowledge that defeat could mean national extinction?

Guide to Further Reading

Paret and Howard have written excellent introductory essays on the genesis and influence of *On War* for their translation. The volume also contains a guide to the reading of *On War* by Bernard Brodie. Paret's major book on Clausewitz (1976) is invaluable. Aron (1976) is being translated.

Articles by Paret (1968), Rosinski, and Brodie (1973) are helpful on the intellectual influences in Clausewitz's life. Paret has also written a bibliographical survey (*World Politics*, vol. 17, no. 2 (1965), pp. 272–85). Michael Howard's *Clausewitz* (Oxford, 1983) is a brief and highly literate introduction.

There is no good biography of Moltke in English. Whitton is inadequate. There is, however, an English edition of his correspondence (Mary Herms (trans.), *Field-Marshal Count Helmuth von Moltke*, London, 1893). Von Caemmerer discusses his strategic thinking and Ritter (Vol. I, 1970) analyses the conflict with Bismarck. The wars of 1866 and 1870–1 are admirably dealt with by Craig (1965) and Howard (1961). For the literature on military thought between 1871 and 1914, see the Guide to Further Reading at the end of chapter 8. Bergounioux and Polivka look at Clausewitz's interpretation in Germany and Irvine (1942) considers his handling in France. Porch (1975 and 1981, chapter 11) puts the French 'spirit of the offensive' in the context of French military disorganisation.

Chapter 8

Technology and its Impact on Tactics

The irony in the arguments for the adoption of the offensive before 1914 was that they had little basis in traditional military thinking. Many military theorists believed that only professional soldiers could deliver an effective attack. By contrast, conscripts and citizen soldiers were considered fit only for the defence. But in the years after 1870, long-service professionals had been ousted by short-service conscripts. Through this means, France, Germany, Italy, Russia and Austria-Hungary collectively doubled the size of their standing armies. On the eve of the First World War, both the French and German armies totalled over 800,000 men each, and that of Russia 1,300,000. Those bewitched by the fashionable theories of ethnic evolution might therefore reasonably contend that an army represented the spirit of the nation. More prosaically, such an army would have to secure a quick victory and therefore would have to attack. Otherwise the absence of so many able-bodied men from productive occupation and the strain on the exchequer through prolonged mobilisation would cause economic collapse.

These large armies were not a further manifestation of the imitation of Napoleon. The French armies of the First Empire had progressively owed more to the heritage of Enlightened Despotism than they had to the nationalist spirit of the Revolution. The laws of 1798 and after were codified in 1811. Under them all Frenchmen aged 20–25 were liable for service. But exemptions undermined the principle of universality: to save on poor relief for destitute wives, married men might be excused; after Napoleon's concordat with the Pope (1801), seminarists were released; and, above all, a man could procure a substitute, either by paying him or by finding a volunteer. Only a fixed number of recruits were taken each year, and so the burden fell inequitably on the poorer 40 per cent of the eligible male population. To meet his progressive manpower losses, Napoleon resorted to foreigners rather than apply truly universal service. In 1808 about a third of the French army was made up in this way, and for the invasion of Russia about two-thirds.

Napoleon was a mercantilist in his thinking on population as much as on trade. But even had he wished it, France could not have sustained a genuinely mass army over a prolonged period. The underlying determinant of the size of armies must after all be population size. The great surge in population expansion took place after 1815. In 1700 the population of Europe was about 110 million. In 1800 it had risen to 187 million, but by 1850 it was 266 million, by 1900 401 million and by 1913 468 million. The populations of Britain and Russia quadrupled between 1800 and 1910, and those of most other countries more than doubled.

Population expansion can only create the potential for mass armies; it does not of itself produce the political determination. Thus, although the general drift is clear, the pattern of change varies. Prussia was the power that even in the crisis of 1848 stuck by short service: the soldier spent two years with the regulars, five in the reserve and eleven in the *Landwehr*. Two problems concerned Wilhelm I. The first was the inefficiency of the *Landwehr*, and the second was the fixed size of the army, which was progressively becoming a smaller percentage of Prussia's growing population. But the ensuing constitutional struggle between Wilhelm and the liberals over army organisation, which spanned the decade 1857 to 1867 and through which Bismarck engineered his rise to power, at heart concerned neither of these problems. The king wanted his army to have the attributes of a professional force: he wanted its ethos to be military, not civilian, and he was therefore determined that recruits should serve three, not two, years. As the liberals saw, the effect would be to militarise society rather than nationalise the army. Wilhelm won (although in 1892 two years' service was restored). Thus, while the exploits of the Prussian army in 1866 and 1870−1 did advertise the virtues of short service and large reserves, the nation in arms found truer embodiment in France's *franc-tireurs*. Moltke himself saw the later stages of the Franco-Prussian War as a clash between a trained army and a militia. France's defeat therefore ensured that 1870−1 constituted an argument for universal service in a standing army and not for the real citizen army, the defensive militia characteristic of Switzerland.

None of the major belligerents of 1914 opted for conscription on these purist lines. None the less in republican France its protagonists were very strong and found voice in Jean Jaurès's classic *L'Armée nouvelle* (1911). Jaurès and his socialist colleagues certainly had an impact on the debate but found it hard to gainsay the logic of professional soldiers. The *Loi Niel* of 1868 had aimed to create an army of 1 million men, but still permitted exemptions and still preserved a relatively long period of service – five years. The law of 1872 established no more than the principle of personal and obligatory service for the entire male population. It set a maximum period of enlistment of five years, but in practice the norm was three years. In 1889, three years was fixed as the longest term, and in 1905 the radicals appeared to have triumphed with a two-year period, without exemptions. The army was to become a vast training school for the reserves rather than a body available for immediate use. However, the lack of long-service soldiers, particularly of NCOs, meant that the training of the reserves was inadequate. Moreover, the French population was not expanding at the same rate as that of her neighbours. In 1911, it had to take 83 per cent of her available manpower to produce the same size army as Germany did with 53 per cent. Therefore in 1913 the three-year term was readopted.

The same struggle was enacted elsewhere. The 1852 recruitment law in Austria fixed eight years with the colours and two with the reserves. In 1868 three years with the regulars was followed by seven in the reserve and two in the *Landwehr*. In 1912 two years became the norm. Italy in 1871−3 favoured four years with the regulars and nine in the reserve, but then in

1875 reduced the four-year term to three. In Russia, the Crimean War had shown the need for a reserve system, but a large army would undermine serfdom (since military service was rewarded with personal freedom). In 1861 the serfs were therefore emancipated, and in 1864 the term of enlistment was shortened to fifteen years. From 1874 nine of the fifteen years were spent in the reserve, leaving only six with the regulars, and in 1906 regular service was reduced to three years. Britain, despite pressure for conscription, stuck by professional long service, although in 1908 she did reform her reserve, the Territorial Army.

The equation between citizenship and military obligation was thus being established throughout Europe. But the *laissez-faire* liberals were probably right. Democratic principles may have been used to underwrite the rise of the truly national mass army, but in time – particularly with periods of service longer than two years – they were ousted by incipient militarism. Neither Britain nor the United States, the most stable liberal constitutions of the period, introduced conscription. Germany, Russia and Austria before 1914 show universal military service being used to strengthen absolutism not democracy. Popular feeling, the enthusiastic fire of liberty, could not be relied on to discipline armies. Instead, from the French Revolution onwards, a contractual society strengthened the hold of the state over the individual. His right to refuse to serve was weakened if the government could claim to represent the general good. Furthermore governments did not allow their conscript armies simply to represent the societies from which they were drawn; they used military service as a means to educate and transform their societies. The intensity of the debate over terms of enlistment in France and Germany is thus understandable; in Austria-Hungary the army was the most obvious symbol of unity in an empire of diverse ethnic groups; in Russia the army reforms of 1874 were designed not least as an assault on peasant illiteracy. Whole societies would go to war in 1914, but those societies had already been profoundly marked by military values.

At the time the implications for the conduct of war were felt by some to be reassuring. J. G. Bloch, the Polish banker, who foresaw many of the features of the First World War in his six-volume treatise of 1898, argued that 'universal military service for short periods presents conditions in which lie concealed the germs of the impossibility of war itself. This impossibility lies mainly in the difficulty of providing for immense masses, as a consequence of the diminution in productiveness, the possibility of economic crises, and popular commotions, and, finally, in the extreme difficulty of directing armies consisting of millions of men.' At the very least the division between peace and war was now much clearer. But in Bloch's analysis, if war did come, it would be truly horrific. By contrast Moltke argued that, by bringing in the educated classes, violence in war would be moderated. Beyond this, universal military service seemed to establish that in future wars would be brief. Short service allowed the creation of the largest army possible, while leaving peacetime productivity unfettered. Moreover, without conscription, as Moltke told the *Reichstag* in 1867, the state's security would be forfeit and therefore all productivity lost. The implicit corollary of all this was that, if the reservists actually had to be mobilised, production would collapse and war itself not be long sustained.

But, as even the revolutionary armies of the 1790s had shown, universal military service gave the state an immense reservoir of manpower. Battle would follow battle. Clausewitz's emphasis on killing-rates and on the consequent tendency to attrition could only be more, not less, relevant. The concept of absolute war was becoming inherently more realisable. Moreover this was expressed not simply in population growth. The relatively peaceful Europe of 1815–70, with the demand of its burgeoning population and with greater facilities for credit, provided ideal conditions for the mounting pace of industrialisation.

The motor of innovation was no longer the textile industry but one of the sinews of war itself, iron. The exploitation of coal, and in particular coking coal, and Watt's invention of a commercially viable steam engine (1776) were the essential ingredients in the development of heavy industry. The peace of 1815 allowed British techniques and technology to cross to the continent. The really staggering development was in Germany. Her coal and lignite production rose from 1·2 million tonnes in 1815, to 9·2 in 1850 and 247·5 in 1913. Her annual pig-iron production stood at 85,000 tonnes in 1823, topped 1 million in 1867 and was approaching 15 million on the eve of the First World War. Even France, the origins of whose industrial take-off lie back in the 1770s, was reaching industrial maturity by 1870. In the 1850s and 1860s Bessemer's converter transformed the speed and cost of the production of steel. Between 1865 and 1879 steel output in Germany and Britain quadrupled, and in France (which started from a lower base point) it increased eightfold. Steel is less brittle, more malleable and more ductile than iron. One of its immediate applications was in the production of artillery. Industrialisation transformed war. The standardisation of machine tools, also a development of the mid-century, allowed the manufacture of large numbers of identical and interchangeable parts. Weapons were therefore easily repaired, far more consistent in their performance and far more readily available. The quality of steel permitted pieces able to take higher charges and therefore of increased ranges. Finally technological innovation allowed greater theoretical performance to be transformed into reality.

In 1815 the dominant small arm of the armies of Europe was the muzzle-loading, smooth-bore musket. It had remained essentially unchanged in its main features for over a hundred years. Its calibre was about 0·75 inches. The large bore was justified by the weight of shot, which allowed it to inflict ferocious wounds at close range. Two hundred yards was its maximum effective range, and its best application was against closed formations at distances a quarter of that. In 1834, Colonel John Mitchell described the firing of this musket: 'In nine cases out of ten, the difficulty of pulling the trigger makes the soldier open the whole of the right hand in order to aid the action of the forefinger; this gives full scope to the recoil; the prospect of the blow makes him throw back his head and body at the very moment of giving fire; and as no aim is ever required he shuts his eyes, from the flash of the pan, at the same instant so that the very direction of the shot becomes a matter of mere accident'. Not surprisingly he concluded that only 2 per cent of all the shots fired by the British army in the Peninsular War had taken effect.

The first improvement in the infantry weapon was the adoption of the percussion lock, in place of the flintlock. In 1807 the Revd Alexander Forsyth, a Scottish minister, patented a lock which exploded the charge by striking rather than by ignition (as the flintlock had done). It was the development of the copper cap in the 1830s that made Forsyth's invention a practicable weapon for military use. The cap contained detonating composition and was placed on the nipple, to be struck by the descending hammer. The principal attribute of the percussion cap was the certainty of fire in all weathers, since there was no longer any powder or pan to be exposed to wet. It also obviated the flash in the pan which Mitchell had so castigated.

The main desideratum to meet the bulk of Mitchell's criticisms was an effective breech-loading rifle. Much inaccuracy derived from the excessive windage (the gap between the musket ball and the sides of the barrel). A rifled barrel, with grooves cut into the bore so as to impart spin to the ball, gave greatest accuracy. But, in the days of muzzle-loading, securing a sufficiently tight fit to allow the rifling to take effect made loading hard work. Soldiers armed with rifles were equipped with a hammer, which they used in obstinate cases to drive the ramrod down the barrel. The rate of fire with a rifle was thus less than half that with a smooth-bore musket, and the exertion of loading often made the firer's aim shaky, so undermining the basic advantage the rifle was meant to impart. An effective breech-loading system would not only remove all the difficulties of loading, but also allow the soldier to fire prone and thus present a smaller target.

The first breech-loading rifle in general military use was the Dreyse, 60,000 of which were ordered by the Prussian government in 1840. The Prussians were understandably secretive about the weapon, and – contrary to the *laissez-faire* orthodoxy of the day – the government tried to monopolise and nationalise small-arms production. Not until 1851 did Prussian units receive the Dreyse as a regular issue, and not until Königgrätz in 1866 did the powers of Europe fully appreciate the qualities of the weapon. The weight of the breech brought the centre of gravity in the rifle nearer the shoulder and thus enhanced its accuracy. It ranged up to 800 yards. But its main attribute was its rate of fire, which could rise to seven rounds a minute. However from this also originated one of its main defects. Sixty rounds were about as much ammunition as a soldier could carry: with the Dreyse this represented a mere quarter of an hour's firing. In addition the Dreyse's needle-fire system of percussion proved delicate. The barrel tended to wear at its junction with the breech-bolt and so the escape of gas at the breech (the perennial and major technological problem with breech-loaders) grew progressively worse.

The Prussians themselves had doubts and many officers were drawn to the more traditional virtues of a Franco-Belgian solution to the problems of windage and slow loading. A pillar in the breech of a muzzle-loading rifle was designed to drive into the base of the bullet so that the latter would expand into the grooves of the rifling. The weapon took its name from the designer of its bullet, Minié, who put a cup in the base of the conical round, so that, when fired, it was the cup – rather than the initial action of ramming down – that forced the bullet into the grooves. The Minié had far greater penetration than its smooth-bore rivals, ranged up to 1,000 yards and had none of the delicate susceptibilities of the Dreyse. Its robustness ensured its adoption in virtually every European country during the course of the 1850s.

However, for all these powers, the Minié and its relatives were an interim solution pending the development of an effective breech-loader. Its successor arm in British service, the Enfield, was converted to the Snider breech-loading system in 1864, thus doubling its rate of fire to six rounds a minute. In 1866 the French adopted the most successful breech-loader thus far, the Chassepot rifle, sighted to 1,600 yards and with a smaller calibre than its predecessors (0·43 inches), thus allowing ninety rounds to be carried. The Chassepot overcame the problem of escaping gas by having a rubber obturator to seal the breech.

The pace of change now became very rapid, as the infantry rifle developed the features that were to characterise it until after 1945. One set of developments centred on ammunition. The adoption of metallic cartridges in the late 1860s simplified problems of loading and extraction. The discovery that a bullet did not have to be soft to take the grooves of the rifling allowed it to be harder and thus it could be smaller without losing penetration. In 1861, Nobel developed nitro-glycerine as a basis for smokeless powder; it ensured virtually complete simultaneous combustion, and consequently a more powerful explosion, greater ranges, less smoke and less fouling in the barrel. The first generation of arms to embody these improvements were also magazine-loaded – the German Mauser of 1884, the French Lebel of 1886, the Austrian Mannlicher and the British Lee-Metford, both of 1889, and the Russian Mossine of 1891.

The armies of Europe on the eve of 1914 therefore placed enormous stress on magazine rifle-fire. However, the emphasis on the rifle was by then already outmoded, and indeed helped to obscure an equally dramatic innovation, that of the machine gun. During the 1860s two practicable machine guns (both multi-barrelled) were undergoing development. America, the home of the machine-tool industry and of mass-produced, standardised arms, threw up the crank-operated, water-cooled Gatling gun. The Gatling could fire 200 rounds a minute and saw service in the Civil War. In France the *mitrailleuse*, which could fire 150 rounds a minute over a range of 1,000 yards, was developed in conditions of such secrecy that in 1870 nobody was fully trained in its use. Furthermore the French reflected a general tendency to see the machine gun as a form of artillery rather than as a weapon for close infantry support. It was thus deployed so far back as to forfeit many of its inherent advantages. Gunners, anxious to protect or enlarge their responsibilities, colluded in this. But between 1883 and 1885 Hiram Maxim developed a machine gun which used the force of the recoil to operate the rejection, loading and firing mechanism: the initial pull of the trigger made the firing fully automatic until the trigger was released. One barrel, not several, was consequently possible, and the Maxim weighed a mere 40 pounds. The machine gun therefore became a much more mobile weapon. Britain adopted the Maxim in 1889, and Germany and Russia followed suit. Its main rivals – the Hotchkiss and the Browning – had mechanisms operated by the gases released on firing, and it was the former which was adopted by both France and Japan. But no clear doctrine on the use of the machine gun followed. For some they were ponderous weapons, suitable only for the defensive, and therefore neglected when tactical doctrine emphasised the offensive: one machine gun's firepower might equal that of fifty riflemen, but the more machine gunners, the fewer bayonets available for the final assault. For others they were mobile fire support, to aid the infantry in the closing moments of an attack, firing in enfilade, and not to be used in defence. Traditional military thinking stressed reliability, robustness and simplicity in weaponry ahead of rates of fire. Rapid shooting wasted ammunition, and the Maxim could fire ten rounds a second. While the British and French might be clear about the machine gun's value as an infantry weapon in colonial operations (here was another compensation for insufficient manpower), they were less sure about its application to continental warfare. The distribution of machine guns was therefore limited: as the 1911 United States regulations put it, 'Machine guns must be considered as weapons of emergency. Their effectiveness combined with their mobility renders them of great value at critical, though infrequent, periods of an engagement.'

However muted the initial impact of the machine gun, technology had wrought a revolution on the battlefield in the years 1840 to 1900. The range and rate of small-arms fire had increased tenfold. But it was a change that was clearer in theory than in practice. Limited visibility or wooded terrain were as genuine constraints on the fulfilment of potential performances as were fear or exhaustion. Thus it is not only military conservatism which explains their slow reflection in tactical developments. In the 1840s the debates on the relative merits of column and line continued. Jomini, in the *Précis de l'art de la guerre*, praised the virtues of the *ordre mixte* and of shallow battalion columns in terms which would have been recognisable a hundred years previously. Generals still tended to rate shock over fire-effect: at the battle of Sobraon (1846) in the First Sikh War Gough, when told that his artillery had run out of ammunition, triumphantly exclaimed, 'Thank God! Then I'll be at them with the bayonet.' Even the advent of the Minié could not overthrow the praise of the offensive virtues of the bayonet. In the Crimea in 1854, the French commander, St Arnaud, condemned the fire-fight. But at Inkerman, a battle fought in the misty half-light of an early November morning, it was the Minié that had ploughed through the approaching Russian columns. Limited visibility and close hand-to-hand fighting notwithstanding, only 6 per cent of the casualties had been caused by the bayonet. The problem with firepower was that it was a weapon of defence not of attack. The tactical dilemma was the need to combine acknowledgement of the supremacy of musketry with the ability to keep moving. Formations would have to be smaller and more dispersed, command delegated to lower levels.

By 1813–14, the Prussians had established the company, not the battalion, as the basic tactical unit. But small-scale attacks, with the fire-fight predominating, had not brought decisive results. Therefore, although the 1847 Prussian regulations advocated the use of company – not battalion – columns, they still regarded the fire-fight as no more than the preliminary to an attack by closed columns. The answer to firepower was to cross the danger zone more quickly. This was exactly the doctrine preached by Napoleon III in Italy in 1859. He used battalion columns, screened by thick skirmishing lines. The French, reflecting their North African experience and also their high ratio of officers, became adept in moving rapidly over ground in short rushes. They now tended to regard the chasseurs as assault troops rather than light infantry. Meanwhile, the Austrians still stressed the defensive, which should have worked to their advantage. But their musketry training was poor, their Lorenz rifles fired in excessively curved trajectories (thus passing over the heads of the advancing French) and they therefore engaged ineffectively at too great ranges. Not unnaturally, the 1862 Austrian regulations concluded that speed and the use of the bayonet should be employed in the attack: breech-loading rifles simply wasted ammunition.

Meanwhile, a fresh element had been injected into the debate in Prussia by Moltke. The exposed points remained the flanks. Therefore, Moltke argued in a memorandum of 1858, the enemy must be forced by flanking marches and enveloping movements into taking the tactical offensive. The Prussian infantry would break the onset with its firepower and then itself go over to the attack. Moltke then fused the strategic offensive with the tactical defensive. In the event, however, the 1861 Prussian regulations were not so defensively minded. Closed formations were still seen as decisive. But the compact company column was to probe, moving rapidly and using cover. When the Prussians finally clashed with the Austrians at Königgrätz, the company columns moved forward, fanned out by platoons and fed the skirmishing line. The rate of fire of the Dreyse inflicted appalling losses on the advancing Austrians: they suffered 45,000 casualties to the Prussians' 9,000.

The French were suitably impressed. Their regulations of 1867 stipulated that two companies were to screen the advance in column of the remaining six companies of a battalion. When in range, all eight were to deploy to give fire. Once the enemy was shattered, the columns would reform and charge. The superiority of the Chassepot over the Dreyse, particularly in range, encouraged the French to emphasise the intermediate, defensive stage of the process. But static riflemen were exposed to artillery. Thus, although Prussian infantry thinking was not very different from that of the French, it was the Prussian artillery that made the difference. Indeed it did more than that, for in 1870 Prussia's tactical doctrine was at variance with the sort of war she was trying to fight. Moltke's emphasis on the tactical defensive and on the application of fire-effect required highly disciplined troops, who could be relied on to check the impulse to close with the enemy. But in 1870 Prussia took the offensive with short-service troops against a more experienced army that was determined to fight a tactically defensive battle. At St Privat the Prussian Guards advanced up a gentle slope for one mile in columns of half-battalions, with skirmishers deployed in front. They suffered 30 per cent casualties, and in one battalion 55 per cent. The Germans learned quickly: barely two months later they successfully attacked a position at Le Bourget in loose lines, using cover and supporting each other as they advanced in bounds.

Other wars confirmed the drift. Trenches and the use of cover came to characterise the American Civil War; Sherman said of the Atlanta campaign, 'I rarely saw a dozen of the enemy at any one time'. The Russians suffered 35 per cent losses in their assault on the Turks in Plevna in 1877. Field fortifications and earthworks, supplemented by the Turks' Peabody — Martini rifles, broke up the Russian columns. The Russians adopted smaller units, and, so as to sustain the attack, fed in fresh formations as the first faltered. Under the guidance of Todleben, the hero of the defence of Sebastopol in 1854—5, they began their final attack with a four-day bombardment and had to reckon on a virtual two-to-one numerical superiority for success.

Prussian thinking between 1870 and 1914 therefore stressed the reciprocal support of advancing and firing, and the need to make effective use of cover. An attack from the front would pin the enemy, while the main thrust could be delivered from the flank. In loose formations, the soldier no longer had the security of a comrade on his shoulder, and tended to fire indiscriminately and to rush forward against unbroken positions. Discipline was at a premium, particularly in semi-trained conscript armies. Small sections, with command delegated to junior officers and NCOs, were therefore best.

The French regulations of 1875 accepted the dominance of fire. The main fight was now to be conducted by the skirmishing line. Nobody in France ever really doubted the necessity of open order, but many did question the quality of the French soldier's training. The solidity of close order had helped compensate for the conscript's lack of skill. The offensive spirit, with its emphasis on moral factors, and deriving its inspiration from du Picq, was a compensation for lack of discipline. The 1884 French regulations reflected this, and it was further developed in those of 1895. At an operational and a tactical level, the French aimed to advance to contact, to identify the enemy's strong points, and then to concentrate their attack against his weakness. Having approached to within 400 metres of the enemy, the fighting line would be reinforced and bayonets fixed. It would then close to 200 or 150 metres. Magazine fire would be opened, the reserves would close up and 'at a signal from the Colonel the drums beat, the bugles sound the advance and the entire line charges forward with cries of *en avant, à la baionette*'.

French military thought tended to pooh-pooh the experiences of the South African or the Russo-Japanese Wars as irrelevant to Europe. None the less it would be wrong to overplay their emphasis on the offensive at a tactical level. The major difficulties arose because some French military writers failed to distinguish between the strategic offensive—defensive and the tactical. The worst effects of Foch and the offensive school were therefore really felt in terms of strategic planning. The 1904 field service regulations emphasised concealment, dispersion and the defensive—offensive.

Those of 1913 spoke of a skirmishing group of four men advancing in bounds of 10 metres. Morale became crucial only for the final attack. The real tactical problem for French generals was that 70 per cent of their army was made up of first-year conscripts or reservists who were ill-suited to skirmishing. In consequence the preparatory phase of the attack was far shorter than that envisaged by the Germans.

The British case underlines the point. Again nobody was denying the impact of firepower. General staffs and military theorists concentrated on the attack because it was in this phase that the problems weapons posed were most acute. Nor, despite the fame of the British Expeditionary Force's musketry in 1914, was there any reason to believe that the professional qualities of the British army would provide a better trained infantry than that of the other European powers. When mobilised, 60–70 per cent of the British Expeditionary Force would be made up of reservists. Immediately after the Boer War, the British stressed flank attacks. But in 1910 the words in *Infantry Training*, 'the decision is obtained by fire', were replaced by 'superiority of fire makes the decision possible'. Doubts about training and about musketry pushed Britain too to an emphasis on human qualities. The 1912 field service regulations reflected the French approach: engagement along the whole front was to be followed by a concentrated assault on one sector. The 1914 reorganisation of the British infantry battalion (into four companies not eight, and into sections of ten men not twenty-five) was designed to abet these tactics. The stronger company was for penetration.

In all the debates about the infantry assault, relatively little weight was put on artillery. The French field service regulations of 1875 to 1900 omitted to mention artillery at all. Partly this reflected inter-arm rivalry; partly it was an acknowledgement of the importance of the machine gun; principally it sprang from a conviction that artillery prepared the attack but did not support it. In any case, technology, when applying the principles of rifling and breech-loading, had found it easier to perfect small arms. The greater the charge and the larger the calibre, the greater the shock of concussion in firing and the greater the strain on the construction of the piece. Throughout the second half of the nineteenth century the rifle had led the way. But in 1890 small arms reached a plateau. It was only in the twenty years before 1914 that the artillery emerged from a similar evolution.

With the successful application of breech-loading and rifling to small arms, there was a military demand to develop rifled, breech-loading ordnance. The maximum effective range of smooth-bore field artillery was about 1,000 yards and its rate of fire about two rounds a minute: rifles such as the Minié could rival it in range and the Dreyse could treble its rate of fire. Thus, in the mid-century, some were prophesying the artillery's impending demise.

Already, however, three developments had occurred which were to aid the renaissance of the field gun. The first was the perfection by Boxer in 1852 of a fuse for the shrapnel shell. Henry Shrapnel had filled a hollow shell with shot in 1784: it was designed to burst over its target, scattering fragments, and thus was particularly effective against dispersed formations.

However, not until Boxer's invention was its performance sufficiently consistent for artillery to be able to counter light infantry and skirmishers effectively. The second was the progressive increase in weight, and hence of range (since a heavier gun could take a larger charge), of the field guns. From 6- and 9-pounders in the Peninsula and Waterloo, 12- and even 18-pounders were being used in the Crimea. But the most important technological breakthrough was the improving quality of wrought iron, made possible by Cort's puddling process developed in the 1780s. Wrought iron's malleability and tensile strength could take the inbuilt weaknesses which breech-loading and the grooves cut for rifling would give artillery barrels. In 1855, after a decade of intense experimentation throughout Europe, Armstrong produced a breech-loading rifled 40-pounder gun by shrinking over one another successive coils of wrought iron. It was adopted by the British in 1859.

In the event the Armstrong gun was – in a sense – a false dawn. The British temporarily reverted to muzzle-loading, as less complex for general military use. In the American Civil War, potentially the first great test of the breech-loading, rifled gun, the ground was so wooded that the range and effectiveness of artillery were limited. The fuses and mechanism of smooth-bore guns were more reliable, and as late as 1864 two-thirds of the Army of the Potomac's guns were smooth-bores. However, for a prescient observer such as Patrick MacDougall, writing in the same year, the Civil War showed 'that a position in open country, which had been prepared for defence, cannot be carried by direct attack by troops moving in close order, exposed to the present field artillery'.

Bessemer's converter (1856) and the Siemens–Martin open-hearth process (1864), both for producing steel from pig-iron, were the essential contributors to a new generation of field guns. Iron guns of increased ranges would be heavier and therefore less mobile. In the 1830s and 1840s Krupp was developing cast steel for the manufacture of guns. A steel gun was light, mobile and could take both rifling and breech-loading. But it remained expensive. However, by 1864 the cost of steel had been brought down and the arguments for rifled breech-loaders were in the ascendant: Prussia ordered 300.

The Austrian artillery was completely re-equipped with rifled artillery, albeit muzzle-loading, after 1859. It was trained to come well forward, to mass and to provide the firepower its infantry spurned. At Königgrätz, Benedek had 450 rifled guns in position, and a further 320 in reserve. The Prussians by contrast had only 492 rifled guns (and 306 smooth-bores), which they kept well back on the line of march. Although they therefore came late to the battle, in the event they played a crucial role, for the Prussian gunners galloped forward and drew the fire of their Austrian counterparts from the hard-pressed Prussian infantry.

Within four years Prussia perfected her artillery. Steel breech-loaders were adopted throughout the army. Percussion fuses which exploded on contact gave the German artillery greater flexibility than that of the French, which had bursting zones limited to 1,350 to 1,550 metres or 2,650 to 2,850 metres. Chastened by 1866, the Prussian artillery was brought forward on the column of march. It accompanied the infantry to the attack, moving in close to prepare the assault and to compensate for the firepower of the Chassepot. Greater precision of fire and greater reliability in performance allowed far more effective support: hitherto the variations in ammunition had rendered overhead fire as demoralising and dangerous for the artillery's own infantry as for the enemy defenders.

The solution to this close support fire was to entrench. The immediate French reaction in the decade after Sedan – before the onset of the offensive mania – lay in fortifications. The Turks' use of earthworks at Plevna reinforced the point: Todleben reckoned that it could take a Russian battery a whole day's firing to kill a single Turk. The artillery's response was the howitzer, a gun which fired at a high angle, rather than laterally as a field gun did, so as to hit targets that were protected to their front.

The adoption of smokeless powder (cordite entered British service in 1890) had an even greater effect on artillery than it had done for small arms. Its burning time was slower and more controllable, and in a long bore this meant more overall thrust with lower maximum pressures on the gun. At the same time steel artillery allowed greater muzzle velocities. Therefore guns could become bigger. The battlefield was no longer obscured in smoke, with the result that the benefit of this increased range could actually be extracted. Simultaneously Wille in Germany and Langlois in France developed a mechanism in which the barrel recoiled on a slide without moving the gun carriage, brakes or buffers checked the recoil, and compressed springs forced the barrel back to its original position. Thus instead of running the gun back up and relaying it after each round, fire could be maintained without pause. The gun-crew now remained close to the weapon's breech, and so a shield could be added to protect them from the sniping of marksmen. Quick-firing field artillery ranged 2–3 miles and maintained a rate of 10 rounds a minute – or even double that in the case of the French 75 mm adopted in 1897.

Massed guns firing deliberately and specifically were now considered outmoded. Smokeless powder made it hard to spot enemy batteries, and therefore counter-battery fire was often wasteful. Instead extended formations needed to be checked by dispersed guns blanketing the area with fire. The field gun should be mobile, to be able to follow an infantry attack and to give direct support as required. In the Russo-Japanese War, forward observers with telephones guided artillery fire on to its target, particularly to suppress machine gun posts. Field batteries included howitzers, to fire high explosive rather than shrapnel, in order to break up defensive positions. But again there was the problem of selection, of deciding what in the longer term was relevant to *grande guerre*. Something of the pattern that was to dominate in the First World War had been made clear, but much – as we shall see – had not.

The revolution in firepower clearly threatened the use of the *arme blanche* and in particular its main exponent, the cavalry. However, cavalry's initial reaction – embodied, for example, in the book by Captain L. E. Nolan, the bearer of the order for the charge of the Light Brigade at Balaclava in 1854 – was to emphasise its speed. Hitherto it had probably galloped only the last hundred yards in a charge; now it should gallop eight hundred.

Demands on the fitness of the horse and the discipline of its rider were unrealistic. In consequence, in 1870, the French cavalry was launched in desperation, over broken ground, without prior reconnaissance, against an unshaken enemy. By contrast the successful charge of von Bredow's dragoons at Rezonville used the cover of ground and the smoke of the battlefield to shelter its approach.

Even if the massed charge could no longer be the sole *raison d'être* for cavalry, the mobility imparted by the horse still ensured for its several crucial roles. Foremost was reconnaissance. Prussian doctrine after 1815 tended to argue that the cavalry should be kept concentrated, ready for the decisive charge with the *arme blanche*. Therefore the patrolling and dismounted duties of light cavalry were neglected. In 1866 the Prussian cavalry was kept in reserve, and failed in intelligence-gathering. Even in 1870 it lost contact with the French after the battles of Spicheren and Worth. But as the campaign developed, so it improved. *Uhlans*, pushing far ahead, not only provided information but also gave a moral impact, suggesting Prussian ubiquity to the French. German doctrine therefore restored some emphasis to the mounted arm. 'It must encircle the enemy like an elastic band', wrote von der Goltz, 'retire before him when he advances in force, but cling to him and follow him when he retires.' The first clash of arms in a campaign would be that of cavalry, perhaps ironically enough charging each other in order to penetrate the enemy's screen.

The second and more independent role for cavalry was the strategic one suggested by the American Civil War – the detached column, ranging deep and far and fast into the enemy's rear, capable of hitting hard at soft spots and then withdrawing. In the heavily populated, urbanised and enclosed areas of Western Europe the possibility for surprise was limited. In the less developed areas to the East it promised more, and the Russians in particular planned to use such formations on the frontiers of Germany and Austria-Hungary.

In both cases the weapon the horsemen would use was as much the carbine or rifle as the sword or lance. Cavalry had to become mobile firepower. J. E. B. Stuart's entire command in the American Civil War was trained in the use of firearms. In 1870, the Prussians added one or two battalions of *Jäger* to each cavalry division. The Boer War confirmed the tendency. The British cavalry brigade in 1914, with its machine guns and the horse artillery's 13-pounders, was the most mobile fire unit in the British Expeditionary Force.

But the cavalryman, like the foot-soldier, needed to integrate the defensive virtues of firepower with the maintenance of the offensive. His arguments for the charge were therefore regularly renewed. Douglas Haig, an advocate of cavalry as mobile firepower immediately after the South African War, still saw the extended nature of the battlefield as widening the options for cavalry in 1907. Its rapidity would become more valuable because of the development of firepower, its moral effect would be greater on the isolated infantryman, and the smaller the calibre of rifle bullet the less would be its stopping power against a galloping horse. 'I ask', he wrote, 'those who have felt the elation of a successful charge or who have known the despondency which attacks those who have been ridden over by the horsemen who they have fired at in vain, whether magazine fire, which makes the shooting so erratic, hurried, and much less easily controlled, and spends the ammunition so quickly, has really so very much changed the conditions of thirty years ago?' Haig's view was swinging to continental orthodoxy: after 1909 the front ranks of British cavalry regiments were equipped with lances, but in Germany the entire arm had had them since 1890.

The essential point was that it was not firepower but the internal combustion engine which would drive the horse from the battlefield. Until then the value of the horse could not be gainsaid. It remained the most flexible means of transport over rough terrain even into the Second World War. Between 1914 and 1920, the British army transported 5,269,302 tons of ammunition to France, but took 5,919,427 tons of oats and hay. This fodder was not so much for cavalry awaiting a breakthrough as for the draught animals supplying the forward units of Britain's first mass army. The railway, which had revolutionised civilian transport in the second half of the nineteenth century, had a dramatic effect on the conduct of war. But it lacked adaptability. Ironically, as the cavalry in the American Civil War and T. E. Lawrence's exploits in the Hejaz in 1917 demonstrated, the greatest threat to its fixed iron tracks was the mounted raid.

Initial military thinking on the value of railways stressed their contribution to the defensive. Britain, obsessed with the bogey of French invasion, had 10,000 kilometres of track in 1850. She could now concentrate her small home army round Aldershot. No longer did it have to be fragmented into small detachments to be immediately on the spot in the event of a crisis. Instead the railway allowed a large force to move rapidly to any threatened point. Prussia, with exposed frontiers to south, east and west, had similar reactions. Friedrich List, the economist, urged the compatibility of commercial and defensive railway construction. Moltke, as a director of the Berlin–Hamburg line in 1841–4, pressed for state control, and von der Heydt, Prussia's minister of commerce from 1848, was responsible for initiating a massive programme of construction, much of it state-owned. Moltke, as chief of the general staff, established close co-operation between himself and the ministers of war and commerce. By 1859, Germany too had more than 10,000 kilometres of track.

The same year had seen the first major application of the railway to war, but it had been offensive not defensive. The French mobilisation of 1859, chaotic though it was, had been greatly speeded by rapid communications to the frontier. However, it was the American Civil War that provided European military observers with their first full insight into the impact of the railway. Relatively undercultivated and unpopulated, with few roads, and embracing an area the size of Europe, the American theatre of war was a prime candidate for the development of the railroad. Troops could be rapidly switched from one centre of operations to another, and at the battles of First Bull Run and Chickamauga actually went into action straight from their trucks.

The major problem in the military use of the railway was that hardy perennial of transport and supply, the division of military and civilian responsibility. Soldiers tended to regard logistics as irrelevant to fighting and therefore not their business. They were, however, annoyed by *intendants* and commissaries who did not appreciate the exigencies of campaigning. If the line was built for civilian use, it often lacked transverse links, which could run parallel to the front and connect the supply lines of independent formations. Much early railway building was single-tracked, and therefore men and supplies could be moved up or alternatively the wounded and prisoners brought back, but not both simultaneously. The Russian use of the Trans-Siberian railway in 1904 demonstrated this: the line kept the Russian army in the field but being single-tracked never really allowed the full flow of supplies its existence might have suggested. Finally, the gauge might change on crossing a frontier, thus causing an invading army to have to detrain, and for this reason the Russians deliberately opted for a wider gauge than their potential opponents in the West, the Germans. Therefore railway lines generated fresh tensions. Supplies could be rushed up, dumped at a congested railhead, but not necessarily be distributed. On 5 September 1870, the Prussian 2nd Army had 2,322 wagons standing on five different lines, loaded with 16,830 tons of provisions: the 2nd Army itself was short of food. The tendency of field commanders to use trucks as 'another form of commissariat wagon whch may be kept loaded for an indefinite period' infuriated commanders of military railways. Regardless of the existence of an overall plan of distribution and supply, and regardless of the inflexibility of the railway, they would try 'to seize and work the portion of the line nearest to them'. These are the words of Sir Percy Girouard, director of military railways in the South African War. But the fault was not all on one side. The railway authorities often seemed to treat the handling of men in the same way as that of supplies. At 9.30 a.m. on 7 January 1871, a French battalion arrived to entrain at Bourges. At 9 p.m. the same evening they were ordered to board the train. At 10 p.m. the order was cancelled. At 4 a.m. the following day they finally entrained. At 11 a.m. the first train left. The following night, the days of 9 and 10 January, the night of 11–12 and the day of the 12th, were passed without moving at all. On 15 January the battalion arrived at Baume. It had travelled 230 miles. It had also set off with only two days' rations.

Admittedly the French army's management of trains in 1870–1 touches such heights of absurdity as to suggest fantasy. France tried to combine the process of mobilisation with that of concentration. Thus units were sent forward before they were complete, and the laggards were left to catch up as best they could. The solution was the development of a supreme co-ordinating authority, with the power to unite the civil and military strands and with a military body of railway workers. As early as 1862 the Northern states in the American Civil War had appointed a military director and superintendent of railways. At times he had 12,000 troops under his command. In 1861, the Prussian army formed a Railway Department. In 1864, a 'central commission for the transport of large troop masses on railroads' was created, and in 1866 the first railway workers were added to the Prussian army. But the Seven Weeks' War demonstrated that there were still problems of co-ordination: the chief of the railway section of the general staff planned railway movements, while the technical problems were attended to by the central railway directorate of the ministry of commerce. Not until 1872 was a fully centralised controlling body established under the aegis of the German general staff. Its peacetime duty was to assess the number of vehicles required on mobilisation, the size of trains, the length of time it would take to load them, and the intervals between each train. Faced with the threat of war on two fronts and with the related need to bring her reserves into the battle as quickly as possible, Germany in particular saw internal communications as crucial for concentration and mobilisation. In 1871 she had 21,471 kilometres of track; by 1913 she had built 63,378 – a third more than France and twice that of Britain. Furthermore much of this construction had a military rather than a commercial application: she had a disproportionate number of lines thrusting towards Belgium and France, and of transverse links just within her frontiers.

Railways thus determined an army's possible line of operations. The track's vulnerability meant that troops had to be committed to its protection. But, although in some ways strategy was rendered less flexible, in others it became more so. Troops arrived fresh on the battlefield: ten days' march could put out 2,000 men in a force of 50,000. The greater the distance, the more the railway's advantages increased. An army corps could march ninety miles in seven days and would probably – after its equipment had been loaded and unloaded – cover no more distance in the same time by train. Quadruple the distance, and the marching time would become months, while the railway movement would only take a day or two longer. Less baggage had to accompany an army corps, as resupply could be rapid and the wounded and prisoners withdrawn. A fleeting strategic advantage could be exploited by swift reinforcement. But by the same token war became more absolute. The difficulty of bringing a nation's resources to bear quickly and at one point had diminished. The railway allowed an army to tap all the resources of manpower and industry. In 1854 the Russian army, fighting in the Crimea on the end of a long land line, had been exhausted by a smaller force fed from the sea. In 1904 it had fallen prey to the same fate. But the Japanese had acted then because they realised that, when the Trans-Siberian railway was completed, the logistic balance would swing in favour of the continental power.

However, beyond the railhead, movement had not undergone a comparable revolution. The railways were vital in the deployment stages of the 1866 and 1870 campaigns, but thereafter local requisition played an increasing role in the feeding of the German armies. Rapid advances widened the gap between the railhead and the forward units, and the distribution of supplies effectively broke down. The Germans moved to feed. But, as potential ammunition consumption increased in the years 1870–1914, so the need to maintain communications became more compelling. Relatively untrained reservists were potentially less adept at foraging in the field. An army corps became a ponderous bludgeon: in 1914 it could not operate at peak efficiency more than twenty-five miles from its railhead. Composed of thirty to forty thousand men, its marching column was fifteen miles long and its baggage more than the same again. Its tail was therefore two days' march from its head, and it was very hard for it to deploy and engage the enemy on the same day. But a smaller unit would make inadequate use of the road and would not have the strength independently to hold the enemy.

The tactical ponderousness of the mass army was compounded by the problem of communications. Again a revolution at the strategic level had not been reflected at the operational. Semaphore telegraph had been used in the Napoleonic Wars for linking fixed points. The electric telegraph had advanced in step with the railway: thus the allied commanders in the Crimea had been linked with their home capitals. But the system lacked mobility, was easily disrupted and could of course be tapped. Prussian field telegraph units, formed in 1856–7, were designed to link general headquarters with Berlin, rather than with the field armies or forward units. Moltke in any case was loath to interfere with the freedom of action of the army commander. The rather inefficient telegraph units of the Wars of Unification were used not as a vehicle for command but to relay information and intelligence. The major breakthrough came between 1897 and 1901 when Marconi perfected a practicable wireless telegraph. Here was a system of communications of potentially far greater value on the battlefield. However, initially it remained too bulky to be suitable for use in forward units. Line was vulnerable and effective telephone or buzzer communications limited to a range of about thirty kilometres. There was a contrast between highly efficient telegraphic links at the levels of high command, and a relatively primitive chain below those of the division and brigade. Lamps and flags were the only supplement to the staff officer or messenger, mounted on horseback or – in the years immediately before 1914 – on a motorcycle or car.

The German army made a virtue of necessity. It stressed the independence and initiative of subordinate units. General headquarters issued directives, indicating the overall intention of the chief of the general staff, but specific orders were left to those leading lower formations, who thus had the flexibility to respond to the situation that actually confronted them. In order to ensure harmony of action, a mass army had to rely on a common doctrine. This was imparted in two ways: first it was acquired by attendance at a war college or staff school, and secondly it was disseminated by the appointment of the graduates of these academies to the staffs of corps and divisions.

In the eighteenth century most commanders had two principal staff officers, the adjutant-general and the quartermaster-general. The former was responsible for discipline, promotions and appointments. The latter organised marches and arranged quarters for the army; he collected maps and intelligence; his, in germination, were the duties of a chief of staff. Puységur, writing in 1733, said 'all the duties of the quartermaster-general are those of the commander-in-chief himself, so that this is the only office proper for preparing its holder for command'. His intelligence and cartographical roles caused his duties to continue into peacetime.

The importance of the *intendant* (who embodied many of the quarter-master-general's roles) meant that in France the adjutant-general was a more important figure. In 1792 a chief of the general staff for the army was appointed, with four adjutants-general as his assistants, and adjutants-general were also the principal staff officers of field formations. In 1796, Berthier, Napoleon's chief of staff, drew up a memorandum outlining the duties of the staff, dividing its responsibilities into four sections. Four years later, Thiébault published a manual for the staff that was translated into English, Spanish, German and Russian. But beyond the standardisation of the staff's presence, Revolutionary and Napoleonic France offered little by way of precept. The *intendant* continued to be a separate function; Berthier, although chief of staff, had no independent operational control; and all intelligence was passed not to Berthier but to Napoleon's Cabinet. The staff lacked initiative and was suffocated by its merging with the imperial household and hence with the government of France.

Elsewhere in Europe the influence of the quartermaster-general remained paramount, and at times there were suggestions of the development from him of a true general staff. Sir George Murray, Wellington's quartermaster-general in the Peninsula, was his principal staff officer; the members of his department represented the army's intellectual cream and many of them had been trained at the Senior Department of the Royal Military College. At home, in Britain, the quartermaster-general's responsibility for preparing plans to counter French invasion gave him a true measure of strategic insight. In Austria, the Archduke Charles reorganised the quartermaster-general's staff to include operational duties and the gathering of intelligence. But his plan to have the chief of the quartermaster-general's staff as an adviser to the Supreme War Council was thwarted. In Russia too the growth of the quartermaster-general's department was marked by increasing independence. The emphasis on its intellectual excellence was such that in 1810 selected officers were sent to Moscow University.

But with the peace, much of this proved a false dawn. Wellington and Napoleon were bad at delegation, and in the end had operated without highly developed staffs. The small armies of the peace had even less need of overall co-ordination. The only true school of generalship was held to be experience, and as the stock of that dwindled it was replaced by personal qualities – courage, *coup d'oeil* and dash. Admittedly in France a *corps d'état-major* and a staff school were established in 1818, but by 1838 the corps had become a closed body, service in which was not rotated with service in line battalions, where seniority dominated promotion, and which was obsessed with the geographical minutiae of survey. In 1848, the Austrians in Italy had 11 trained staff officers for 70,000 men. Benedek, as chief of the quartermaster-general's staff, did polish the existing functions of the staff but made no attempt to update them. In Britain the story was similar. Long-standing pressure for a staff college was rewarded only after the multiplicity of conflicting departments had come crashing down in the Crimea. But even then no general staff emerged: the widespread nature of colonial commitments meant that prior planning could prove futile. Adaptation and improvisation were the keynotes, and the size of the armies small. Russia performed better than most, as perhaps she had to, given the size of her army. In 1832 a staff academy was opened under the control of the quartermaster-general, and in 1836 his department was reorganised and staffs for field commands established. Major staff reforms were carried through after the Crimea. The chief of the general staff became subordinate to the minister of war, and in the field the chief of staff was both the co-ordinator and also the second-in-command. But logistics were neglected, the organisation was over-centralised, and the low level of general education left Russia a poor field of choice.

What these powers had achieved was in the end little more than the creation of an administrative department to assist the general officers of the army at headquarters or in the field. France had tried to establish a special pool of officers to assist generals in the exercise of command, but had allowed it to atrophy. None of them had created a capital staff – a central organ to assist the ministry of war or head of state in strategic and operational terms. Only with this supreme body to determine overall doctrine could real direction be imparted to the staff officers of field commanders.

However, in Prussia the quartermaster-general's department had evolved somewhat differently. In 1802–3 a member of the department, von Massenbach, had pressed for technical training for staff officers. In 1803 an instruction for the quartermaster-general's staff embodied his ideas. Staff officers were to be selected by competitive examination, they were to be promoted by merit not seniority, and, so as not to become remote from everyday soldiering, they were to rotate staff appointments with line duty. The staff was to prepare plans and thus to act as a central planning body. Gneisenau gave practical application to much of this by stressing that staff officers should share operational responsibility with their commanders, and by encouraging flexibility and initiative within the framework of the overall objective. However, both he and Blücher remained prey to the monarch's will, which found increasing expression through the growth of the adjutant-general's department into a military Cabinet. Then in 1821 Rühle von Lilienstern became chief of the general staff department of the war ministry. His senior in rank, von Müffling, was already serving in the department and, to avoid friction, was moved out and appointed chief of the army general staff. In 1825 Rühle's department was dissolved. Thus almost by accident the general staff secured its independence of the ministry of war. Müffling reorganised the staff into three main divisions, dealing respectively with personnel, with training and mobilisation, and with technical and artillery matters. None the less in the 1840s and 1850s the general staff was still overshadowed by the king's military Cabinet.

It was Moltke's appointment in 1857 that marked the general staff's emergence as the main voice of the army. Consulted neither in the constitutional crisis on army reorganisation nor in the plans for the Danish War in 1864, the general staff reached maturity later in that year. Moltke's abilities allowed it to take advantage of the constitutional position staked out by Müffling. In June 1866 the chief of the general staff was given the right of direct communication with troop commanders, without passing through the war ministry. The importance of the railways placed a premium on planning and doctrine. In 1870, German general headquarters was divided into three sections – movements, railways and supply, and intelligence. The staff officers with field formations were in a sense Moltke's representatives, with wide powers of initiative and discretion in operational matters. After the Franco-Prussian War, Moltke's personal prestige and the general staff's independence of parliamentary control consolidated its position in the state. In 1883 the chief of the general staff was given the right of direct access to the Kaiser, even in peacetime. Thus the achievement was a mixed one. Germany had created a supreme co-ordinating body: its officers, trained in staff-rides and war games, were encouraged to display initiative and enterprise. But it was not subject to full political control. In could plot and plan in a military cocoon, where professional virtues could exclude political or diplomatic considerations.

However, the triumphs of the Prussian general staff in 1866 and 1870 ensured that it became a model for all Europe. In 1871, Austria-Hungary dissolved its closed general staff corps, and confined its staff appointments to those who attended the war college. Beck, appointed chief of the general staff in 1881, strengthened its operational and transport sections, and – as in Germany – established its independence of the minister of war. In 1905–6 Russia reorganised its general staff, appointing a German expert to its head. The tsar hoped thus to provide a direct link between himself and the army in order to bypass the war ministry, which was answerable to the Duma. However, the chief of the general staff, Sukhomlinov, was appointed war minister in 1909 and rendered the chief of the general staff a cypher. In the United States, Elihu Root established a staff college in 1901, and a general staff followed in 1903.

However, in creating a strong body of professional doctrine, a state exposed itself to a power of enormous political potential. The consequent problems of control were highlighted in two distinct ways by the examples of France and Britain. For France, the key issue was the subordination of the army to the Third Republic. Civilians were therefore wary of a centralised staff. In consequence, although Niel had begun reform before 1870, it was not until 1876 that the Ecole de Guerre was established, not until 1883 that the staff was opened and its officers rotated into the line, and not until 1890 that the first proper chief of the general staff was appointed. However, many problems remained: the Ecole de Guerre selected its students from the army's lieutenants and captains, and therefore the élite of the officer corps was marked out early in its career. The general staff thus developed a bureaucratic attitude and professional self-regard which led ultimately to the Dreyfus affair. So anxious was the staff to cover over its own failings in the interests of army morale that it could no longer see clearly the needs of the Third Republic. The aftermath of the affair left the staff grievously weakened and the *conseil supérieur de guerre* (a consultative body for corps commanders) was dispersed. Only in 1911 did fear of Germany cause a fresh start to be made. The chief of the general staff became France's supreme military officer, the *conseil supérieur de guerre* was restored, and a joint military and political co-ordinating body, the *comité supérieur de la défense nationale*, was created. But these measures were both little and late. The high turnover of commanders-in-chief and of chiefs of staff (France had seventeen between 1874 and 1914) meant that, although political subordination may have been guaranteed, France went to war without any clear tactical doctrine.

In Britain, the issue of political control arose in the context of foreign policy. A general staff was not created until 1906. Increasingly interpreting Germany as the main enemy, the British army could at least begin to concentrate on one issue. Therefore, from 1910 the general staff planned to aid France against Germany even though there was no diplomatic commitment to do so. Thus British strategy in 1914 was to some extent predetermined. However narrowly soldiers understood their duties, their collective wisdom was hard to direct. General staffs planning possible wars were novelties in the years 1870 to 1914: proper political and constitutional direction was understandably difficult.

However, without general staffs, the mass armies of pre-1914 Europe would have been uncontrollable. Furthermore, professionally they and their officers were highly competent. Contrary to oft-repeated views, tactically the military image of the next war in Europe was surprisingly accurate. Auger in France and Henderson in Britain both saw the dominance of firepower and trenches. Two works in their editions of 1883, Clery's *Minor Tactics* and von der Goltz's *The Nation in Arms*, reckoned that the infantryman should carry a spade. The frontal attack, von der Goltz thought, would become more and more enveloped, the wedge it created being shattered by the firepower of the defence. The battle would become less an attack, more a gradual chipping away at the enemy lines over several days, with many pauses and high losses. Schlieffen, Moltke's successor as chief of the German general staff, reflected a similar vein in his memorandum of 1905: 'All along the line the corps will try, as in siege warfare, to come to grips with the enemy from position to position, day and night, advancing, digging in, advancing again, digging in again, etc., using every means of modern science to dislodge the enemy behind his cover'.

Schlieffen's memorandum went on to conclude that since frontal attacks were well-nigh impossible, the maintenance of the offensive depended on flank movements, envelopment and encirclement. But Schlieffen embodied the professional tradition: his thinking – and that of his contemporaries – was faulty not at the level of tactics but of strategy. He concluded that industry could not lie idle for long. Across the water a British staff officer's assessment of 1901 reckoned that as a democratic, trading empire Britain could only fight a short war. France's manual, *La conduite des grandes unités* (1913), made the same point: 'the great numbers . . . the difficulty of supplying them, the interruption of the social and economic life of the country, all urge . . . a decision . . . within the shortest possible time'. For none of the great powers was a war of exhaustion politically or economically possible. The volume and capabilities of modern technology would make war more intense and more destructive. The British directorate of military training expected the army to suffer 65–75 per cent casualties in a year's fighting. But it did not expect fighting to last as long as a year. The failure to relate war to politics, to integrate what was possible tactically with what had occurred socially in Europe, meant that the ethos of 1866 and 1870 prevailed: war would be a search for absolute victory but it would be short. The failure of analysis was not primarily military; it was political. The American Civil War had become a war of exhaustion, and it caused Kitchener to conclude that the First World War would also be a war of exhaustion. In France Joffre and Galliéni tended to agree. Von Moltke the younger, a nephew of the victor of 1870, was another of the few who realised that the strategic context might have changed. He told the Kaiser on his appointment as Schlieffen's successor in 1905: 'We have now thirty years of peace behind us, and I believe that our views have largely become peacetime views. Whether it is at all possible to control by unified command the mass-armies we are setting up, and how it is to be done, nobody can know in advance.'

Guide to Further Reading

The officers of European armies between 1870 and 1914 were prolific in their writings, and also highly literate. Good representative authors are von der Goltz for Germany, Colin for France, and Henderson for Britain. Bernhardi is an excellent guide to the state of play on the eve of the First World War. Jay Luvaas (1959) has looked at their work in the light of the reaction to the American Civil War, and has also provided a general essay in Howard (1965).

The suggestions on specific armies made at the end of chapter 5 hold good for this chapter. In addition, Showalter's writings (particularly his book of 1975) have exhaustively tackled the Prussian army's response to the challenges of technology. Porch (1981) is the most recent treatment of the French army after 1871.

E. M. Lloyd provides a general, but dated, survey of infantry tactics. The problems of fire, movement and the offensive are considered for the Prussians by Showalter (1974 and 1975), for the French by Zaniewicki, Arnold and House, for the British by Travers (1978 and 1979) and Spiers (1981), for the Austrians by Rothenberg (1976) and Wheatcroft (in Best and Wheatcroft), and for the Russians by Bellamy (albeit briefly). Hutchison discusses machine guns. The artillery needs more work, but Spiers (1979) deals with the British. William L. Taylor provides a general treatment of the cavalry. Showalter (1976) looks at the Prussian cavalry, and Bond, in Howard (1965), and Badsey consider the British.

Pratt's standard work on railways has now to a large extent been replaced by Westwood. Showalter (1973) looks at the telegraph.

Irvine, in *Journal of Modern History* (1938), provides a valuable model for the interpretation of the history of general staffs. Hittle's book, which attempts a synthesis for a number of nations, lacks rigour and is disappointing. Görlitz provides a readable history of the German staff, but Craig (1955) and Ritter (1970–3) are more substantial. Craig in Howard (1965), looks at Austria before 1866, and Irvine, in the *Journal of the American Military History Foundation* (1938), considers France before 1870. The evolution of the British staff can be traced through Ward, Bond (1972) and Gooch (1974).

Chapter 9

First World War

The development of firepower seemed to have created a tactical impasse. The professional problem of how to mount an attack was particularly acute for the German general staff. Convinced that war on the French frontier would provoke war on the Russian (or vice versa), it had to seek a rapid and decisive engagement against one in order to release the army to face the other. The solution embraced by Schlieffen, as chief of the general staff from 1891 to 1905, was to avoid the fortifications erected on both borders, and instead to seek the flanks, to envelop and to encircle.

Schlieffen's thinking was inspired by Hannibal's victory over the Romans at Cannae in 216 BC. The Carthaginian had weakened his centre and strengthened his flanks in order to achieve envelopment: the Romans had been drawn in to the front and had thus exposed themselves even more decisively to the crushing of the wings. However, Schlieffen failed to distinguish between Hannibal's application of battlefield tactics and his own concerns, which were those of operational strategy. Schlieffen's definition of encirclement owed more to Napoleon than to Hannibal: 'You must not reach for the flanks at the extremes of the enemy's front, but in the full depth of a different disposition. The destruction of the enemy must be achieved by an attack against his rear.' The tactical concerns of Hannibal in 216 BC were in 1905 reflected in the application of the firepower of machine guns and quick-firing artillery to enable movement. Schlieffen's advocacy of envelopment contributed little to this.

The German plans formulated for use in the event of war in Europe were preventive rather than aggressive. Frightened of France, not only of a France anxious to revenge 1870 but also of the inveterate and implacable foe of 1806, the general staff had a professional duty to consider ways of fighting her. The additional spectre was that of a two-front war, with the German army having to turn simultaneously both east and west. From these defensive origins, Schlieffen formulated an offensive plan of reckless audacity. He aimed to knock out France in six weeks, in order to be free to turn against Russia. The attack in the west would swing on the pivot of Alsace-Lorraine, putting its weight on the right wing, which would wheel through Belgium, envelop Paris and drive the French armies against the border in the south-east (see Map 13).

Schlieffen's plan was inflexible at a number of points. But its besetting sin was its political naïvety. This was no more than a reflection of the pure professionalism of its author. His task had been to draw up a plan to deal with the French army before the Russians could mobilise. This he had done. But in the process he accepted the violation of Belgian neutrality, while failing to consider the response of Britain and in particular the possible dispatch to Europe of a British Expeditionary Force. Between 1897

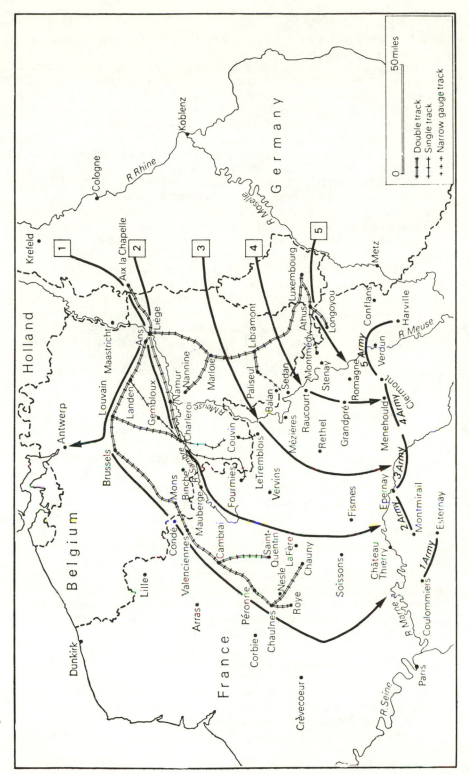

Map 13 *The German advance in the West, 1914*

and 1911 the navy received a growing share of the German budget, but Schlieffen gave no more consideration to its role than he did to that of naval operations as a whole. The plan was a purely military product, conceived in a vacuum by the German army. Not even the general staff of Germany's ally, Austria-Hungary, was privy to its full implications.

Schlieffen's successor as chief of the German general staff bore a distinguished name: he was the nephew of Helmuth von Moltke. Moltke the younger was in many respects far more realistic than Schlieffen. He appreciated that war in Europe might be triggered by a Balkan crisis rather than by France. But, despite the Eastward trend of political rivalry, he could see no alternative to the Western direction of Schlieffen's design. Gripped by a sense of fatalism, he saw the plan not as a formula for victory but as a last resort. Moltke made two major adaptations to Schlieffen's conception. He drew troops off from the west to protect the east: this was wholly justified by Russia's reform of her army after the war with Japan and by the Russo-French agreement in 1912 that Russia would attack in East Prussia by the fifteenth day of mobilisation. Secondly, he placed more troops on the left wing in the west, giving a balance in favour of the right of three to one, not Schlieffen's seven to one. Moltke feared that a French attack in Alsace-Lorraine would cut the German army's communications. He accepted that, if the French army was to be beaten, it could have to be fought where it was found. It would not necessarily conform to the thrust of Schlieffen's plan. However, in the event, the success of the German left wing drove the main French body westwards into the path of the advancing right wing.

The most surprising feature of the Schlieffen plan was its inherent military weakness. Above all there was no allowance for 'friction'. Kluck's 1st Army, which was on the extreme right, was required to cover three hundred miles in its great wheel, sustaining a marching rate of fifteen miles per day without pause for three weeks. The regimental field kitchens could not keep up: one regiment was without bread for four days. At times the advance was seventy to eighty miles ahead of the railway. The direction of the march took the armies away or across the main rail links, and therefore the further they went the greater became the supply problem. Logistically the right wing could have been no stronger than it was.

Clausewitz had reckoned that experience eased the cares of 'friction'. But the German army had not fought since 1871. None of the seven army commanders had commanded a formation larger than a regiment in action. Moreover Schlieffen was relying on the improvisation of reserve corps to furnish sufficient troops not only to carry out the advance but also to occupy the rear areas and to besiege Paris. In spite of all these constraints, Schlieffen had tried to plan the campaign right through to its victorious denouement. He expected the enemy to conform to his initiatives, and he left his subordinate commanders without the flexibility to exercise individual initiative.

The younger Moltke, like his uncle, appreciated that the plan could cover only the initial concentration. But in the event he found himself unable to find a balance in command and control. Part of the problem was that his attention was divided: while he was attempting to co-ordinate the advance in the west, he had also to supervise the overall situation in the east. But more serious was the deceptive state of wireless development. Marconi's breakthrough gave the commanders of 1914 the illusion that they were in contact with their forward units. In practice field telegraphy was still at an innovatory and experimental stage, and it caused as much confusion as it resolved. The German headquarters was the first during the First World War to find that it lost touch with its armies. It had only one receiving set; the 1st Army had two transmitters. The code employed was slow in decipherment, and the French were adept at jamming (and intercepting) transmissions. Other forms of communication proved as inadequate. Dispatch riders mounted on motor cycles found themselves lost on crowded roads. Air reconnaissance suffered from the lack of trained observers. Meanwhile the older, tested methods had been allowed to decay. In the years before the war, the German cavalry had stressed its role as fire support, not as scouts. The supply problems hit the horses hardest, and by 4 September they were suffering from sore backs. Moltke received a report of the disembarkation of the British Expeditionary Force on 13 August 1914, but had no idea of its whereabouts for the next nine days. From 7 to 9 September he received no report of any value, and not until 11 September did he fully appreciate the fate of Kluck's 1st Army.

What had in fact happened on 7–9 September was the climax of the battle of the Marne: in it the Germans had lost all hope of defeating France in six weeks. As the German right wing emerged from the bottleneck of Belgium, its numerical weakness forced Moltke to contract his front, and swing east of Paris. Kluck's army was to guard the German flank against a thrust from the capital, while the remainder continued the planned drive to the south-east. However, by the time Kluck received his orders he was already ahead of Bülow's army on his left and across the river Marne (see Map 14). He therefore pressed on. In a highly romanticised episode, Galliéni, the hero of French North Africa, commandeered the taxis of Paris, and threw the garrison into Kluck's flank and rear. The British withdrawal had made the Germans neglectful of their front. The gap between Kluck's and Bülow's armies opened as the former turned to meet Galliéni. The British cautiously entered it. Meanwhile Joffre, the supreme French commander, capitalising on the railway lines radiating out from Paris, effected a rapid transfer of French troops from the eastern frontier westwards, to central France. Kluck, the enveloper, was himself effectively enveloped. The victory was complete, and the Germans withdrew, eventually to the Aisne. Both sides continued to push towards each other's northern flanks, and these battles of late 1914, miscalled 'the race to the sea', were finally checked when the coast was reached. Neither the Germans nor the Franco-British forces had carried through a decisive envelopment battle. No flanks were left: in the west there was only a continuous front from the Channel to the Alps. The problem that remained was the one that the general staffs had been addressing before the war – how, given the development of firepower, to mount a frontal attack.

Events on the eastern front in 1914 were similarly characterised by the search for a decisive envelopment (see Map 15). Russian preparations

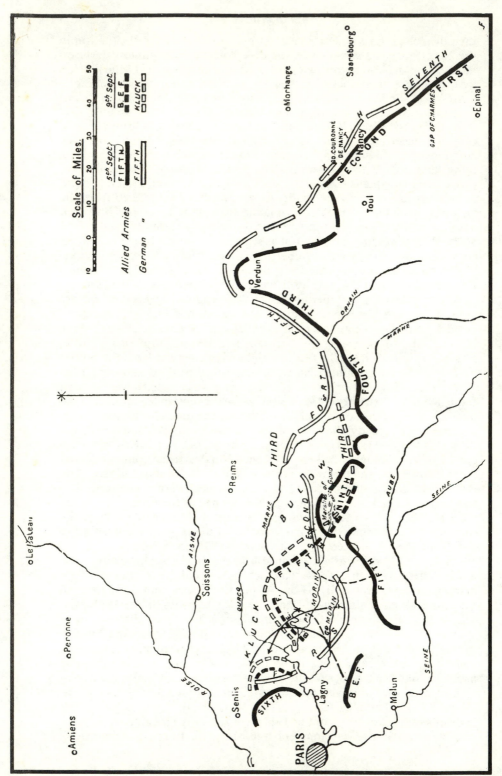

Map 14   *The battle of the Marne, 1914*

were bedevilled by their lack of rolling stock and railway line. Therefore positioned two-fifths of their forces well forward in Pol Vienna, Conrad planned a massive pincer movement on this salient, w. the Germans advancing from East Prussia and the Austrians through Galicia. This too was a plan devoid of realism. Conrad was sufficiently buoyed by vague German talk of a quick victory in the west to reckon on their rapid availability in the east. Furthermore Austria-Hungary's initial quarrel was with Serbia, not Russia, and it was thither that she directed her initial concentration. While the Austrian army's chaotic mobilisation was compounded by its division over two fronts, the Russians proved far more efficient than expected. Between 1910 and 1914 they managed to increase the available flow of trains from 250 to 360 per day, and they thus mobilised two-thirds of their army in eighteen days. For them Galicia was the dangerous salient, and on 3 September 1914 they smashed the Austrians at Lemberg.

However, the Russians had not avoided the pressure to disperse their effort. Their commitment to aid France (which in the event indirectly contributed to the Marne) compelled an offensive against the Germans in East Prussia. Again communications proved a central problem for an advancing army: Russian wireless traffic, transmitted in clear, was picked up by the Germans, while telegrams to Samsonov's 2nd Army were sent to the Warsaw post office and from there were ferried in bundles by car to his headquarters. The Germans' delay in attacking the Russian centre hastened the Russian advance. The Russians found themselves enveloped, and by 30 August 1914 the Germans had taken 92,000 prisoners and 400 guns in the battle of Tannenberg. Hindenburg, the German commander, and Ludendorff, his chief of staff, maintained that they had planned and executed a 'Cannae'. The fact that luck as much as judgement gave them the victory was in a sense irrelevant. The important point was that Hindenberg and Ludendorff continued to believe that envelopment battles could be effected, whereas Falkenhayn, Germany's war minister and Moltke's successor as chief of the general staff, did not. Hindenburg's and Ludendorff's case was stronger on the eastern front. Although there – as in the west – positions stabilised by the end of 1914, similar numbers of troops were holding double the length of front. The line was not continuous, was more thinly held and thus remained more fluid.

Even had the armies of 1914 been furnished with unlimited space in which to manoeuvre, the mobility would have been circumscribed by the difficulties of supply. As in 1866 and 1870, railways were crucial for the mobilisation and concentration of armies, but they could not maintain the rate of advance required to supply attacking troops. In 1866 and 1870 requisition had compensated. However by 1914 a major new element had been added to the supply problem, and it was one for which requisition could never be a palliative. The introduction of quick-firing artillery, machine guns and magazine rifles created enormous demands on ammunition supply. In 1905, a British field artillery battery could fire between 3,600 and 5,400 shells an hour. A conventional horse drawn supply system could sustain that rate of fire for two hours. The lorry, the long-term answer to mobile supply, only increased in use during the war itself. In

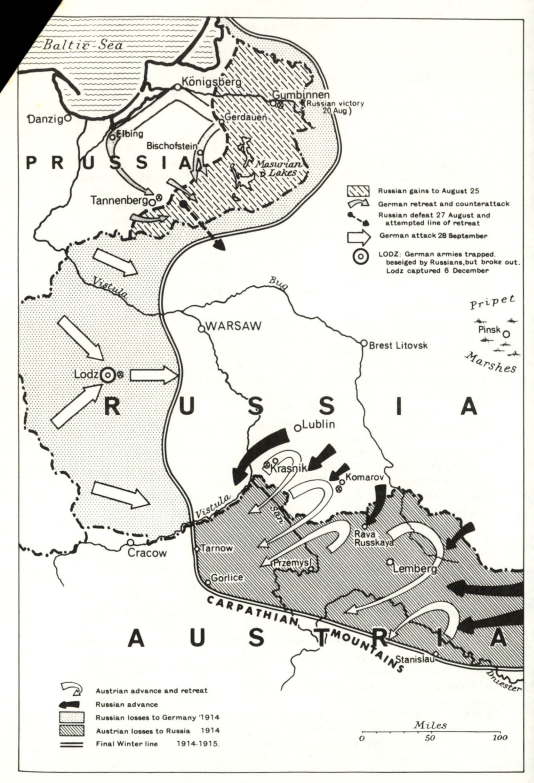

Map 15 *The eastern front, 1914*

August 1914 the British army possessed eighty for all theatres (although this figure had grown a thousandfold by the end of the war). Lorries were crucial to French supply of the Verdun battle in 1916. Broadly speaking, however, the horse remained the central and most flexible feature of forward transport units in the field. More ammunition therefore meant more horses. In 1870 there was one horse for every four men, in 1914 one for three. But a horse consumed ten times as much as a man in weight of food. Thus Kluck's army, with its 84,000 horses, required 2 million pounds of fodder a day. More munitions therefore also demanded more fodder for the draught animals. And so movement was slowed by a series of interacting brakes.

Ammunition supply created a problem in the rear as well as at the front. The powers had planned on a maximum of nine months' fighting at pre-1900 rates of ammunition consumption. The expenditure of 1914 therefore outstripped the capacity of domestic munitions industries. Britain was perhaps the most culpable as she had experienced the demand of the quick-firing gun in South Africa. But the scale was very different: in the Boer War the British army had fired a quarter of a million shells; by February 1915 it had expended four times that number. In 1914 the War Office was putting out contracts to private companies which did not possess the plant to meet them. In August orders were placed for 176 million rounds of small arms ammunition, when existing capacity could produce 3 million rounds a week. By June 1915, when Britain established a Ministry of Munitions, high explosive shell production was 92 per cent in arrears. The other belligerents faced similar crises. Three-quarters of France's production lay in the north-east and was thus lost within the war zone. The French army required 100,000 shells per day, but daily production of 75 mm ammunition stood at 14,000. The Russian army calculated it needed 250 million shells a month, when Russia's annual production was only 550 million. In December 1914 the Austrian army wanted 1 million rounds, but so far only 116,000 had been manufactured. Although Germany too faced an armaments crisis by October 1914, it was minor compared to that suffered by the other powers. For her the problem came in 1916 with the strain of Verdun and the Somme. In August 1916 Hindenburg introduced a programme aiming to triple machine gun and artillery production and double munitions output by the spring of 1917.

Long before then the other belligerents had learned to cope by a combination of nationalised industry and the state control of procurement. Russia's shell production for her 76·2 mm gun rose eightfold in 1915, and doubled again in 1916. By September of that year she was producing 4·5 million rounds per month, against Germany's production of 7 million and Austria's of 1 million, both of whom were fighting on other fronts. British shell production rose from half a million rounds in 1914 to 6 million in 1915 and 45·7 million in 1916.

None the less, the existence of a genuine crisis at the end of 1914 gave unsuccessful field commanders – particularly in Russia and Britain – a scapegoat on which to blame problems in the field in 1915. Tactical inflexibility was compensated for by weight of shell. Sir John French, the commander-in-chief of the British Expeditionary Force – despite his cavalry origins – was convinced that in its opening months the war would be dominated by trenches and heavy artillery. Thus by January 1915 he could conclude 'Breaking through the lines is largely a question of expenditure of high explosive ammunition. If sufficient ammunition is forthcoming, a way out can be blasted through the line'.

By seeing in shell supply the key factor in trench warfare, French ducked the inherent tactical problems facing the attacker of 1915. The difficulty of amassing sufficient strength – not only in men but also in artillery – for an attack meant that offensives were mounted on too narrow a front. They could thus be enfiladed by the defending artillery. The reserves to support the push were often too far in the rear to exploit any success in time. The best attacks therefore had the reserves well forward and already moving up at zero hour. However, on the eastern front in particular manpower might be too thinly distributed to allow the formation of a reserve. Aerial reconnaissance, which in trench warfare had usurped the role of cavalry, made it hard to concentrate the men and shell for an attack without being spotted in the process. These difficulties were only those of the preparation for an attack: fresh problems emerged as the infantry advanced over the top into no man's land. The machine gun, with its range of 2,500 to 3,000 yards, proved an enormous boon to the defence. It produced concentrated fire on a narrow front, and its weight and fixed elevation gave it an accuracy not shared by the rifle. Machine guns were organised in pairs, and, by 1916, in batteries of four to eight guns, in order to create fields of fire. The attackers would none the less probably have sufficient momentum to penetrate the defence's first line. They could not, however, overrun the full depth of the position in one bound. The defenders would withdraw towards their own reserves and artillery support: they would hold at the flanks, so as to enfilade the salient the attackers had formed. Meanwhile the attackers were enlarging the distance between themselves and their reserves and supports. In particular the lack of a man-portable wireless meant that communication between forward units and their rear was extremely vulnerable. In a static trench system, deep-laid telephone line assured excellent links with the rear areas. Fresh line would be laid above ground by the advancing units, but it would regularly be cut by shell fire. Thus the defender could call up artillery support; the attacker could not. Local breakthroughs could not be exploited by the rapid commitment of fresh reserves. The general was starved of information: like an eighteenth-century commander he was in a sense powerless the moment the battle began. Therefore he naturally enough tried to prepare for every contingency by putting all his effort into his plans. The loss of tactical flexibility was in this way exacerbated. It was confirmed by the tendency to conclude that the artillery bombardment was the best method to guarantee subsequent success.

Artillery, particularly heavy artillery, was the dominant arm of the First World War. In the Russo-Japanese War artillery fire caused 10 per cent of casualties; in 1914–18 it inflicted 70 per cent. The British Royal Artillery had 72 field and 6 heavy batteries in France in 1914. Four years later its strength stood at 568 heavy and 440 siege batteries.

In 1914 the artillery armaments of the major powers were dominated by the quick-firing field gun – Germany's 77 mm, Russia's 76·2 mm, France's 75 mm and Britain's 18-pounder. An infantry division had about fifty such guns. They were designed with a flattish trajectory, for their role was to provide a high rate of direct fire in close support of an infantry attack. Despite the lessons of the Russo-Japanese War, howitzers, capable of high-angle, indirect fire, were in short supply. The British had eighteen in an infantry division, the Germans twelve, but the Russians only three or four (and they were light pieces) and the French (who were caught in the midst of a debate as to the appropriate calibre) none. No power had adequate stocks of heavy artillery. Ironically the Germans had 575 heavy guns (against Russia's 240 and France's 180) for the 'wrong' reason – because they had expected to use them in besieging the forts of Belgium. Finally shell supply, like the emphasis on field guns, reflected the need to create conditions in which the foot-soldier could move. The emphasis was on shrapnel, whose scattering fragments were intended to force enemy skirmishing lines to ground and so allow one's own infantry to advance. Artillery in 1914 was designed as infantry support. However, in order to break up deep enemy positions, high explosive rather than shrapnel was required. Thus by 1915 the balance in the relationship between infantry and artillery was tilting to the opposite extreme. It suggested that artillery alone could drive infantry from trenches.

The attitudes which underlay the artillery procurement decisions before 1914 very often continued as factors in the structure of the arm for at least the first two years of the war, and in some instances throughout the war. As the Germans possessed more howitzers and heavy guns, from the outset they fought for ground from which observers could direct fire. The allies looked for reverse slopes, which provided protection against the direct fire of field guns but still lay within the range of high-angle howitzers. As a cheap and rapidly procured expedient to compensate for the lack of high-angle fire, they resorted to grenades and mortars, the weapons of eighteenth-century siege warfare. Furthermore, in the attack, the field gun retained a value since the forward burst of shrapnel allowed the infantry to stay close to the barrage.

Broadly speaking, the problems of the attackers in the western front were those of the British and the French. From January 1915, the Germans were searching for victory in the east. In the west, the advance of 1914 had left them strategically on the offensive: they occupied the industrial heartland of France, and they held high ground round Ypres and the Somme, overlooking the allied positions. Tactically they could now take the defensive without forfeiting the overall initiative. In the New Year, Falkenhayn ordered the preparation of a deep defensive position, which would allow the main body of troops to be kept out of the front line and therefore clear of the principal artillery attack. This decision determined the basic character of trench warfare in the west until March 1918: it became an interaction between the allied artillery attack and the German defensive battle.

Neuve Chapelle, the first British set-piece attack, launched on 10 March 1915, was characterised by many of these features. The bombardment lasted 35 minutes, and was delivered by 240 field guns, 36 howitzers and

64 siege guns. The attack at 8.05 a.m. by 30,000 men was only delivered on a 2,000-yard front. The German forward positions were thinly held, the machine gun nests being 1,000 yards back to give them clear fields of fire, and the main body lying 7,000 yards back. The attack got into the first line, but it had not yet encountered the principal German formations. Furthermore it was held up on the flanks. Because communications had to be relayed through battalion, brigade and divisional headquarters before they reached the corps commander five miles back, the orders to renew the attack were not issued until 3.30 p.m. and did not arrive until darkness at 6 p.m. By this time the German defensive positions were re-established, and the British initiative had been lost.

The British and French concluded that the solution was a long, methodical bombardment, with the subsequent infantry attack confined to the gaining of only limited objectives. The artillery was to provide the fire, while the infantry – moving forward in successive waves – was to occupy the devastated ground. Attacks therefore proceeded by timetable: surprise and flexibility were deliberately sacrificed. More positively, the sophistication of artillery tactics flourished. By 1917, through intelligence techniques, such as sound-ranging, flash-spotting and aerial observation, and through technological improvements in meteorology, ballistics and shell fuses, the gunners had developed methods for predicted fire and for making the barrage shorter and more accurate. The role of the artillery came increasingly to include the suppression of the enemy's artillery.

However, on the other side of the line, the operations section of the German headquarters was engaged in some radical, long-term tactical thinking. The principal threats were identified as the build-up of allied artillery and the related danger of an attack and breakthrough on a wide front. The Germans proposed to thin their front line, and to create the main line of resistance and a line of reserve trenches further back. The attack would therefore be filtered by a line of outposts, and then would be drawn deeper into the position and away from its support to be smashed between the main line of resistance and the line of reserve trenches. Counter-attacks would be launched by local reserves before the enemy could consolidate his gains. If a counter-attack could not be made immediately, it would be postponed until it could be launched with full deliberation. Ideally the German line should be sited behind the crest of a slope, so that it lay out of British or French artillery observation but within German view. The observers themselves were to be back from the line so as to be able to direct German fire with coolness and circumspection. The most important debate within this general framework was the degree of rigidity to be imparted to the front line. Traditional thinking rejected the idea of creating a line with no firm intention of holding it because of its adverse effects on morale and because of the difficulties of organising a retreat. It was a debate to be conducted in battle itself.

On the Somme in 1916 the strength of the German defences was weighted towards the front not the rear of the position, and the whole system was only 2,000 yards deep. Belts of wire 30 feet broad, traverses and dug-outs of a corresponding thickness and depth, characterised a tough outer crust. On 1 July 1916 the British attacked this position on a 14-mile front, while the adjacent French moved forward on a 9-mile front. The artillery preparation had been immense: the British had an 18-pounder every 25 yards and a heavy gun every 58 yards. They had brought up 3 million rounds, and fired over half of them in the seven-day preliminary bombardment. The German surface positions were devastated. But, deep in their dug-outs, the soldiers survived and, as they clambered out to meet the allied attacks, they found that the shell-holes provided securer defensive positions than the original trench line. The Germans, following the Moltkean tradition, were better at delegating command, and allowed greater initiative to their battalion and divisional commanders. The forward officers could control the reserve as well as the frontal troops in their sectors. They thus fought a more flexible battle, adapted to local circumstances, and marked by mobility throughout the depth of the position. By contrast, the British attack remained bound by its original planning. The new German positions were unknown to the British artillery. The barrage moved forward on timetable, lifting 100 yards every two or three minutes. A slower rate would have wasted ammunition, would have broken up the ground over which the infantry had to advance and would have allowed the Germans to bring up their reserves. Thus the needs of the artillery dictated the linear inflexibility of the British attack, ensuring a divergence between firepower and movement. On the first day of the battle the British army made minimal gains for almost 60,000 casualties, and in the subsequent four and a half months of fighting the total rose to 415,000.

However, German losses were at least comparable and probably higher. On 5 September 1916 Hindenburg responded by ordering the creation of a new line of defence designed to cut out the Noyon salient and so free thirteen infantry divisions. Its guiding tactical principles – above all a fluid defensive – offensive rather than a rigid frontal defence – were those formulated in the course of the Somme battle. They were promulgated in November and December 1916, and Ludendorff devoted the New Year of 1917 to intensive training in their practice. The new positions, which collectively came to be called the Hindenburg line, were chosen to aid artillery observation. Their foremost sector was 8,000 yards deep, with the outpost line on the skyline, and the main line of resistance (consisting of three trench lines) 600 yards back. The potential battle zone was obscured from allied artillery observers and lay between the main line of resistance and the second trench line, 1,500 to 3,000 yards in. Machine gun shelters were built of concrete and were designed to give all-round, not simply frontal, defence. In March 1917, the Germans withdrew to the new line.

The French Champagne offensive of the following month demonstrated a failure to adapt to the continuing evolution of German tactics. Nivelle, Joffre's successor, set a timetable for the artillery that was far too fast for the infantry. He aimed to reach 8,000 yards in three bounds in eight hours, and so overrun what he construed to be the full depth of the German position. But not the least of the virtues of the Hindenburg line was its low troop density – half that of a similar area on the Somme in the previous year. Principally this minimised vulnerability to artillery fire, but it also enabled ten divisions to be held 10,000 yards back and a further five 10,000 yards behind those.

Nivelle's failure in Champagne was offset by the limited British successes at Arras and on the Vimy ridge in the same month. Here 2,687,000 shells were fired over an 11-mile front, with a gun for every 9 yards. The British counter-battery work was excellent, and German front-line troops were caught still in their dug-outs, while the reserves were brought up too late. The German response was to scatter their machine guns and so break up the attack, while providing fire-support as a preliminary to the counter-attack. For every two divisions in front, one reserve division was deployed close in, with its leading regiment 5,000 yards from the foremost position. German pilots – not least Richtofen's famous Flying Circus – harried the allied aerial reconnaissance and so hampered the gathering of intelligence.

The Arras offensive was therefore checked as soon as it tried to expand the initial salient. Plumer's attack in the Ypres salient on 7 June 1917 did not make the same mistake. It harnessed ends to means in brilliant fashion. Three million shells were fired on a 6-mile front for 7 days, and then 19 mines (which had taken over a year to prepare) effectively lifted the Messines ridge out of the ground. The attack was successful partly because of the surprise, partly because of the acceptance of the dominance of *matériel* over tactical flexibility, but principally because it set itself only very limited objectives.

At the end of July, the British mounted their main offensive of 1917, the third battle of Ypres. A year's production of shells for 55,000 workers was brought up in 320 train-loads. One gun was distributed for every 6 yards of front, and over 4 million shells were fired. The German response was to abandon their trench lines for the relative safety of no man's land. But the British artillery was now more adept at responding to the German defensive battle. As the battle progressed, it stopped aiming for the trenches, and thus no longer created shell holes to aid the defence. Instead it laid its emphasis on counter-battery fire, so as to suppress the Germans' attempt to hamper the British troops' assembly before their attack. With the infantry launched, the artillery then prepared to check the German counter-attack. The infantry itself consolidated its gains on chosen ground, and thus forced the Germans to counter-attack on unfavourable terms. So the Germans once again had to hold their front line in strength, and to opt for methodical but delayed counter-attacks.

The trench, combined with barbed wire and machine guns, had strengthened the defence. The role developed for artillery was to open a path in this defensive network in order to permit a breakthrough. One technological novelty that fleetingly seemed to offer similar tactical advantages without forfeiting surprise or breaking up the ground was gas. By 1914 the French, British and Germans had all looked at the possibility of using irritant gases. However it was the Germans, spurred on by the munitions' shortages and by the relative ineffectiveness of shell against trenches, who decided to release chlorine gas from containers, allowing the wind to carry it over the enemy positions. On 22 April 1915, at Ypres, gas created a 4-mile gap in the British line. The Germans were confounded by their own success: they had never intended to create the opportunity for a strategic breakthrough and they had no reserves available to exploit the opportunity. Furthermore the prevailing wind over north-west Europe was south-westerly or westerly, and therefore in future the advantage in the use of gas was to lie with the French and British. However the wind was a fickle ally: Haig planned a gas attack at Loos in September 1915, but the wind dropped in the early hours of the morning of the offensive. Thereafter gas was little more than a valuable adjunct to trench warfare. Gas shells could be delivered with greater accuracy, independently of the wind, and they were particularly important in 1917–18 in disabling gun crews and so neutralising (if not destroying) enemy batteries.

The major problem posed by the strength of the defensive was the one that the tactical thinkers before 1914 had been struggling to resolve. To restore power to the offensive it was necessary to integrate fire and movement. The growing dominance of artillery in preparing the attack had merely widened the division between the two. In retrospect, the tank can seem to have been the obvious technological novelty to recombine fire with movement. But the masses of fast-moving tanks of the Second World War can obscure the true origins and nature of the First World War tank. All the major European nations had experimented with armoured motor vehicles by 1914. It was the trenches, and the need to destroy machine gun nests and to crush wire, that impelled the tank's subsequent development. Modern tank designers argue that their craft consists of blending three elements which can often in part prove mutually exclusive – firepower, protection and mobility. The early tank stressed the first two to the detriment of the third: its average speed was 5 m.p.h. Sir Ernest Swinton, the tank's prime mover in Britain, saw its roles as first to penetrate, second to enfilade trench lines and third to support infantry. Tanks, he wrote, 'are purely auxiliary to the infantry, and are intended to sweep away the obstructions which have hitherto stopped the advance of our infantry beyond the Germans' first line and cannot with certainty be disposed of by shell-fire'. Their task was to break in rather than break out.

Haig, the British commander-in-chief, contrary to the views of those who see him as the embodiment of military reaction, proved over-anxious to use tanks. Following Swinton's precepts, he prematurely put forty-nine into the battle of the Somme on 15 September 1916 in detachments of two or three machines. The first relatively independent use of massed tanks was at the battle of Cambrai on 20 November 1917, when 381 machines were launched over favourable terrain and in close conjunction with the advance of the infantry. Surprise was assured: because the tanks crushed the wire, no preliminary bombardment was required to cut a path. The tanks overran three German lines and penetrated five miles. The year 1918 witnessed increasing allied use of tanks: the French, concentrating on the production of lighter models, had over 3,000 by the armistice, and the British manufactured 1,359 in 1918 alone. But the tank had not revolutionised warfare. Over 400 machines went into action at Amiens on 8 August 1918, the so-called 'black day of the German army', and they reached as far as a German divisional headquarters, but by the 12th only six were still functioning. Their successes were dependent on effective co-operation with artillery and infantry.

In tactical terms, therefore, the model First World War offensive was a well-prepared attack that maintained an element of surprise but that above

rdinated the efforts of artillery and infantry. A spectacularly suc-
llustration of this was Brusilov's offensive launched against the
is from Russia's south-western front on 4 June 1916. The
edged weakness of the Russian artillery forced Brusilov to com-
by means of carefully prepared alternatives: direct liaison
between the infantry and the artillery was established at every level from
regiment to corps, the guns were kept as far forward as possible in order
to range to the full depth of the Austrians' positions, twice in the bombardment the fire moved forward prematurely in order to force the
Austrian guns to reveal their position, and – finally and perhaps most significantly – the alleged shell shortage kept the barrage brief but intense.
Therefore, rather than trust solely to weight of shell, the Russians
advanced their trenches to within 75 yards of the Austrians: they were into
the Austrians' line before they could recover from the artillery attack.
Preparations were made on a front so wide that it could not be enfiladed,
and at twenty places so that the Austrians could not detect where the main
thrust would come. Failure on one sector was thus offset by success on
another. Brusilov had his reserves well up and moving forward at zero hour.
By 16 September, the Austrians had lost 750,000 men, of whom 380,000
were prisoners. The strategic consequences were immense: the Austrian
effort against Italy slackened, the Central Powers transferred eighteen
divisions from the west and five from Salonika, and Romania finally –
but in the event misguidedly – threw in her lot with the Entente. Operationally, however, Brusilov's offensive turned sour. Brusilov himself
wanted to switch the attack to another sector but instead his success was
reinforced. The enemy rallied, the Russians were halted and eventually
they suffered a million casualties. The problem that Brusilov highlighted
was that of finding a viable strategy given the limited tactical possibilities.

Many commentators on the western front, particularly Frenchmen,
argued that the tactics of the infantry remained the hub of an effective
offensive. From early in the war they called for an elastic defence and
small unit attacks. Joffre opposed crowding the front line. In 1915, André
Laffargue challenged the tendency to see the artillery as the decisive arm.
Surprise in the attack, he argued, could be gained only by the infantry.
The artillery bombardment should be sudden and cover the full depth of
the position. The first wave of the infantry should press on without being
checked or without the restraint of set, limited objectives. Small groups
within each platoon, equipped with their own firepower in the form of
light machine guns and grenades, should tackle the defensive strong
points. Once across the front line, the leading sections should infiltrate,
looking for gaps, and leaving the clearing and consolidation of the main
line to support units. Machine gun nests would be taken in the flank. Fire
and movement would thus be reintegrated. In 1916 Nivelle made his reputation at Verdun organising counter-attacks with his infantry in small groups,
supported by a rolling barrage and bypassing centres of resistance. But, as
his offensive of the following year demonstrated, such flexibility still
threatened to become the prisoner of poor timing and of the timetabled
artillery barrage. Both dictated linear attacks in waves, making it hard to
exploit local successes, and putting the emphasis on redeeming failure.

The German defensive battle was by 1915 already developing in the same direction, linking fire with movement and emphasising efficient use of ground. Steel-helmeted assault troops, equipped with light mortars, machine guns, grenades and flame throwers, had begun to appear in the van of the counter-attack. In 1917 Ludendorff made the group of eleven men, commanded by an NCO, and equipped with a light machine gun, the basic tactical unit. On the eastern front, at Tarnopol on 19 July 1916, the Germans used a hurricane bombardment against previously located targets. After two hours, the bombardment lifted before the Russians could bring up their reserves, and the attack went forward, exploiting weaknesses and eventually advancing eighty miles. The emphasis in the artillery attack was on disruption rather than destruction, and it demanded sophisticated ballistic techniques to eliminate the need for preliminary registration. Above all, it allowed the infantry to determine the rate of advance. These principles – the hurricane bombardment, the fast advance spearheaded by stormtroopers, and the supporting formations clearing centres of resistance – were systematically applied at Riga on the eastern front on 1 September 1917, at Caporetto on the Italian on 24 October, and at Cambrai on the Western on 30 November. But the most spectacular successes were Ludendorff's five offensives in the west in spring 1918.

As before, twelve months earlier, the Germans devoted the New Year to training and dissemination, with the stormtroopers teaching the tactics of small unit attacks. The collapse of Russia allowed the Germans to boost their divisional strength in the west from 150 to 192. In the attack itself the stormtrooper formed part of the second wave, to penetrate the weak points identified by the probes of the first wave. Two additional features of German tactics are worth stressing. First, the general staff tradition of delegation within a leading idea embraced not merely the divisional commander but also the NCO, and so minimised the problems of battlefield communications. Secondly, fire support was well integrated, the guns moving up with the advance, and aircraft attacking machine guns on the ground. However, despite all these positive attributes, the Germans' success was in part a product of British weakness. They opened on 21 March 1918 with an attack on Gough's 5th Army, whose 14 infantry divisions were scattered over a 42-mile front, and had only one 18-pounder for every 100–200 yards. The British had not fully understood the German doctrine of the defence: their trench lines were developed more as jumping-off points for an attack, they lacked wire, and their machine guns were not properly sited. The weight of the defence lay well forward and therefore within German artillery range. Consequently, the Germans took 140 square miles on the first day, and eventually three major wedges were created. But the allied line held. As with the Brusilov offensive, the problem was the strategic application of a tactical success.

The constraints that faced soldiers in the First World War were tactical. Having accepted those constraints, the task which faced them was that of finding a viable operational doctrine which still left open a possible strategic objective. The generals gradually realised that limited attacks with limited objectives proved most successful. They should therefore aim to kill as many of the enemy as possible and thus exhaust him. Falkenhayn appreciated this as early as 1915: Sir William Robertson and Joffre followed suit. The year 1916 witnessed the first great battles of attrition, with the Germans aiming to bleed France at Verdun, and the British responding by attempting to break the old German army in four months' fighting on the Somme. On 19 June 1917, Haig told the War Cabinet that, if fighting continued at its present intensity, Germany was within six months of the total exhaustion of her manpower.

The strategy of attrition held a treble danger. The first was the reluctance with which generals brought up to the idea of a decisive victory approached it. Falkenhayn's limited attacks in the east early in 1915 were upset by Hindenburg, Ludendorff and Conrad, all of whom saw their objective as the total defeat of the Russian army. Falkenhayn himself had difficulty sustaining the strategy without ambiguity. At Verdun his subordinates were not checked when they preferred to interpret their task as the capture of the fortresses rather than the bleeding of France. On the other side of the line, Robertson would not fully accept a strategy of attrition until April 1917, and then only by default. Rawlinson, commanding 4th Army at the Somme, saw the battle as a gradual advance, while Haig still sought a breakthrough. Similarly, the British commander-in-chief may have presented Passchendaele in terms of attrition, but he simultaneously retained hopes of a breakthrough to the Belgian coast. The second risk in a strategy of attrition was that battles fought for limited objectives could allow the tactical possibilities to dominate and so obscure the strategic dimension. Indeed Ludendorff argued that 'Tactics have to be considered before purely strategical objects, which it is futile to pursue unless tactical success is possible'. In March 1918 Ludendorff achieved the greatest tactical success of the war. But he allowed individual battles to multiply as the British reserves were brought in, while collectively the fighting lost its overall coherence and direction. The third and final risk was also illustrated by the March 1918 offensives. The tactics of trench warfare favoured the defensive and thus the attacker seeking the attrition of the enemy might himself suffer greater casualties. The maintenance of the German army's tactical proficiency, given the loss of trained men in the punishing battles of 1916 and 1917, was a remarkable achievement. But it carried its own indications of weakness. In order to maintain the impetus of the advance, Ludendorff spurned the allied idea of 'leapfrogging' the forward units, and so units were whittled away as losses among the stormtroopers mounted. The success of 21 March still cost Germany 39,329 casualties (of whom all but 300 were killed and wounded), as against British losses of 38,512 (of whom only 17,512 were killed and wounded).

The failure to find a consistent mode of operations was – on the face of it – remarkable. General staffs had been created between 1870 and 1914 precisely to deal with these sorts of issue. But on the allied side the outbreak of the war had marked the effective collapse of the machinery for planning. In Russia, the Grand Duke Nicholas was given command of the armies although he had not been privy to war plans since 1908. The *Stavka*, reflecting a prewar split in the officer corps, remained weak in its relationship with the individual army groups. In Britain, staff officers

hastened to posts at the front, leaving a vacuum in the rear which Kitchener – now created secretary of state for war – was in no hurry to fill.
France, faced by so dramatic and immediate a military threat, delivered
itself into the hands of Joffre. He endeavoured simultaneously to be his
country's principal strategic adviser and its effective field commander on
the western front. However, by late 1916 the allies had come some way
towards the solution of these problems. Sir William Robertson's appointment as chief of the imperial general staff in December 1915, Kitchener's
death in June 1916 and Lloyd George's creation of a War Cabinet in December 1916 together created – although not admittedly without continuing rancour – a more effective dovetailing of political objectives and
military planning. In France, the replacement of Joffre in December 1916
allowed the division of the offices of supreme commander and commander-
in-chief on the western front, and the subordination of both to effective
political control. The Supreme Allied War Council, created in the autumn
of 1917, carried the same principle into the overall strategic direction of
the war. But the western front itself continued to lack a united allied command until Foch was appointed generalissimo in the midst of the March
1918 crisis.

Thus the problem of finding an allied strategy was compounded at two
levels. On the one hand it was enmeshed in a domestic squabble for primacy in the administration and direction of a wartime state. On the other
the diplomatic view of the strategic objectives of the war looked beyond
the armistice to the peace settlement, and so was divorced from a military
perspective that interpreted strategy as the most direct means to the
achievement of victory. In Britain the initial willingness to become
engaged on the peripheries of Europe, although it has been criticised as a
selfish reversion to a more familiar mode of conducting war, may none
the less have been consonant with military objectives. The Dardanelles
campaign of 1915 was designed to open up the eastern route to Russia,
and it was hoped that the Salonika venture would encourage the neutral
powers of the Balkans to enter the war on the allied side. Thus the objective remained the support or procurement of allies in order to defeat Germany and Austria-Hungary. But the Palestine campaign of 1917–18 was
concerned far more with diplomatic policy, with the settlement of the
Middle East *after* the collapse of the Ottoman empire, and harked back to
a prewar struggle with France for supremacy in the region. It can be taken
as an indication of civilian dominance in British counsels. The campaign
had scant relevance to the main battle in north-west Europe, where the
bearer of the principal military burden, France, was engaged in a desperate struggle to repel an invader. For the soldiers, the heart of the problem
throughout the war remained the defeat of the German army. The
demand that the primary effort should be devoted to the western front
could never be gainsaid; nor was it. However, the problem for the leaders
of democratic states was that such logic led ineluctably to a strategy of
attrition, and that was politically unpalatable.

While the allied conduct of the war was marked by the gradual reasser-
tion of political control, for the Central Powers the reverse occurred. The
German army grew progressively more powerful both in domestic terms

and in relation to its allies. Bethmann Hollweg, the German chancellor, and Falkenhayn at least saw that, if Germany was to win, she would have to split the allied coalition. Falkenhayn seemed to appreciate that his commitment to a strategy of attrition might imply the acceptance of a negotiated peace rather than total victory. However, in August 1916 Hindenburg succeeded Falkenhayn in the supreme command, and brought in Ludendorff as his quartermaster-general. Gradually the army became the controller of Germany's war effort. In the interests of war production, the general staff assumed overall responsibility for industry, and in December 1916 Hindenburg and Ludendorff secured the passage of the Auxiliary Service Law, which mobilised all German male adult labour. The army added its weight to naval pressure for the declaration of unrestricted submarine warfare. On 1 February 1917 Bethmann Hollweg reluctantly acceded. Although aimed at Britain, the consequence was to bring the United States in on the allied side. Finally in July 1917 Bethmann Hollweg was prevailed upon to resign. The duality of chancellor and chief of the general staff embodied in Bismarck and Moltke was overthrown: policy was now truly subordinate to war.

However, what resulted was not a blending of policy and strategy, but an imbalance between the two. Hindenburg and Ludendorff continued to foster Germany's more grandiose war aims, when militarily speaking the major victory needed to consolidate a German-dominated central Europe was no longer possible. Furthermore the division between politics and the conduct of war was not simply evident in the crude divergence between diminishing means and escalating ends. The strategy of attrition also revealed a tension for Germany within the conduct of war itself. She was mobilising the entire nation for a war effort that could aspire to only limited tactical gains. By 1918 her strength was ebbing: Germany had never possessed the resources to allow her to embrace a strategy of attrition. The demands of war, and to a lesser extent the blockade, was weakening her economy; her industrial output in 1918 was 57 per cent of her 1913 level; insufficient rolling stock contributed to a transport crisis. The army itself began to suffer: Ludendorff had to nominate 56 of his 192 divisions 'attack divisions', and give them preference in the issue of supplies and equipment. Even then, hungry German soldiers took to looting in allied rear areas and so contributed to the breakdown of the 1918 offensives. Only a negotiated peace was really possible with limited military success, but neither Hindenburg nor Ludendorff was willing to acknowledge this. After the war, Ludendorff turned Clausewitz on his head: 'warfare', he wrote, 'is the highest expression of the national "will to live"', and politics must, therefore, be subservient to the conduct of war'.

By contrast, the allied strategy of 1918, while embracing much of Ludendorff's tactical thinking, did not lose sight of the strategic dimension. Shallow attacks with massive artillery support were designed to achieve only limited objectives and to avoid the creation of salients. Each was successive and related so as to exhaust the Germans' reserves. The infantry, freed from the inflexibility of the artillery barrage by the tank and by the technical improvements in the guns themselves, could move forward in 'blobs' and 'snakes', rather than 'waves'. Furthermore the strategy of attrition was being applied at two levels: Haig and Pétain were concentrating on wearing down the German army in the field, while Lloyd George was building up reserves and waiting until the Americans arrived.

A fortnight after the battle of Amiens, Foch and Haig realised that they could now set their divisions more distant objectives, neglecting their flanks and without fear of counter-attack. The situation in the west coupled with the collapse of Bulgaria to break Ludendorff's nerve. At the end of September he initiated the process which led to Germany's request for an armistice. On one level the German army had been defeated. But in the course of the subsequent negotiations, Ludendorff's resolve hardened once again. When the armistice finally came into effect on 11 November, the German army was intact in the field, strategically still on the offensive, well outside its own frontiers. Thus it was able to argue that it had been betrayed by a domestic collapse. By transferring responsibility, it emerged with its *amour propre* intact. And so the objectives of the allied generals were thwarted: the pride and professionalism of the German army survived the First World War.

Guide to Further Reading

The literature on the First World War is marked by a wealth of detailed literature and a shortage of good surveys. Furthermore it is a war whose main features remain the subject of fierce controversy. In these circumstances scholarship still has much to give. A. G. S. Enser's *A Subject Bibliography of the First World War* (London, 1979) provides guidance on specific topics. Of the general accounts, Cruttwell remains by far the best. Ferro is brief and good on the social aspects, while Hardach covers the economic dimension in a thoroughly competent way.

Liddell Hart's account of military operations (1934) is one-dimensional and without serious discussion takes for granted the superiority of the naval blockade over the futility (as he sees it) of the western front. But no more recent operational account is as succinct or helpful. Ritter (1958) is essential on the Schlieffen plan. Broad discusses the development of the British artillery attack, and Wynne and Lupfer look at the German defensive response. Winter considers the nature of trench warfare. Shelford Bidwell and Dominick Graham consider British generalship and tactics in *Fire-Power: British army weapons and theories of war 1904—1945* (London, 1982). Shell shortage in Britain is discussed by French and Trebilcock. For Russian production problems, and much else on the eastern front, see Stone. Feldman is the best guide to Germany's economic mobilisation.

The debate about war aims, begun by Fritz Fischer's enormously important and influential book, *Germany's Aims in the First World War* (London, 1966), has not yet been fully reflected in accounts of the strategic direction of the war. Hunt and Preston provide a beginning, but some of their contributions are more helpful than others.

Chapter 10

Blitzkrieg

Qualitatively and quantitatively there had never before been a war like the First World War. Its scale redefined what men meant by war: the connotations of violence and futility, loss and suffering were now etched in the collective consciousness of twentieth-century Europe. Furthermore, at an individual level it was the formative military experience of the generals of the Second World War.

But, although the experience was shared, the conclusions men drew were divergent. The politics of the interwar years provide a stark contrast: pacifism and disillusionment found themselves cheek-by-jowl with the overt militarism of ex-servicemen's organisations and of Fascism. Tactically, the dominance of the trench was taken as proof that the defence was the superior means. France embodied this conclusion in the construction of the Maginot line. Nor was she alone: Germany built the *Westwall*, Greece the Metaxas line, Russia the Stalin line and Finland the Mannerheim line. None the less, many soldiers were keen to restore power to the attack. To do so they had to construct arguments on the largely unproven technology of the tank and the aeroplane; they had to extrapolate too much from the limited evidence garnered in 1914–18. Economic dislocation followed, as prototypes proliferated while peace caused the industrial plant for mass production to wither. For, if there was one lesson from the First World War on which all were agreed, it was that economic mobilisation would be crucial in any future European war. Britain, the USSR and France avowed this quite openly, both in their interpretations of the causes of victory and in their preparations for the next war. On the German side, the economic aspects of rearmament and the search for a rapid victory through *Blitzkrieg* contained their own implicit acknowledgement.

France had been the scene of the heaviest fighting and, although nominally victorious, the casualties she had suffered, coupled with the disruption of her industry, left her with a sense of loss. Politically her army was out of sympathy with the Third Republic. Pay was caught by inflation and the slump, and morale remained low. In 1921 a committee on the lessons of the war produced the *Instruction provisoire sur l'emploi tactique des grandes unités*. Its conclusions were effectively re-endorsed in 1936. The *Instruction* contended that the dominant lesson of the war had been the importance of *matériel* and therefore of industrial mobilisation. The tactical expression of material superiority was the artillery. Its role was to destroy and to neutralise, that of the infantry to advance and to occupy. Thus, once again, rather than integrate mobility and firepower, soldiers opted to discount the former in favour of the latter. Tanks and aircraft were simply support weapons. Thus, too, the idea of the nation in arms was extended to the entire labour force. Industrial productivity was as vital to a sustained

war effort as fighting itself. In 1928 the term of service was fi*
year, and, although the falling birth-rate forced the Third F
raise it to two years in 1935, the effect was to render the arm*
ous training establishment, capable of only defensive fighti*
fessional army was branded with the costly offensives of 1914. 1..
task of the army, expressed in the term *couverture*, was to cover the mo*
ilisation of the French nation for total war. In particular it must, as it had
not in 1914, protect the vulnerable industrial heartland in north-east
France. From 1928 the Maginot line, a fortified line along the German
frontier, gave practical effect to this doctrine. The line terminated with
the Ardennes, which were accepted as impenetrable, and to the north, for
the purposes of defence, Belgium was regarded as part of France. Both
assumptions proved unwarranted, but the Maginot line itself was well
adapted to an untrained reserve army fighting a defensive battle, and was
the supreme expression of one view of the First World War.

Mechanised forces were fundamentally out of sympathy with this
thinking. Tanks, the skills needed to man them, and the offensive style
with which they were associated, were all felt to require a professional
army. In 1934 Charles de Gaulle published *Vers l'Armée de Métier*. Its
significance is conveyed far more in its French title than in its discussion
of armoured warfare – which only took up about a quarter of the book
and which relied heavily on the thinking of France's great tank pioneers,
Estienne and Doumenc. De Gaulle was in the tradition of du Picq. He
wanted a regular mechanised army, 100,000 strong and capable of taking
an early offensive. France, by tying the whole nation to a defensive
policy, was committed to total war. De Gaulle argued that she should
retain the ability to wage a limited war, or even to launch a rapid, pre-
emptive strike.

In 1935 Paul Reynaud championed de Gaulle's book. However,
although the contentious matter lay in the political arguments, it was
more at the tactical level that the opposition confronted de Gaulle. French
dependence on foreign oil, improvements in anti-tank weapons and the
poor state of the French arms industry after a decade of neglect were all
adduced as reasons against mechanised forces. These points were not
without force: Estienne's design of heavy tank, the B1 *bis*, had seventeen
different engines, but none of them was in mass production. Thus,
although tank development did occur, beginning with the establishment
of the 1st *Division Légère Mécanique* in 1934 and carrying through to the
approval of two armoured divisions in December 1938, it remained scarred
by a lack of doctrine. The cavalry had taken a leading role in the *Division
Légère Mécanique* and it therefore emphasised scouting and reconnaissance. The infantry's interests were reflected in the armoured division:
Estienne's medium battle-tank with its 75 mm gun was to support the
breakthrough and was therefore tied to the speed of the foot-soldier. In
1936 mass production of new types of tank and tracked vehicle began. But
the result was that in 1940 there were ten such types in use, and there had
also been a similar proliferation of formations – motorised, light mechanised, light cavalry and armoured divisions. Moreover, the operational
task of those units owed nothing to Gaullist thought: it remained mobile

defence, to plug any gaps in France's outer crust. Therefore, by 1939 the thinking embodied in the 1921 *Instruction* and in the doctrine of *couverture* was badly out of line with tactical and technological developments in warfare. In particular it ill accorded with a growing respect for a possible German *attaque brusquée*. Even more seriously, its defensive thrust rendered the French army capable only of fighting west of the Rhine, while diplomatically the Third Republic had given undertakings to Eastern Europe.

Britain too, in the interwar years, could be accused of allowing her military thinking and her foreign policy to diverge. Although she retained commitments to Europe, psychologically she turned her back. Even before the end of the First World War, the War Cabinet had been disproportionately concerned for the future of the empire. With no obvious European enemy (unless it be France), the 1920 budget had reasonably reckoned on the absence of war for ten years. The Royal Navy was once again to be the main defence of Great Britain against an invasion, and the army — in a policy reiterated as late as December 1937 — was to concentrate on its imperial role. So little thought was devoted to the conduct of European warfare that not until 1932 was there even a War Office committee on the lessons of the First World War.

Basil Liddell Hart, a wartime captain, was the principal intellectual advocate of this policy of 'limited liability'. He also fundamentally affected the interpretation of the First World War through his own writings and through his close relationship with the wartime prime minister, Lloyd George. Broadly speaking he argued that the naval blockade had broken Germany and that therefore the British Expeditionary Force need never have gone to France. His fear for the future was that France's continuing commitment to total war would again suck in Great Britain. His book, *When Britain Goes to War* (1935), held that maritime pressure, abetted by European allies and only a limited British effort on land, had historically been the British way in warfare. He supported this position by two supplementary arguments. First the trend tactically now favoured the defensive, and the moment was therefore not propitious for forays into Europe. Secondly he criticised the European tradition in strategic thought: the emphasis on mass at the decisive point was bloodthirsty and militaristic and neglected manoeuvre, subtlety and surprise. These were the themes of a book that came in its later editions to be called *Strategy. The Indirect Approach* (first published 1929).

In these circumstances the Royal Air Force, not the army, became Britain's offensive arm for continental war. The expansion of air forces during the First World War had been prodigious: at the beginning of 1918 Germany had 200 squadrons, France 260 and Britain 100. But there were enormous difficulties in formulating a doctrine of airpower. Technically the development of flight was too rapid for service thinking to keep pace: the progression from the Wright brothers to the intercontinental ballistic missile occurred in one man's lifetime, and the chiefs of the air staff even in the 1950s had embarked on their professional careers before separate air arms had been created. In the First World War, airmen had been gleaning low-level operational experience not serving on the staff. On this slender basis they were required in the interwar years to shape thinking on military aviation from first principles. Lord Trenchard, the British chief of air staff from 1919 to 1929, is a case in point: his service life began as a soldier and he had never been to staff college. A third complicating factor was that no sooner had doctrine become set according to the precepts of the First World War than the greatest technical changes occurred. In the mid-1930s, the advent of radar, of the monoplane, and of the long-range heavy bomber recast the capabilities of air forces.

The First World War suggested a number of obvious applications for airpower – reconnaissance, close air support for ground forces, and interdiction bombing against an army's rear and communications. Air forces remained linked to and dependent on armies: ground troops were still needed physically to occupy territory.

Britain, however, drew a different lesson from the war. In 1916 German airship and bomber raids on Britain reached a peak. They caused minimal damage, but they evoked sufficient anger to suggest retaliation in kind. Allied experience of bombing was limited. The Royal Naval Air Service had developed precision bombing techniques against German airship sheds on the Belgian coast, and in 1917 the French created an independent bombing force. The idea of striking at civilian targets in Germany, adumbrated in the 1917 Smuts reports on air defence, commended itself for other reasons. An independent air force would help lessen the emphasis on the military effort on the western front. In 1917 an aircraft production surplus was likely, and the Air Board – whose main role was to allocate aircraft between the army and the navy – could thus channel aircraft to a separate air arm. On 1 April 1918 the Royal Air Force came into existence. It was the only truly independent air force in the world. But it had been born out of bureaucratic pressures rather than strategic logic, and thus, to ensure its survival in peace, it had to find a role. That role could not be the army-oriented ones of reconnaissance or close support. Instead its task was justified by the circumstances of its birth – strategic bombing.

The evidence from the First World War for the efficacy of strategic bombing was slender. Its great advocates in Britain and the United States, Trenchard and Mitchell (the latter was even court-martialled in 1925 for his intemperate support of an independent air force), had gained their experience in interdiction bombing. Trenchard supplemented his thinking with the RAF's independent use of airpower in colonial operations in the 1920s. Two principal targets were proposed for strategic bombing. The first was civilian morale: Trenchard once argued that the psychological effect of aerial bombardment would be twenty times greater than any material damage it might do. The second was the economy. Here was a direct lesson from the First World War: if full industrial mobilisation was required to fight a prolonged total war, a direct attack on productivity would shorten it. The Royal Air Force had therefore assumed the mantle of bombardment and blockade previously carried by the Royal Navy. The doctrine of strategic bombing, like the French interpretation of the nation in arms, proceeded from an acknowledgement of the economic aspects of twentieth-century European war. Its underlying conception, again like that of France, was defensive. Bombers were to deter an enemy from attacking by threatening his cities. However the implications of deterrence (should it fail) were also more total than aggressive war conducted by field armies. The ethics of strategic bombing were therefore doubtful. None the less, Liddell Hart argued in 1925 that, as bombing would produce a quick victory, it would minimise losses and therefore the end would justify the means.

The great European advocate of strategic bombing was neither Trenchard nor Mitchell, but an Italian, Giulio Douhet. His book, *The Command of the Air* (1921), was not published abroad until between 1932 and 1935, and its influence outside Italy was thus to corroborate rather than to formulate. Like Trenchard, Douhet assumed that there was no effective defence against the bomber, and assumed too that civilian morale would be shattered. War would therefore be shorter and more humane. Italy had pioneered the use of airpower in Tripoli in 1910, and her domestic geography made her naturally receptive to Douhet's ideas. The mountainous peninsula was unsuitable for tanks and well-adapted for defence. Mussolini and the commander of the Italian air force, Balbo, embraced 'Douhetism' as deterrence: bombers could launch strikes across the Alps against any North European opponent.

During the 1930s some of the logical and technological fallacies in strategic bombing doctrine ensured the waning of 'Douhetism'. The assumption that the. bomber would always get through had caused air defence to be neglected. Belatedly it now received attention. The monoplane fighter, the development of radar, and the provision of effective communications between the two together constituted the crucial breakthrough. In 1936 the RAF created a separate Fighter Command. The threat of the bomber had not actually deterred Hitler in his conduct of foreign policy. In 1937 Britain realised that she was more vulnerable to air attack than Germany and that therefore she must switch the emphasis in production from bombers to fighters and anti-aircraft guns. Indeed strategic bombing doctrine had far outstripped the technological possibilities: Trenchard had made little attempt to enlist the support of science, and night-bombers, long-range heavy bombers, bomb sights and navigational aids were not put into production until the mid-1930s. These factors in combination meant that Britain did not yet have the ability to launch a strategic bombing offensive on Germany. Strategic bombing doctrine was also undermined by its implications for foreign policy. Air attacks could be launched on Britain from Europe, and the emphasis on airpower rather than seapower thus put British defences on the Rhine and not in the Channel. Implicit, therefore, in the thinking of the RAF was a requirement for ground forces. The doctrinaire reluctance to integrate air forces with armies commanded fewer adherents in the late 1930s.

None the less the RAF's espousal of strategic bombing was not without its consequences. The belief that the RAF possessed a continental reach helped obscure the fact that Britain's diplomatic obligations in Europe lacked a military doctrine to support them. In September 1938 the British army could not have backed a strong stand against Hitler at Munich. The Treasury had favoured the air force over the other two arms: throughout the 1920s it was accorded priority, and even in 1939 the RAF received 41 per cent of all military expenditure. Thus the navy and army were left in second and third places in the financial pecking order. Operationally, the tri-service approach of the British thus contrasted with the continental tendency for the army to dominate in defence decision-making. Its negative legacy was poor service co-operation in Britain. The undercurrent of an independent bombing doctrine remained: in 1938 Bomber Command still claimed that by attacking the Ruhr it could bring the German war machine to a standstill in two weeks. Not until 1942–5 could the RAF launch this sort of offensive, and, even if it was effective, it was not independently successful. Whether or not Trenchard's bequest was thereby justified will be discussed in chapter 11.

The irony of Britain's emphasis on strategic bombing and of her neglect of continental land warfare was its implicit derogation of the tank. Britain had done most to develop the tank in the First World War and had produced its principal tactical theorist in Major-General J. F. C. Fuller. Fuller, the planner of Cambrai, was abrasive and intolerant. Bearing the imprint of the pre-1914 French school of tactics, he contended that battlefield success was achieved through the demoralisation of the enemy. With this in mind, and influenced by Germany's success in the March 1918 offensive, in May 1918 Fuller drew up his 'Plan 1919'. The scheme was of some long-term theoretical importance, but of no short-term significance, despite the encouragement its progenitor received from Foch and Fuller's fellow Francophile, Sir Henry Wilson. Fuller called it, significantly, a 'psycho-tactical' plan. His intention was that it would be the formula for allied victory in 1919. Medium tanks were to launch a surprise attack on a 90 mile front, penetrate at certain points only, and then head for the area between the German divisional and army headquarters. The central idea was the strategic paralysis of the front line troops through the disruption of their command organisation. The remaining enemy positions would be cleared by heavy and medium tanks, and yet more medium tanks would conduct the pursuit. The RAF was to reconnoitre, to give tactical assistance and to bomb.

Even had the war continued for another year, Fuller's conception would have remained visionary. It called for a tank designed for exploitation, capable of 15–18 m.p.h. across country, and with a range of at least 150 miles. No such tank was in production until 1923. Furthermore the plan demanded a total of 4,352 heavy and medium tanks, a number far in excess of the production possibilities. Indeed economic performance was perhaps the biggest constraint on the development of armour. The cut-back in arms industries in the 1920s placed an emphasis on continuous, low-level output, with insufficient plant for massive short-term production.

But it does not follow that Fuller was an advocate of total war. On the contrary, like de Gaulle, he argued that tanks were a substitute for manpower. Their crews would require more training than could be given to short-service conscripts, and therefore costs would keep armoured forces small. Furthermore the speed of an armoured attack would allow insufficient time for the full mobilisation of reservists or of industry. Thus, in many respects, Fuller's thinking was consonant with Liddell Hart's arguments for limited war. But, whereas Liddell Hart held that manoeuvre – the 'indirect approach' – could be a substitute for battle, Fuller accepted that the first stage in a breakthrough must be a battle for penetration.

With his vigorous style, Fuller tended to gloss over the obstacles to the full flowering of his ideas. He felt smaller armies without horses would be less dependent on 'natural' supply, and therefore a self-contained force would have more space to allocate to 'military' supply. Even allowing for the existence of small armies with minimal food requirements, this line of thought totally neglected the problem of petrol supply, which in the event proved a far more inflexible constraint on operations than fodder for the horses. By putting the machine at the centre, Fuller felt that his model army had minimised the problems of friction. 'The machine', one of his followers, G. C. Shaw, wrote in 1938, 'can brave the elements; it needs no accommodation; it suffers no sickness; it has no emotions – it is insentient.' But Fuller's projected success for the tank still rested on the assumption that the enemy troops remained ill-trained conscripts prey to moral forces, and in particular that the moral impact of the tank would remain as great as it had in 1918. Furthermore he did not reckon with the application of the machine to the defence in the shape of the anti-tank gun.

Liddell Hart, although more adept at self-publication than Fuller, was not comparably pioneering in the development of tank tactics. Indeed his initial interests were in the infantry, with the result that his appreciation of the tank's potential lay dormant until awoken by Fuller. However, these early concerns were not without their impact on armoured doctrine. From his study of the March 1918 offensive, Liddell Hart developed the idea of the 'expanding torrent'. He argued that deep strategic penetration, relying on its own speed and moral superiority to numb the enemy, would overcome the need to attack on a broad front. Whereas Fuller tended to neglect the other arms, Liddell Hart stressed that they remained complementary: the infantry should be motorised to accompany the tanks and to deal with strong points. A possible alternative to self-propelled artillery for such a fast-moving force was the dive-bomber.

Despite the story Fuller and Liddell Hart would have us believe, the slow development of tanks in Britain was not solely attributable to the purblind conservatism of the army's senior officers. Tragically the first major check proved to be Fuller himself. Rarely do armies entrust a theorist with operational responsibility, but in 1927 Fuller was given command of the Experimental Mechanised Force on Salisbury Plain. The only positive feature that arose from his resignation over the terms of the command was that it gave him the opportunity to write his most concrete and influential discussion of armoured warfare, *Lectures on F.S.R. III* (1932). Sir George Milne, the chief of the imperial general staff, then decided to mechanise the whole army and thus to proceed slowly on a broad front, rather than to create rapidly an élite 'new model' force which would produce distortions and differing capabilities within the army. Positively this meant that in 1939 the British army was the only army in the world whose transport was entirely motorised. Negatively it led to the disbandment of the Experimental Mechanised Force. In 1929 the War Office published its first manual on mechanised war, the so-called 'purple primer' drafted by Charles Broad. It allowed independent attacks by armoured brigades on favourable terrain. However, rather than accept Liddell Hart's emphasis on the tank's mobility, it preferred to stress the exploitation of firepower. Thus the distinction between mobile all-tank forces and heavy tanks committed to infantry support became increasingly important. In 1931 Broad was entrusted with the formation and training of a tank brigade. This was put on a permanent footing in 1933 under the command of Percy Hobart. Hobart perhaps over-played the independent capabilities of armour in movements of deep penetration. Certainly he produced a reaction, partly designed to maintain the morale of the other arms, but aided by the decision to mechanise the cavalry rather than to expand the Royal Tank Corps. The cavalry's main task had become reconnaissance, and this role thus also came to be associated with mechanised forces. The 'cavalry spirit', including as it was bound to do a reluctance to part with the horse, was not an unmixed blessing for the prospects of the tank. In 1938–9 the secretary of state for war, Hore Belisha, influenced by Liddell Hart, established that the army was to have two types of division, a motorised division based on the light machine gun and a mechanised armoured division built round the tank. However, such a project could only be long term. In 1940 Britain had but two armoured divisions.

This palpable weakness had arisen not least because the army had spent the 1930s preparing to fight not in Europe, but in the colonies. Tanks were therefore of only limited value. Even as the possibility of European war grew, the army's main priority remained its contribution to air defence and specifically to anti-aircraft guns. The very rapid expansion of 1939 produced chaos. The debates of the 1930s left the War Office with no agreed weapon designs for specific tactical tasks. In many ways the advocates of an independent use of armour had been too successful. Their stress on mobility meant that the requisites of combat – thick armour and heavy guns – were confined to the Matilda, a slow-moving tank for infantry support, which even then had an inadequate 2-pounder (or 40 mm) gun. They had discussed airpower largely in terms of reconnaissance, to find the line of 'least expectation', rather than of close air support. Thus the RAF's own reluctance to face up to co-operation with the army was confirmed. When, far too late, in June 1939, the War Office requested the staggering total of 1,440 aircraft for close air support and tactical interdiction, it received the soon-to-be customary trilogy of replies: the RAF opposed any dissipation of effort, any division of its forces, and any transfer of aircraft from its own command. The independent armour enthusiasts had fostered the belief that tanks could win battles on their own. The damage thus done to inter-arms co-operation was carried through into the desert campaign of North Africa. Liddell Hart's own writings were riven with an internal contradiction. His advocacy of the tank in the 1920s had been developed in a vacuum. He was arguing against a commitment to Europe, and thus in operational terms he had shackled the offensive capability of the tank to mobile defence. Even in 1938–9 he felt it was impossible to carry through extensive mechanisation in the time available. His advocacy of the tank at a tactical level was coupled with its implicit neglect at the strategic.

Russia, in the wake of the Bolshevik seizure of power in October 1917, provided more favourable ground in economic and political terms for the germination of mechanisation. The doctrine and nature of the Red Army were only settled after fierce arguments beginning in the Civil War and reaching a climax in 1923–4. Trotsky, the effective victor of the Civil War and commissar for war, argued for a defensive territorial force. Therefore in 1924 the army was organised into forty-two territorial divisions and twenty-nine regular. Trotsky was pragmatic. He accepted that the USSR was as yet too weak to support the world revolution: her strategic thinking must be defensive while her strength was husbanded. As for tactics, they were dictated by circumstantial factors such as geography, and could not be subject to a durable law.

Frunze, his short-lived successor as commissar for war, argued that the Civil War should be the basis for a unique communist doctrine, itself a reflection of the structure of its parent society. 'The course of the historical revolutionary process', he argued, 'will force the working-class to go over to the offensive against capital whenever conditions are favourable.' Frunze had powerful professional support. The relative fluidity of the eastern front in the First World War provided evidence in favour of mobility. The Red Army's first victories, those of the Civil War, had been won by the cavalry, exploiting its power of manoeuvre in massive independent operations. These tendencies in the doctrine of the new army were confirmed by the contributions of former tsarist officers to its formulation. In order to ensure professional competence, Trotsky had insisted on their retention, and, by 1929, they had written 198 of the 243 contributions to Soviet military literature. In the Civil War their loyalty had been ensured by the presence of political commissars, and no order was valid without their counter-signature. In 1925 Frunze moderated the powers of the commissar and in 1934 the commissar's role became purely advisory, with the military commander being given complete authority over his unit. Therefore, by the early 1930s the prevailing tone, with its emphasis on specialist skills and with a revival in the status of the officer corps, was becoming progressively that of a regular and settled army.

One of the Civil War cavalrymen, Voroshilov, succeeded Frunze on the latter's death in October 1925. He injected a crucial new element into the doctrine of the offensive. For him mobility would be imparted not by cavalry but by mechanisation. In 1926–7 this seemed a pipe-dream: Russia produced only 500 vehicles that year, and there were 30 light tanks between the Urals and the Pacific. However, in 1928 Stalin inaugurated the first five-year plan. The Soviet drive for industrialisation was motivated not simply by a desire for economic competitiveness or self-betterment. Russia was the crucible of world revolution, and therefore its defence was interpreted as essential to the survival of Bolshevism. The emphasis accorded to heavy industry in the five-year plans was directly related to the requirements of total war, and Russia's performance in this sector of the economy proved impressive. As early as 1932 her aircraft production was the largest in the world, with an annual output of 2,595 and it held this position until 1939, when 10,382 aircraft were manufactured. Even more significantly for land warfare, the USSR produced 3,300 tanks in

1932. The world's first mechanised corps was created, and the Academy of Mechanisation and Motorisation established. In 1935 the Red Army had 7,000 tanks and Russia possessed 100,000 lorries.

The great advocate of the integration of this industrial development with Russia's foreign policy and with her military doctrine was her most outstanding general of the 1930s, Tukhachevsky. Future war, he argued in 1928, would be total war; all society and all industry would be mobilised in the search for victory. He wanted his army fully mechanised, and he also wanted it made up of long-service regulars capable of resuming the revolutionary offensive. Between 1933 and 1936 encirclement was the keynote of Red Army exercises. The 1929 field service regulations had preached that encircling attacks should be staged by the cavalry and tanks. However, if the flanks were too extensive, all arms – with artillery support – should mount a breakthrough attack. From the outset, aircraft were intimately involved with ground operations: close air support and deep interdiction were their primary roles, and in 1931 Russia pioneered the use of paratroops. The 1936 field service regulations, published under Tukhachevsky's signature, stressed a central principle of Russian thinking – the co-operation of all arms. The artillery, tanks and aircraft were to break open the enemy's defensive system, and the infantry were to seize and hold it. The tone was very different from that of Liddell Hart: 'Only decisive offensive in the main line of advance, closed with a relentless pursuit, will lead to the complete annihilation of the manpower and resources of the enemy'. The artillery were to suppress the enemy's anti-tank guns. The first stage of the attack was to be directed against the enemy's weak points, the second was to reinforce this success, the third was to see the mechanised troops exploit the breakthrough and encircle the enemy, and the fourth and final phase was the pursuit. To achieve all this the tanks and mechanised forces were to be organised in corps, and by 1936 the USSR had four such corps, together with six independent mechanised brigades and six independent tank regiments.

Thus in 1936 the Red Army had the most advanced doctrine and the greatest capability for armoured warfare in the world. The organisational debate of the early years had been settled: a large regular army, based on conscription and supported by a healthy arms industry, now only needed time and training in which to consolidate. But then came set-back. The Spanish Civil War broke out in the same year. It was eagerly studied for evidence on the performance of the new weapons technologies. Superficially the tank fared badly: the terrain proved unfavourable, the tanks outstripped their support and they were then broken on the fire of anti-tank guns. Russia rejected the independent use of tanks. The mechanised corps were disbanded, and the mechanised brigades subordinated to infantry divisions. Stalin also condemned the independent use of airpower, and in consequence insufficient attention was devoted to the development of new types. Moreover, Stalin's memories of the Civil War debates were revived by domestic jealousies. The credibility of the army and of its leaders was undermined by the NKVD. In 1937 the supremacy of the commissar over the field commander was restored. In June Tukhachevsky and others were falsely accused of plotting a coup. Half the officer corps perished in the subsequent purges. The cavalry leaders of the Civil War were returned to command, and the notion of an élite mechanised army was shattered.

Evidence of the damage was forthcoming in December 1939. The Red Army's invasion of Finland revealed poor training, insufficient co-ordination between the arms and weakness in leadership. Prompted also by the German victories of 1940, a re-evaluation began. The commissar was once again subordinated to the military commander. The army was reorganised into tank divisions (composed of six tank battalions, three motor rifle battalions and three field artillery battalions) and motor rifle divisions (six motor rifle battalions and three tank battalions). Two tank divisions and one motor rifle division constituted a mechanised corps, and about twenty such corps were envisaged. But the process of restructuring was still not complete in June 1941. The loss of officers in the purges lowered training standards and left four corps without operations or intelligence sections on their staffs. Doctrine was poorly defined; it stressed attack to the virtual exclusion of defence, particularly anti-tank defence. Consequently production and procurement were left in disarray. Radios were scarce, and most units used civilian land lines: in June 1941 the 22nd Tank Division operated through the local post office. In late spring most mechanised formations had only half their complement of vehicles. By this time the outstanding medium tank of the war, the T34, with its 76·2 mm gun, was into full production, but its distribution had no systematic basis. Massive stocks of obsolescent types dominated the Red Army. One organisation had been dismantled; nothing had yet replaced it.

The German adoption of the tank was very different from that of the Russians. Far from being the result of a search for a new doctrine, the tank's attractions lay not least in the ease with which it fitted into the shape of existing thought. The British argument that blockade had been the decisive instrument in the First World War was eagerly swallowed by the German army: it confirmed that the causes of defeat lay not on the battlefield. Thus the intellectual tradition of Schlieffen survived. The emphasis on a decisive early victory through an attack aimed at the enemy's rear continued. It was now supplemented by the tactical lessons of the German defensive counter-attacks and of the March 1918 offensive, both of which had emphasised the search for the enemy's weak spots and the need to maintain the momentum of the attack. The Versailles settlement only served to confirm the drift: Germany was left with an army of 100,000 men, without aircraft or tanks, and without a general staff. However, its fundamental strategic problem – the possible need to defend both eastern and western borders simultaneously – remained unchanged. So small a force could not undertake the static defence which the French envisaged fighting on the Maginot line. It had instead to concentrate, and to fight a mobile defence.

The formative influence on the German army between 1919 and 1926 was Hans von Seeckt, the head of the *Heeresleitung*. He treated the army as an élite, a basis for expansion. Flying clubs and ex-servicemen's organisations were used as covers for military formations; military departments were hived off to civilian ministries; and Russia, in exchange for technical aid in the establishment of her arms factories, provided training facilities. Seeckt's own experience of the First World War had been predominantly on the eastern front. He had served in the most rapid and decisive campaign of the war, Germany's conquest of Romania, and thus he saw Schlieffen's teaching as having continued relevance. Germany's professional army, particularly if it remained numerically weak, should use speed to strike pre-emptively; her conscripted opponents would be caught at their most vulnerable while still mobilising for total war. The air force would be a prime agent of disorganisation: having gained aerial supremacy, it would switch the attack to the enemy's communications. The tactical framework for this strategic conception was refined by Ludwig von Beck, chief of the general staff from 1933 to 1938. Beck too preferred conducting a strategic defensive with the tactical offensive. He envisaged air attacks suppressing the enemy artillery, and then the ground attack would move fast, circumventing the strong points, aiming for the flanks and rear. The tanks would have three tasks, to support the infantry, to conduct a mobile defence and to be the independent agents of deep penetration. He wanted over a third of the army to be mechanised, giving a total of twelve armoured brigades. None the less the infantry would remain the mass for decision. Beck, in line with the lessons of 1918, was stressing the effective co-ordination of all three arms.

The ground was thus far more receptive for the development of armour than the tank advocates, particularly Heinz Guderian, subsequently liked to maintain. It was true that both Seeckt and Beck had limited tactical foresight and continued to have faith in the superior mobility of cavalry. But the effect of this, combined with the cavalry's own disdain for mechanisation, was to leave others unfettered to develop the tank. The German armoured divisions profited from being the progeny of a technical arm, the motor transport battalions. In 1922 Guderian was appointed to the Inspectorate of Transport's staff, and in 1923−4 he and Brauchitsch worked on co-operation between tanks and aircraft. Tank production itself could only go ahead in Russia: not until 1928 did Guderian actually get inside a tank. However, his ideas were already crystallising. He argued in 1929 that the speed of an attack should be determined by the speed of the tank, and that therefore independent armoured divisions with their own mechanised infantry and artillery were required. In 1931 Guderian was appointed chief of staff to the Inspectorate of Transport Troops and in 1934 the inspectorate became the basis for a Motorised Troops Command Staff. The following year, three Panzer divisions were created, each containing a tank brigade, a motorised rifle brigade and its own support arms. Already, the British and the French were reasonably clear about the likely direction of German tactics.

The principal drag on the development of mechanisation was the small size of the arms sector in German industry after the low demands of the 1920s. The tanks lacked armour, their maximum speed was 12 m.p.h. and they had no wireless. Guderian spurned the division between light and heavy tanks: he wanted vehicles that were strong enough to penetrate and speedy enough to exploit. They should travel at 25 m.p.h., be armed with

75 mm guns, and be equipped with wireless. He did not get them until 1938−9 (they then remained − as the Panzer marks III and IV − the main armament of the German Panzer divisions until 1943). Circumscribed by the lack of raw materials, it was impossible for the German army in the 1930s to mechanise, as the British were doing, on a broad front. Guderian therefore argued even more strongly for the independent use of armoured divisions, in circumstances and on terrain favourable to the tank. The deep penetration exercises of Hobart's brigade proved instructive. 'The armoured divisions', Guderian wrote in 1935, 'will no longer stop when the first objectives have been reached; on the contrary, utilising their speed and radius of action to the full they will do their utmost to complete the breakthrough into the enemy lines of communication.'

However, Beck was more conservative, and saw the mass army, not armour, as the decisive instrument in battle. His case was augmented by the reintroduction of conscription in 1935, and in 1936 he opted for Panzer brigades operating as infantry supports. Guderian secured timely support against Beck in the person of Hitler himself. Hitler was fascinated by technology and in *Mein Kampf* had expressed his conviction that motorisation would prove decisive in the next war. The powerful advance of the machine fitted well into Fascism's self-image. However, the confrontation between Hitler and Beck arose not over tactical doctrine but over the Führer's conduct of foreign policy. Exceptionally for one brought up in the Schlieffen tradition, Beck's concerns ranged beyond operational matters to the political and economic dimensions of strategy. Convinced that Germany could not overrun Czechoslovakia without causing a general war in Europe, and convinced too that the army was not strong enough for such a war, Beck resigned in August 1938. He was to re-emerge as the leader of the opposition to Hitler, and to die in the aftermath of the bomb plot of 20 July 1944. In November 1938 Guderian was appointed commander of mobile troops and given direct access to Hitler. But tank production never rose as high as Guderian wanted. In order to create nine Panzer divisions, he had to reduce the number of tanks in each from 433 to 299. Thus Beck's emphasis on a combined arms approach found expression in the more balanced composition of the Panzer division itself.

A crucial component of the German armoured attack was the support given it by the *Luftwaffe*. The air forces of both sides had concentrated on providing ground support during the March 1918 offensive, and their effectiveness found reflection in Ludendorff's call for masses of aircraft in his book, *Der Totale Krieg* (1935). From 1933 to 1936 the newly created *Luftwaffe* gave attention to the idea of deterrence and began the development of a four-engine bomber. But its chief of staff, Wever, acknowledged that the *Luftwaffe's* strategy should fall in with the objectives of the armed forces as a whole. Raids to hit the enemy's civilian population and to break its morale were but part of a more general mission to check the flow of supplies to the front line. As important were the battle with the enemy air force and the maintenance of support for the army and navy. The *Luftwaffe's* thinking was thus a balanced and comprehensive doctrine for air war. However, Wever's death in 1936 coincided with the onset of procurement problems for the *Luftwaffe*. The speed of rearmament foreshortened the processes of research and development and at the same time exacerbated shortages of materials. As was natural for a continental land power, the needs of the army tended to become pre-eminent. Many *Luftwaffe* officers, including Kesselring (Wever's successor), had begun their careers in the army, and therefore favoured co-operation between the two services. The main instrument of this co-operation was the *Stuka*, a dive-bomber, whose worth was established in the Spanish Civil War. In Spain too the techniques of maintaining close links between forward ground formations and aircraft were developed. Guderian's own background as a signals officer proved pivotal: his style of fighting – commanding from the front and demanding rapid co-operation from all arms – hinged on the effectiveness of his wireless links. He involved the *Luftwaffe* in all the planning stages of his operations, and a *Luftwaffe* officer in radio communication with the aircraft overhead accompanied each mechanised formation. The *Luftwaffe* itself probably put more emphasis on interdiction bombing than on close air support. But the raids against communications and rear areas were conceived as a complement to the ground attack. Once local air supremacy was gained, the *Luftwaffe* construed its primary task as the ability to respond rapidly so as to maintain the momentum of the army's advance.

The *Luftwaffe's* neglect of strategic bombing suggested that Germany was not preparing for a long war, in which full economic mobilisation would take effect and the bombing of industrial targets would therefore prove important. The attribution of Germany's defeat to her economic collapse caused many army officers to argue for the balanced development of a war economy, for reinvestment and redeployment within industry to create armament in depth. But such pleas were rendered hopeless by the breakneck tempo of Hitler's rearmament. The individual services colluded, setting themselves programmes whose demands outstripped not only the production possibilities but also the availability of raw materials. By 1936–7 the ceilings of economic performance had been reached. The forces had created large quantities of equipment for immediate use but in 1939 the economy itself was not yet fully adapted to the needs of war production. No service's rearmament programme was complete on the outbreak of war. The navy's needs in particular played little part in Hitler's calculations: in 1939, despite a fivefold increase in strength since 1933, it had only eleven major surface vessels and fifty-seven U-boats, and it did not expect to be ready for war with Britain until 1943 at the earliest. Hitler failed to appreciate that his attempt to overrun Poland would trigger war with Britain and France. However his forces fought so successfully that they glossed over Germany's lack of preparedness. *Blitzkrieg*, therefore, may have had some meaning at a purely operational level, but as an overall strategic and economic concept it was nonexistent. It was not defined by any *Wehrmacht* directive: instead it flowed from the reaction between Hitler's political will and the self-image and aspirations of the German armed forces.

It was victory that gave *Blitzkrieg* the status of doctrine. Poland was defeated in one month, Denmark and Norway in two months, France in six weeks, Belgium in seventeen days, Holland in five days, Yugoslavia in eleven days and Greece in three weeks. In less than two years, Europe was overrun in a succession of short and in consequence relatively bloodless campaigns. The polish was heightened, but underneath the veneer much of the wood was cracked and flawed. The conquests were not part of a grand design, but were Hitler's personal response to a series of crises. The army had developed the tactics for a short war because that was its tradition, but remained convinced that it should be preparing for total war. In any case much of its thinking on the use of armour – particularly since it had had insufficient opportunity to perfect it – was at an experimental stage. Its supply arrangements constantly threatened to break down: for the *Anschluss* in 1938 Guderian had to telephone the Austrian garages and ask them to stay open so as to be able to refuel his tanks. Transport was still predominantly horse-drawn. Field divisions were created at the expense of reinforcement and training regiments. The *Wehrmacht* therefore had to secure a quick victory or be confined to advances in short bursts. Thus the Panzers, although only 10 per cent of the army, shouldered a disproportionate burden in securing its triumphs.

The opening campaign of the Second World War, Germany's invasion of Poland on 1 September 1939, was not the deep strategic thrust that has – perhaps erroneously – come to be associated with *Blitzkrieg*. To the north, East Prussia gave a natural wedge on Poland's flank. The attack thus became a converging one, with Schlieffen's influence showing itself in the weak centre and strong wings. Much of the responsibility for the rapid success lay with the *Luftwaffe*, whose initial destruction of the Polish airfields gave the Germans air superiority, and which was thereafter able to support the ground operations by concentrating on interdiction.

The attack in the west has become characterised as the classic example of *Blitzkrieg* (see Map 16). But this obscures the origins of the German plan, which was drawn up in November 1939 and which, like the invasion of Poland, owed much to Schlieffen. Indeed, to all intents and purposes, the opening days of 1914 were to be re-enacted in a vast wheel through Belgium. The attack at Sedan, thrusting through the Ardennes and across the river Meuse, was intended as no more than a diversion. However, an advance through Belgium was exactly what the allies expected. Although obliged to cover the entire front down as far as Switzerland, the main weight of their effort lay in the north-east, so that they could move rapidly to the aid of Belgium and Holland. France had 3,524 of her 4,688 tanks in this sector, whereas Germany could only muster 2,574 out of 3,862. The French tanks were superior in firepower and armour (although not in speed) and they were supported by a better anti-tank gun. Manstein, an army group chief of staff, argued that a German attack through Belgium would hit the main allied force, and that therefore the Sedan operation should become the principal thrust. Like the March 1918 offensives, this would be a battle for penetration, not envelopment. In January 1940, an areoplane carrying plans was forced down on the allied side of the line. Fortified by the possibility that the allies now definitely knew his intentions, and with his strength growing as the attack was postponed, Hitler adopted Manstein's proposal. Seven of Germany's ten Panzer divisions

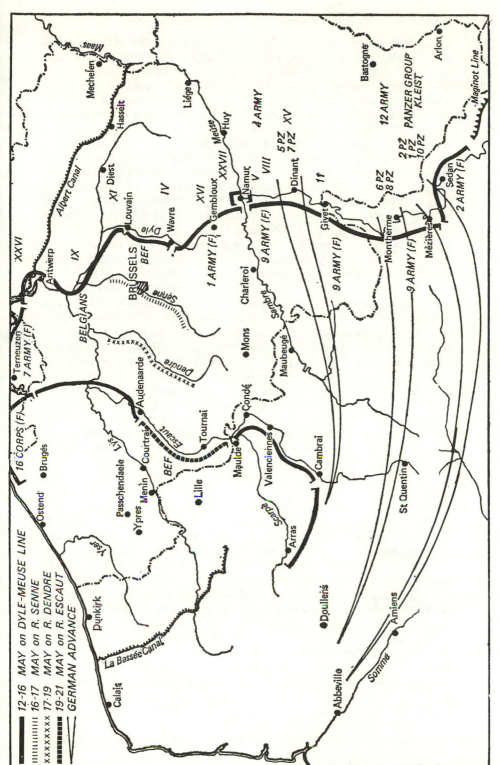

Map 16 The battle of France, 1940

Legend:
12–16 MAY on DYLE–MEUSE LINE
16–17 MAY on R. SENNE
17–19 MAY on R. DENDRE
19–21 MAY on R. ESCAUT
GERMAN ADVANCE

were concentrated in the sector Sedan to Namur, and five of these were at Sedan itself. Thus the allies' plan was completely wrong-footed. They proved slow to identify the direction and weight of the German thrust. The Germans had secured superiority at the decisive point. Above all, however, the attack now aimed at deep strategic penetration across the allied flank and rear, and the allies' advance into Belgium only served to reinforce its effectiveness.

On 10 May 1940, the attack broke. Surprise was complete. The allies had not regarded the Ardennes as penetrable. Certainly the long German columns, constricted by the terrain, were vulnerable to interdiction. But the allied air forces were not united in their efforts. The RAF concentrated on home defence and on the possibility of bombing the Ruhr, and thus contributed only 416 aircraft to the battle. The French emphasised tactical support, but their 1,200 aircraft were outnumbered by the *Luftwaffe*'s 2,750. The French artillery was never properly deployed, and therefore its superiority was not exploited. Gradually, France put 2,200 tanks into the Breda/Sedan sector. But at first they tried to plug the gap too close to the point of breakthrough, committing their tanks in uncoordinated attacks. Then, on 15 May, they withdrew to consolidate. This had the effect of enlarging the German bridgehead on the Meuse. Thereafter the Germans sustained the momentum of their breakthrough in a deep but narrow thrust towards the Somme and Abbeville. The Panzers were commanded from the front, their flanks becoming increasing vulnerable and relying on the *Luftwaffe* for protection. Hitler's nerve began to fail. The perversity of advancing so rapidly over the battlefields of 1914–18 dogged him. To the south much of the French army remained unbroken. The limited British counter-attack at Arras on 21 May confirmed his fears. On 24 May the Germans halted, sixteen miles from Dunkirk. The British now reaped the reward of having held the RAF back. It was committed to the battle, securing local air superiority and proving invaluable in the embarkation of the British Expeditionary Force from Dunkirk.

Although Hitler's nerve had wavered, it had held longer than that of the French. Rent by national and service divisions, the Third Republic was psychologically shattered by the momentum of a thrust which had retained the initiative despite the danger to its own communications. Fighting had only been sporadically sustained: 2 million of the 2,300,000 losses suffered by the allies were prisoners of war. Furthermore the victory was Hitler's in a truly personal sense: his commanders had been reluctant to embark on a campaign in the west. But its very decisiveness masked a deep weakness in Germany's war effort. Glibly put, Germany had no strategy. All revolved around Hitler. If there was any link between *Blitzkrieg* in military terms and its economic implementation, its conscious expression was confined to the mind of the Führer. Switches in war production were governed by his commands; military decisions were reached not by war games or staff appreciations but by stormy interviews with Hitler himself. The collapse of France convinced Hitler that he was a great commander, and that Germany's generals did not understand war. However, his own grand strategy was reactive. He took opportunities as they were offered, but found it hard to sustain for long the concentrated effort that any one scheme might demand. His style of war was therefore in total antipathy to the thoroughly competent professionalism of the German general staff.

The division between the army's staff and Hitler was to continue throughout the war. On 4 February 1938, Hitler took over supreme command of the armed forces, and appointed Keitel head of *Oberkommando der Wehrmacht* (OKW, the command organisation for all three services). However, since Germany was a continental land power, the army's command (*Oberkommando des Heeres* or OKH) regarded itself as the nation's planning staff. Intense rivalry developed between the two. OKH had been left powerless, but OKW lacked a full planning and operations staff and therefore tended to be no more than a funnel for the plans of the individual services. Thus no one body co-ordinated strategic planning. The Norwegian campaign, in which the navy had a strong interest, was planned by OKW, the invasion of Russia by OKH. Two problems that became of increasing importance during the war, the strategy for the Mediterranean and the conduct of air defence, were never subject to staff studies. The military implications of foreign policy decisions were never considered. The staff of OKW, Keitel and Jodl, became Hitler's personal staff rather than a professional advisory body. Jodl described Hitler's headquarters as 'a cross between a cloister and a concentration camp . . . for it was not a military headquarters at all, it was a civilian one and we soldiers were guests there. It is not easy to be a guest anywhere for five and a half years.'

This shaky command structure, this economy capable of sustaining only short campaigns, was now being asked to fight a prolonged war. For the continued survival of Britain, with her maritime links, and her economic and industrial support from the Commonwealth and the United States, left Hitler with the sort of war that he did not want. But he was reluctant to face the consequences. His attempt to use the *Luftwaffe* in a task for which it was not designed, that is to say the defeat of Britain by the independent use of airpower, demonstrates his failure to think through the relationship between operations and grand strategy. Instead he ducked the issue, turning eastwards, towards and beyond the original focus of German interests in 1914, towards the concerns of *Mein Kampf*, towards Russia. He justified his decision in July 1940 by arguing that, if the USSR was eliminated, Japanese power in the Far East would receive a corresponding boost and the USA would thus be increasingly diverted towards the Pacific. Britain would then truly stand alone. In the event, however, the German army could not smash the USSR, and the USA was not prepared to be drawn against Japan ahead of Germany. The bluff of 1939 was called: Germany would have to fight a long war.

Guide to Further Reading

Messenger provides a thoroughly competent survey of the main tactical developments. Watt gives a 'liberal' interpretation of the general staffs of Europe before 1939, while Howard (1965) contains essays on specific aspects of interwar military thinking. On the major innovations, Ogor-kiewicz is thorough but at times slightly over-enthusiastic on armour, while Higham and Collier provide histories of airpower. Higham is the more stimulating of the two. Paskins and Dockrill, chapter 1, provide an excellent short account of the evolution of bombing theory.

Young deals with France. The best short guide to British policy is Howard (1972), chapters 4–6. Bond (1980) looks at the more specifically military aspects. Liddell Hart is discussed by Bond (1977), and on Fuller read Trythall and Reid. The fullest account of Russia is Erickson (1962), but many readers may wish to settle for the shorter treatment in Mackintosh.

Much recent work in German on Germany has found expression in English in Seaton (1982). On the tactical aspects of *Blitzkrieg*, Addington is not wholly satisfactory but provides a start. The memoirs of the Panzer officers, Guderian and von Mellenthin, should be treated with caution but still repay reading. Read Overy (1978) and Murray on the *Luftwaffe*. The economic aspects of German rearmament and war production were first treated (in an intellectually exciting fashion) by Milward (1965). However, his interpretation has now been thoroughly overhauled, most recently by Deist and Overy (1982).

The bulk of the reading on the Second World War will be discussed at the end of chapter eleven. However, Stolfi's article on the campaign in France is important, and on Hitler's relationship with the general staff consult Warlimont. Messerschmidt and van Creveld (1974) discuss Hitler's strategy in a short compass.

Chapter 11

Total War

On 22 June 1942 Hitler invaded Russia. As with the overrunning of Poland, the plan owed much to the influence of Schlieffen. The Germans were unnecessarily frightened of a possible Russian withdrawal (the Russian emphasis was in fact almost exclusively on taking the offensive), and aimed to achieve a massive envelopment west of the river Dnieper. To do this, they formed up in three Army Groups, North, Centre and South (see Map 17). The weight lay in Army Group Centre, thrusting towards Moscow. However, this reflected the aspirations of OKH rather than of Hitler. While OKH wanted to break the Red Army, the Führer looked to the economic targets of Leningrad to the north and of the Ukraine and the Caucasus to the south. Therefore, when in late July the principal objectives of the three Army Groups – Leningrad, Moscow and the Donets basin – still did not lie within reach, Hitler reaffirmed his original priorities. The consequence of the subsequent clash with OKH was compromise. The Panzers of Army Group Centre were taken to boost the drives north and south, but in October were brought back to renew the assault on Moscow.

However, the invasion had been launched late in the year. In August 1940 Germany had increased her army from 120 to 180 divisions, but war production could not cope with the demands for equipment, with the results that the attack was delayed, and that 40 per cent of the German divisions had to use captured French vehicles. The lack of economic preparation for a long war was therefore beginning to tell, and became even more evident as the campaign progressed. Russia was a much bigger theatre of operations than those so far experienced by the German army. For the invasion, the *Luftwaffe* had assembled the massive total of 3,000 aircraft. But this only ensured two machines per mile of front, when in France the ratio had been ten per mile. Such German transport as was motorised was not tracked but wheeled. Therefore roads were crucial to sustain the advance. In Russia, however, the railway remained the foundation of long-distance transport. Roads were few, and, while the Germans battled for their possession, the Russians concentrated on guarding their rolling stock. Moreover the prewar emphasis on equipping the Panzer divisions left other formations short of vehicles. Thus, as the advance continued, a gap – often as much as two weeks' movement time – opened between the Panzers and their support.

When winter closed in, the German army had still not achieved its objectives. It was an extraordinarily cold winter. A bare 25 per cent of German aircraft were fit to fly at any one moment. The tanks, worn out by the distances they had covered, ground to a halt. The Russians, who as a result of increasing Japanese–American hostility were more secure on

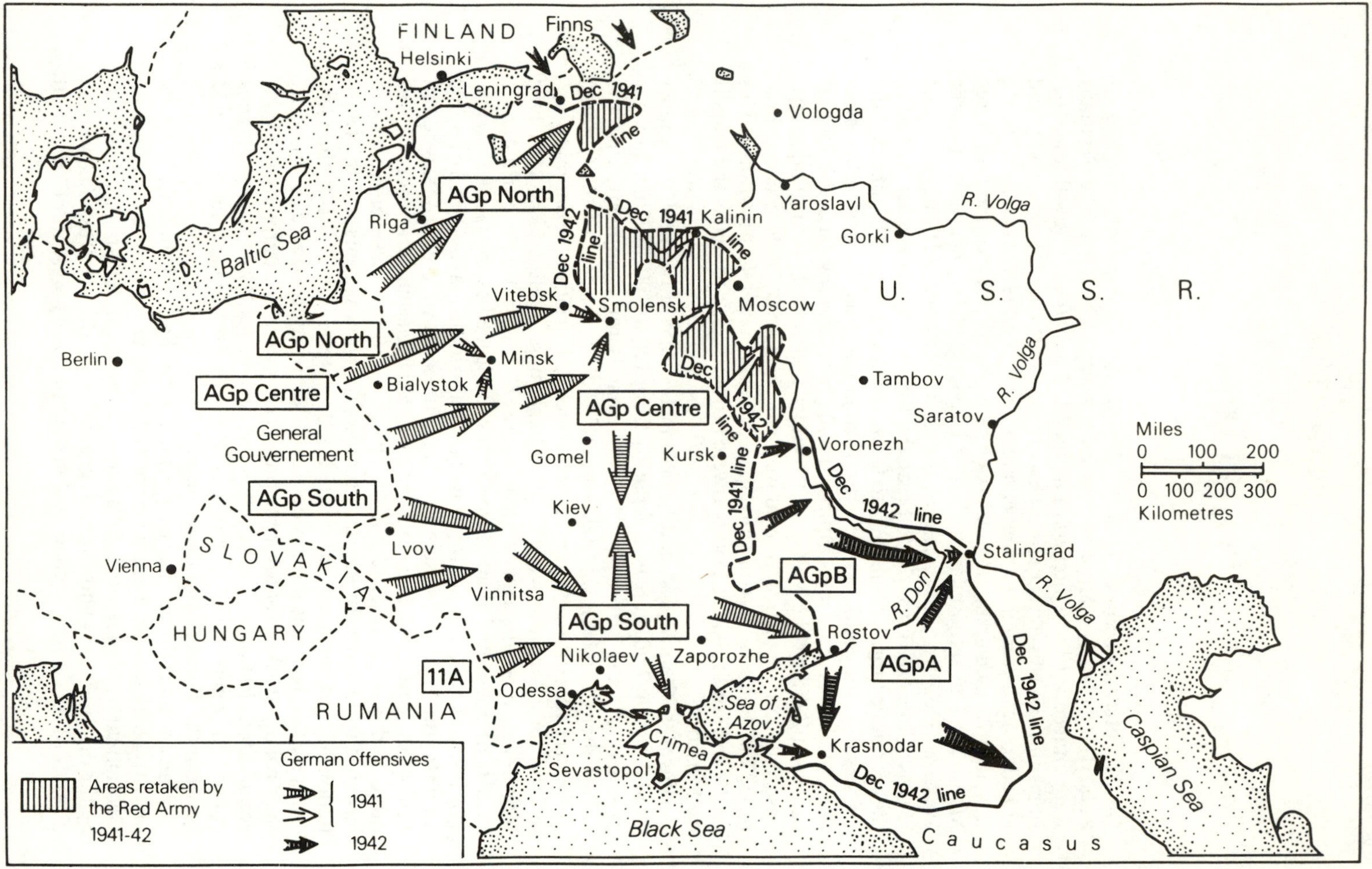
FINLAND
Finns
Helsinki
Leningrad
Dec 1941 line
Vologda
Yaroslavl
R. Volga
Gorki
AGp North
Riga
Baltic Sea
Dec 1941 Kalinin
line
Dec 1942 line
U. S. S. R.
Vitebsk
Smolensk
Moscow
AGp North
Minsk
Berlin
Bialystok
AGp Centre
Dec 1942 line
Tambov
R. Volga
Saratov
AGp Centre
General Gouvernement
Gomel
Kursk
Voronezh
Miles
0 100 200
0 100 200 300
Kilometres
Dec 1942 line
AGp South
Kiev
Dec 1941 line
Stalingrad
SLOVAKIA
Vienna
Lvov
AGpB
Vinnitsa
R. Don
R. Volga
AGp South
HUNGARY
Rostov
Dec 1942 line
Nikolaev
Zaporozhe
AGpA
11A
Odessa
Sea of Azov
RUMANIA
Crimea
Krasnodar
Caspian Sea
Sevastopol
Dec 1942 line
Black Sea
Caucasus
Areas retaken by the Red Army 1941-42
German offensives
1941
1942

Map 17 *The eastern front, 1941*

their Far Eastern border, were able to throw fresh and well-trained divisions into the battle for Moscow. By the end of the year German losses totalled 830,403. The Russian army had lost half its original strength of 4,700,000 but relatively speaking the blow to Germany was greater. A quarter of her army had gone – the victorious cream of 1939 to 1941.

In January 1942 Stalin hoped to expand the successful Russian counterattack round Moscow into a major offensive, directed first against Army Group Centre, but later to move outwards to the flanks. The Soviet Union still lacked the logistic base for such an effort, and her army's frontal attacks were checked. But, despite the enormous casualties, the Russian army had begun to recover its sense of direction. In July 1941 Stalin had become supreme commander, and the direction of strategy was entrusted to a resuscitated *Stavka*. The system remained highly centralised, with Stalin sitting Hitlerlike in his Kremlin bunker. However, the difficulties were offset by the *Stavka* representatives, who were the intermediaries with the front commanders, relating Moscow-issued directives to operational requirements on the ground and linking the work of adjacent fronts. Foremost among the representatives was Zhukov. Zhukov was the fireman of the eastern front, moving to Leningrad in September 1941, to Moscow in October, and – on his appointment as deputy supreme commander – to Stalingrad in August 1942. Together with Vasilevskii, the chief of the general staff, Zhukov shaped Russia's tactical doctrine. They rebuilt the tank corps for exploitation, put the emphasis in the rifle division on firepower rather than manpower, and established air and artillery formations as *Stavka* reserves. In the 1942 battles the Russian army showed itself mobile in defence, able to pull out of the German encirclements. The army's professional pride was restored, and was clinched on 9 October 1942: the political commissar, who had recovered his equality of status in the summer of 1941, was once again subordinated.

The German plan for the summer of 1942 was to pursue Hitler's ambitions in the south by breaking through to the river Don, encircling Stalingrad, and then driving towards the Caucasus. The battle for Stalingrad opened at the end of July. Stalin's determination to defend the city that bore his name exposed once again the split between OKH and Hitler. For OKH the objectives were more immediate, whereas at first Hitler attached little importance to the Stalingrad stage of the plan. The fighting in the city, most of it by night, became fierce and desperate, sucking in the Germans, so that on either side they left long flanks held by weak Rumanian divisions. On 13 September 1942, Zhukov and Vasilevskii persuaded Stalin to mount a counter-attack against these flanks, and then to encircle and annihilate the German troops at Stalingrad. While the fighting in the city itself reached a climax in mid-October, the Russians gradually built up their strength in the area to over a million men, supported by 60 per cent of the available Russian armour and half the artillery reserve. On 19 November, in freezing fog and snow, the attack from the north-east of Stalingrad went in, followed the next day by that from the south-west. On 23 November the two thrusts linked, and over a quarter of a million Germans were trapped. Hitler told the German commander Paulus to stand fast. Göring's attempts to supply Paulus by air failed. Germany had too few reserves left available to relieve the Stalingrad garrison, and on 31 January 1943 Paulus surrendered.

The key to Russia's survival and to her subsequent run of victories was her industrial strength. By the end of 1941 the USSR had lost 63 per cent of her prewar coal production, 71 per cent of her pig-iron, 68 per cent of her steel and 60 per cent of her aluminium. Weapons production for July −December 1941 was halved. Despite these appalling blows, the stubborn defence of forward positions, although criticised in tactical terms because it created enormous pockets to be encircled by the Germans, covered the withdrawal of 1,523 plants and 10 million people. The evacuation was put in hand two days after the war with Germany broke out. The displaced factories were relocated in the Urals and in Western Siberia, areas which had been earmarked for military production in the 1928 five-year plan, and fresh deposits were opened to compensate for the loss of raw materials in the west. The speed with which production was resumed was partly a consequence of the standardisation of equipment. Whereas the Germans had twelve types of armoured fighting vehicle, the Russians had but two. The tooling of factories and the supply of parts proceeded quickly because the production problems had been resolved. The T34 tank took 8,000 man-hours to produce in 1941, but 3,700 in 1943. Standardised and interchangeable parts also eased the problems of repair in the field. On the second day of the Kursk battle, 5 July 1943, the Russians had 3,800 tanks in the salient. By 13 July, their tank strength was down to 1,500, but on 3 August it had recovered to 2,750. Russian industry also adapted so well to the demands of total war because it was already state controlled and was already heavily weighted towards the manufacture of armaments. Her production curve was rising again by March 1942, and in 1944 her gross industrial output was 104 per cent of her 1940 figure. The arms industries stood at 251 per cent of the 1940 total. In 1944 the USSR manufactured 122,000 guns and 29,000 tanks.

The transition of the German economy was more painful. The victories of 1939 to 1941 had been gained without the full development of a war economy. This was not because of a lack of investment: spending on rearmament increased at a consistent rate, and by 1941 60 per cent of the German workforce was employed for military purposes (as opposed to 20 per cent in 1939). But output did not reflect the resources devoted to it. Many sectors of German industry were reluctant to co-operate. They resented state intervention, preferred to rely on skilled labour rather than automated processes, and were often wedded to small-scale manufacture. The disproportionate role of the armed forces in procurement reflected a situation whose main problem was one of co-ordination. The running of the war economy was split between several competing interests. Consequently the production of military equipment, which peaked in July 1941, fell 29 per cent by the end of the year. The January 1941 production target for armoured vehicles was 1,250 but only 700 were delivered for the entire quarter. Artillery production declined 67 per cent from its peak in April. The replacement levels of crucial equipment in early 1942 was very low. A tenth of the lorries lost in the first Russian winter were replaced. By 1942

Army Group South had lost 50 per cent of its original firepower, and the other two Army Groups 33 per cent.

On 10 January 1942 Hitler ordered increases in the production of guns and equipment. His targets provided a fresh argument for administrative reform in German production, and Todt, the minister of armaments and munitions, was given overall control of the war economy. Committees were established for the key sectors in order to pool and allocate resources. Todt's policy was not disrupted by his death in an air crash, but was continued and developed by his successor, Albert Speer. Better management resulted in a better use of resources: in 1942 40 per cent more aircraft were produced than in the previous year, with only 5 per cent more labour and less aluminium. The consequence of this saga was that the German war economy did not reach its peak until June 1944, when its output was triple that of February 1942. Speer concentrated on equipment for the eastern front and for the defence of Germany. Thus from tanks and medium bombers, the emphasis went to guns and fighters. In 1941, Germany manufactured 7,000 guns and 3,744 fighters; in 1944 she produced 40,600 guns and 28,925 fighters.

Enormously impressive though this performance was, it was insufficient to overcome a number of fundamental problems. The original lag in defensive weapons' production was never made up. Germany's equipment losses mounted as the war progressed. In 1944 she manufactured the equipment for 250 infantry and 40 Panzer divisions, but she had only 150 divisions in the field. In any case engines needed fuel, and this too was a diminishing asset. In 1941 Germany was fighting a war on two fronts with an annual oil allocation that was only 70 per cent of Britain's prewar domestic allocation. Thus in 1944 tactical flexibility was further hampered by the inability to manoeuvre. The training time of the fighter pilots needed to protect the oil industry from allied bombing was curtailed for lack of fuel, and so both their effectiveness and their chances of survival diminished. Finally, the weapons with which the Germans were fighting were often technically inadequate. The enormous and immediate needs of 1938–9 had discouraged research and development on new designs. The jet was developed in August 1939, but was then neglected until 1944. At least five years were required to test and perfect aircraft, and the Germans were therefore outclassed in the air by 1943. The alternative was to go into production without proper testing. In this way the Panther and Tiger tanks were rushed into the Kursk battle before their respective vulnerabilities were resolved.

Germany's adaptation to the needs of total war was even more problematic for her strategy than her domestic economy. For Hitler the distinctions between a long and a short war, or between a total and a limited war, were irrelevant. He was, however, conscious of the problems that a major war would pose Germany given her lack of such vital raw materials as rubber, oil and iron ore. But, although the economy consequently lay at the heart of Hitler's thinking about war, he could never relate his anxiety for resources to the necessities of the military situation. He was drawn to Eastern Europe and to Russia in his search for *Lebensraum* not least because he hoped thereby to make Germany self-sufficient. 'Modern warfare', he declared, 'is above all economic warfare, and the demands of economic warfare must be given priority.' The priority was immediate: operational decisions reflected Hitler's need for raw materials. In the drive south after Dunkirk, Hitler was more concerned to secure the iron ore of Lorraine than he was to complete the rout of the French army. Throughout the war, he displayed an exaggerated concern for the security of Norway (the exit point for Swedish iron ore) and for that of the Balkans (the source of oil, bauxite and copper): the allies, aware of Hitler's fear, exploited it, and German troops were uselessly tied to the protection of these theatres. In Russia above all, Hitler's commands to hold ground, so resented by his generals for military reasons, were motivated by concern for the resources of the areas under threat – the industry and the ores of the Donets basin or the iron and manganese of the Dnieper bend. Thus the split between Hitler and the army widened. OKH argued that the war had to be won in operational terms before economic resources could be exploited. The consequence was to harden Hitler's contempt for the professionalism of the German general staff. He failed to concert his strategy with his forces or with his allies.

Hitler's thinking about the war was confined to two levels. On the more exalted plane, war was total because of its high moral character. Politics could not be a moderating influence, because politics were themselves a form of war. His ideological and grandiose objectives, expressed in racial and semi-mystical terms, made the war absolute. His second concern was with low-level tactics rather than with strategy or logistics. His tendency to neglect the higher direction of the war in favour of the lower was reinforced as the initiative passed from Germany to the allies. His involvement became pettifogging. In January 1945 he decreed that no divisional commander could attack or withdraw without allowing the opportunity for the Führer himself to intervene. He became fascinated with new gadgets which might prove war-winners, independently and dramatically capable of reversing the flow of fortunes. So the evolution towards total war was not reflected in a fundamental reordering of Hitler's strategy. His strengths in *Blitzkrieg* – the ability to improvise, the exploitation of crises – became liabilities in a war which required sustained effort and deliberate planning. By 1943 he did acknowledge that Germany was on the defensive. His solution was to argue that the allies were an unnatural coalition, liable to fragment under pressure. Those of the West, being liberal democracies, were more vulnerable than the solid totalitarianism of the Soviet Union. In any case he had little space to trade in Western Europe. Therefore, he increasingly put his efforts into the west, switching from the Kursk battle to deal with the allied landings in Sicily, directing the V-bombs against Britain, and in December 1944 launching a major offensive in the Ardennes. In the east he favoured a rigid defence. Manstein and Guderian fretted, wanting a mobile defence, and still planning battles of envelopment, by withdrawing in the centre and leaving the wings strong. Hitler's priorities undermined Germany's tactical superiority in the east. The army's strength was sapped: from having 70 per cent of its divisions in Russia in June 1941, only 53 per cent remained on 1 May 1944. Of 2,299 tanks and assault guns produced in November and December

1944, only 921 were directed to the east. Germany was increasingly treating Britain and the United States as enemies of importance equal to the USSR. The decisive land battles of the Second World War may have been fought on the eastern front; certainly it was here that *Blitzkrieg* was broken. But the German navy, oriented against Britain from the outset, and embroiled in the battles of the Atlantic and the Mediterranean, argued another alternative which never embraced the notion of a rapid victory.

The interwar conviction in Britain that the blockade had won the First World War served to reinforce the view that European war would be total war, requiring full economic mobilisation. Hitler's conduct of diplomacy and domestic policy in peace allowed him to embark on war without a change of gear. For Britain foreign policy in peacetime was a distinct activity, and war was approached with suitable gravity. Thus, from the outset, Britain, unlike Germany, reckoned on a long fight. In February 1939 the chiefs of staff had sketched out a remarkably prescient British strategy: Egypt should be held as a base from which to mount an offensive against the Axis's weak point, Italy; the storm of a German attack would be weakened by stubborn defence; meanwhile the economic effort would be built up and the support of the Commonwealth mobilised; the United States would deal with Japan; when finally the moment came to tackle an already weakened Germany, the command of the sea would give Britain the choice of points of attack. It was calculated that it would take three years to transfer to a full war economy. Hence, in 1940, Churchill could afford to be confident if the immediate crisis was surmounted.

The central feature of the British approach to the war economy was that it stressed the war rather than the economy. Whereas Germany tailored its military effort to the alleged capabilities of its industry, Britain allowed the war to create its own demands, regardless of whether the economy could take the strain. From the outset Britain, and later the United States, set high production targets and forced industry to conform. Other sectors of industry were taken over: 70 per cent of Spitfires were made by Nuffields, the car manufacturers. The aid of scientists was systematically enlisted, with the Royal Society preparing lists of the best qualified, and with Churchill himself being heavily influenced by Lord Cherwell. But the prewar predictions of the Treasury had been right: Britain had to choose between a major military effort or economic stability; she could not have both. By 1941−2, the economy was ailing, targets were not being met, and the Treasury reckoned Britain lacked the gold reserves to fight for more than another two years.

The question that dominated British minds was the future stance of the United States. Guided by Roosevelt, she looked progressively less neutral. in the summer of 1940 she doubled her war fleet, and in September she introduced selective military service and began the mobilisation of her industry. In the New Year of 1941 the two powers held joint staff talks. They agreed that, in the event of America entering the war, she would focus on Germany and the Atlantic, adopting a defensive strategy against Japan in the Pacific. In March 1941 the lend-lease bill gave Britain and − in due course − the USSR access to the industrial might of America. Thus, long before the Japanese attacked Pearl Harbor on 7 December 1941, the United States had become the arsenal of the allies. As in the United Kingdom, the aid of science was formalised, in this case through the National Defense Research Committee. The bazooka, the proximity fuse, the landing craft, the DUKW and the high frequency radio were all the fruits of this liaison. Again too, production targets were set: the United States manufactured 29,497 tanks in 1943 and 96,318 aircraft in 1944. Moreover this effort did not prevent the United States, unlike Germany, from continuing to have guns *and* butter. Twelve per cent of the American population was mobilised, but her industrial output doubled and the individual standard of living rose.

In gross economic terms, the Axis now had no chance: in 1938 the allies had possessed a total population of 359,940,000 and almost 60 per cent of the world's manufacturing capacity, whereas the Axis had a population of 195,380,000 and 17 per cent of the world's manufacturing capacity. The problem that the allies faced was not economic but political. Their union was unnatural: the communism of the USSR marked it off from the capitalist democracies, while the latter were in their own turn split by American suspicion of British imperialism. Each had a different view of the possible shape and structure of the postwar world. A strategy that projected itself that far forward might rend the alliance asunder. Therefore, the utilitarian bond, the common desire to defeat the Axis, ensured that the priority in strategy should be military victory. On 24 January 1943, Roosevelt announced that Germany would be forced to surrender unconditionally. The British feared that this policy lost sight of Russian ambitions in Eastern Europe, and that it also hardened Germany's resolve. But realistically the alliance could bear no other strategy. Clausewitz's theoretical ideal of absolute war had found embodiment. The objective to be achieved in the waging of war and the means for fighting total war had gravitated towards each other.

Despite the latent political problems of the alliance, it developed a far more effective direction of the war than had the Axis. Russia could of course be left, broadly speaking, to fight her own war. Her effort was blended with that of the Western allies in the great conferences at Teheran (November–December 1943), Yalta (February 1945) and Potsdam (July –August 1945). The problem of regular staff collaboration on a day-to-day basis was therefore confined to Britain and the United States. The tone was set by the constant close contact between Roosevelt and Churchill themselves. Churchill was advised by the Chiefs of Staff Committee, who in turn co-ordinated the individual theatre commands. The chiefs of staff were in regular liaison with the prime minister, and thus tended to bypass the other political officers. On her entry to the war, the United States established a similar structure. A body called the Joint Chiefs of Staff was created, on which the army's representative, George C. Marshall, was very influential, but whose chairman was Admiral Leahy. Leahy had direct access to the president, and the joint chiefs thus increasingly gained political influence. One of its principal functions was to prepare the American view to put before a united British and American venture, the Combined Chiefs of Staff, set up in Washington in the winter of 1941–2. The role of the combined chiefs was to create an overall strategy by relating the efforts of one theatre to another, and by allocating resources between them. Therefore much of the economic direction of the war lay within the competence of the military. Moreover, the need for the theatre commanders to negotiate with the combined chiefs added to the political dimensions of a job already rendered delicate by the multinational composition of their forces and by the demands of their own home governments. Eisenhower, at the Supreme Headquarters of the Allied Expeditionary Force, demonstrated that his task was more akin to that of a chairman than that of a strategist.

The third great advantage enjoyed by the allies – after industrial supremacy and superior staff organisation – lay in the quality of their intelligence. Although the Germans in North Africa and Russia gained valuable tactical information from radio intercepts, at a strategic level their knowledge was poor. Conflicting bureaucracies, in the case of intelligence the armed services, the Foreign Office and the party organisation or *Sicherheitsdienst* (SD), lay at the root of this as of so many other problems in the Nazi state. In addition, the dazzling offensives of 1939 to 1941 had encouraged its neglect. After 1941 Russian political solidarity gave scant opportunity to compensate. The allies on the other hand concentrated during the early years of the war on building up an intelligence picture. At first they had few pieces, but, as information came in, the cumulative effect snowballed. Their sources were many and overlapping – aerial photography, agents on the ground – but at their heart lay signals intelligence. Radio communications came of age in the Second World War. Wireless sets were now sufficiently mobile to be used at a tactical level, and their range was enormously extended by high frequency transmission. However, their messages were public and, to avoid passing information to the enemy, had to be encoded. In 1926–8 the German forces adopted the Enigma machine for this purpose. In July 1939 the Poles, who had been endeavouring to break the Enigma codes, passed the fruits of their labours to the British and the French. This, the 'Ultra' secret, lay at the heart of allied wartime intelligence. At one level it was no more than part of an interlocking picture, providing in particular a continuing idea of the Axis order of battle. In other areas its influence was more dramatic: it could be said to have won the battle of the Atlantic, it tracked Rommel's supplies across the Mediterranean to North Africa, and it monitored the success of allied deception schemes for the invasion of Europe. None the less it remained no more than a tool. The value of raw intelligence depended on the attitude of its users. They could see in it no more than they wanted to see, and, as the Russians did before the German invasion or as Montgomery did at Arnhem, they could disregard information that illaccorded with their own perceptions.

Although the allies were agreed that the defeat of Germany was to take priority over Japan, they were less clear about the appropriate means to achieve that aim. In 1941 only the USSR seemed to be fighting the Germans directly. The position of the United States was compromised by the fact that it had been Japan, not Germany, that had precipitated her entry into the war. None the less the Americans were keen to land in Northern

France, and thus close to Germany, as soon as possible. Marshall talked of gaining a foothold in 1942, as a preliminary to a major invasion in 1943. The American argument gained vehement support from the beleaguered Russians. However, the British counselled prudence. They were already engaged fighting the Italians, and to a lesser extent the Germans, in the Mediterranean and North Africa. They argued against re-entering Europe before the sea battle in the Atlantic had been won. The losses to German submarines prevented the concentration of sufficient shipping for an invasion, and, even after the balance in the battle of the Atlantic turned in April 1943, the allies remained short of landing craft. The British pressed that in the interim the contribution of the Western allies should continue to be made in the Mediterranean and North Africa. Opening the Mediterranean would avoid the Cape route to the Far East and so save tonnage. Attacking Italy was indirectly weakening the German position in Northern Europe, and would divert troops from the eastern front. Strategic bombing constituted a direct attack on Germany, which would weaken her for the *coup de grâce*. Churchill supplemented these arguments by pointing to the Balkans, an area which the allies had favoured as early as 1939 and whose attractions were heightened by 'Ultra'-derived information on Hitler's concern for the region. The Americans suspected that the British were frightened of fighting once again over the battlefields of the First World War. But they found it hard to voice their views against a staff organisation, which by 1942 was profiting in political acumen and professional polish from three years' war. Moreover the case had sufficient practical merit to overcome suspicions that British strategy owed too much to maritime and imperial sentiment. The North African theatre was one in which the allies could exploit their economic and intelligence strengths.

The armies of the desert were small and therefore mobile. But the distances and the inhospitable terrain rendered supply fundamental. That of the Axis had to cross the Mediterranean, monitored by 'Ultra' and passing British-held Malta, and then to follow the lengthening line of communications of an advancing army. The route lay even more exposed for lack of air cover, since the *Luftwaffe*'s first priority was the eastern front. By contrast Tedder's Middle East Air Force worked out a coherent doctrine for the effective support of ground operations. The air commander was equal in rank to the theatre commander, so that the army could request, but not require, RAF support. Permanent liaison between the two established a sound working relationship. Rather than give close air support, the fighters tackled German fighters, leaving the bombers to attack the supplies and rear bases. Therefore, at Alamein (October 1942), Rommel was prey above all to his supply problem. He wanted 10,000 tons of petrol, he was promised 6,000, but he actually received 600. The success of the aerial battle in the Middle East was characterised by the fact that its command was independent but its conduct and effectiveness were interdependent.

The Western allies' direct attack on Germany, the strategic bombing offensive, similarly had to be seen as interdependent to be regarded as successful. Strategic bombing did not independently achieve the surrender of Germany. However, Britain in 1942 still boasted some well-placed advocates of Douhetism. In April, Lord Cherwell affirmed that five months' bombing would render a third of the German population homeless. Harris of Bomber Command endorsed him, and Churchill, an early convert to the efficacy of airpower and casting round for crumbs of comfort, supported them. But the assumption on which the prediction rested was that the German economy was already at full stretch. In the event, strategic bombing between 1940 and 1943 served principally to stimulate Germany's output and to harden her resolve. These trends were reinforced by the gradual way in which the tempo of the bomber offensive mounted. Only 17 per cent of the total tonnage of bombs dropped on Germany in the war was released before 1944. In the latter year, bombing began at last to be effective. German production peaked and then dropped by 30−40 per cent in the second half of 1944. But even this decline could in part be attributed to the shortage of labour and to the loss of raw materials.

A successful strategic bombing offensive was still technically impossible in 1941. In that year only 30 per cent of bombs arrived within five miles of their targets. Major developments were required in three areas − navigational aids (where the main breakthroughs, Gee, Oboe, H₂S and Pathfinders, came in 1942), long-range heavy bombers (the Lancaster and the B17) and long-range fighters. In August and October 1943, the USAAF with no escorts for its bombers suffered up to 20 per cent losses in its raids on Schweinfurt. Not until December 1943 did the Mustang enter service, and thereby provide the bomber with fighter cover over Germany itself.

By these means targeting became progressively more accurate. British doctrine, however, had already hardened in 1941. The gloomy intelligence reports on the effectiveness of the industrial raids, coupled with the inability to tackle the *Luftwaffe* by day, encouraged the RAF to switch to area bombing by night in a bid to break German morale. The ethics of this decision were as doubtful as its effectiveness. But in concrete intelligence terms the latter point could never be definitively assessed. When the Americans joined the offensive, they preferred precision bombing by day, aiming for targets of such economic importance as the aircraft and oil industries. These fundamentally different approaches in practice became complementary. Once again independence gained through interdependence.

The exclusive focus on the strategic bombing offensive had a number of consequences which in military terms were deleterious. The RAF was reluctant to switch aircraft to the battle of the Atlantic, it was loath to train bomber pilots for airborne operations and it scorned interdiction raids. And yet, on the air force's own terms, the strategic bombing offensive was a failure. None the less, in many other ways its achievements were considerable. In 1942, it gave the British and Americans their only means of retaliating directly against Germany. It required 2 million Germans to man anti-aircraft batteries rather than swell the front-line forces. It forced the *Luftwaffe* to switch its fighters from the eastern front, and later from Northern France, to the protection of Germany. Finally, without it, Germany's economic expansion in 1942−4 would have been even greater. Industry had to disperse and thus production was delayed. Raids on marshalling yards isolated goods and by 15 March 1945 German railway car loadings had been cut by 85 per cent. Transport was further hampered by the attack on oil production. In April 1944 Germany produced 175,000 tons of aviation spirit, but then from June until the end of the war she manufactured only a further 197,000 tons. Therefore, Germany, unlike the United States, could not develop her war economy in optimum conditions. Arguably these achievements vindicated the prewar advocates of strategic bombing, albeit not on the terms that they themselves set.

Indirect support for this position is given by the consequences for Germany of her failure to develop an effective strategy for airpower. The *Luftwaffe* foundered in its Blitz on London because it was not equipped technically or doctrinally for the task. The subsequent realisation that it needed an adequate heavy bomber came too late. Instead Germany had to rely on the *Junkers* 88, a medium bomber with a range of 620 miles (a third that of the Lancaster) and a bomb load of 3,960 pounds (against the Lancaster's 14,000 pounds). The *Ju* 88's radius meant that the Germans could do little to interrupt the recovery of Russian production. The commitment to a short war had ignored the long-term importance of the industrial effort. After destroying 4,000 aircraft (many of them on the ground) in the first week of their invasion, the Germans switched their attentions elsewhere. They failed to appreciate that the maintenance of air supremacy would be a constant battle. But not least among the products of the Russian factories was aircraft. By the end of 1941 the Russians on the Moscow front had twice as many aircraft as the Germans, and in June 1944 they had a sevenfold superiority opposite Army Group Centre. Therefore the neglect of the more independent strands of Wever's doctrine for air war ultimately left even the ground forces exposed.

The theme of integration, between nations, between services, and between the individual arms of those services, is a characteristic of the allied war effort. The individual arm pushed its own development to the full realisation of its potential. The problems arose when it had to be blended with other arms which had been doing the same thing. The integration was not achieved without deep political struggles in the command structure, but the staff organisation remained sufficiently resilient to cope, and the net effect was considerable all-round strength. By contrast the European victories of the Axis were above all the achievement of the German army. Indeed, even within the army, the cutting edge was the Panzer division. In practice the *Wehrmacht* consisted of much more than tanks, but the caricature is instructive. The Germans had, largely by accident, shaped their forces round a single leading idea. The allies tended to have a multitude of ideas, frequently competing and at times hindering their cause, but ultimately producing a simultaneous strength in several facets of war.

The development of airborne operations provides an illustration of these points. Paratroops possessed the typical features of *Blitzkrieg*. They were élite troops, used with surprise and flexibility, lacking heavy equipment and often depending on their moral effect for success. In the Low Countries in 1940, German airborne troops secured airfields and bridges, and seized the fortress of Eben Emael, commanding the Albert canal. But their losses were high: in Holland, the officers suffered 40 per cent casualties, and the other ranks 28 per cent. Germany's paratroops were an arm of the *Luftwaffe*. Herein lay the secret both of their success and of their failure. Close liaison meant that air support, the heavy artillery of the parachutist, and resupply were good. But General Student, Germany's outstanding exponent of airborne operations, thus came to believe that they could achieve independent success. In May 1941 he led the airborne invasion of Crete. The Germans were not supported by an accompanying seaborne landing, and they were outnumbered two to one. But with a combination of good luck and poor British tactics Student was triumphant. However, again losses were high. The irony of Crete was that the victorious Germans never again employed paratroops in a major role, whereas the allies set about the creation of airborne forces. The weaknesses that followed were the consequences of strident independence that had not been effectively harnessed. The RAF's reluctance to be distracted from bombing meant that air support was poor and that initially pilots were inadequately trained: at Sicily in July 1943 less than 200 of 3,400 troops arrived over the drop zone, and 47 of 347 gliders landed in the sea. The airborne forces themselves, anxious to establish the claim to an independent existence, emphasised major undertakings of strategic significance rather than low-level tactical operations. The disaster at Arnhem, in September 1944, was caused not least by the fact that an ambitious and distant target put the airborne formations so far ahead of the ground support that they found themselves fighting a prolonged battle independently. Their successes, in the Normandy landings or in the crossing of the Rhine, were those of 'vertical envelopment', in which they secured an objective but were not long isolated from the main army.

The ultimate test of allied inter-arm co-operation was amphibious operations. The allies appreciated from the outset that the invasion of Europe would require the mutual support of all three services. They were fortunate in that Britain's maritime heritage had bequeathed her some experience of seaborne invasion, and that this was supported by the United States commitment to an island-hopping reconquest of the Pacific. The problems were enormous. Dieppe, a trial cross-Channel attack on 19 August 1942, showed the demands on shipping and the need for air support. It demonstrated the intelligence requirements – knowledge of the beaches, tides and weather. Operation Torch, the American landings in North Africa in November 1942, brought in two further elements. One was the need for fire support from the accompanying warships. The other was the value of deception in gaining surprise. By monitoring German signals traffic, it was possible to know the success of ruses pointing to attacks elsewhere and to establish the likely strength of the defenders opposing the real landing. For Sicily, on 9–10 July 1943, the Mediterranean provided a more hospitable environment for amphibious operations than did the Atlantic or the Channel. 2,590 vessels, including 1,734 classed as landing craft, put ashore 181,000 men along 26 beaches. Success was attributable principally to two assets – aerial supremacy, and again the success of deception, which ensured that the landings were virtually unopposed. The choice of Salerno as the beach for the invasion of Italy in September was also largely determined by the need to ensure air superiority.

The D-Day landings in Normandy on 6 June 1944 were the outstanding amphibious operation of the war. The initial force was made up of five landing divisions, together with three airborne divisions, and was supported by a total of 6,939 vessels. Naval gunfire gave the allies artillery support fiften miles inland. However, the crucial feature was again aerial supremacy. In the two months before the invasion, the allies flew 4,500 reconnaissance sorties a day. On 6 June itself, the *Luftwaffe*, mustering a mere 319 aircraft to the 12,837 of the allies, was shot out of the skies in ten hours. By the end of the month it had flown 13,829 sorties to the 163,403 of the allies. The allies applied their aerial superiority in two ways. The first was interdiction. The bombers interrupted their attack on Germany to strike transport and railway networks, and so prevent the reinforcement of the Germans in Normandy. The second function of the air forces was the provision of close air support. Each allied division had a quota of 260 aircraft compared to the Germans' total of 19 per division in 1940. Working in close liaison with forward units, they reconnoitred and, as aerial artillery, bombed. On occasion their efforts were so thorough as to break up the ground and so impede the very attack they were supporting.

The second major achievement derived from earlier experience was the use of deception. The Germans awaiting the landings had two sets of problems. The first concerned the most appropriate tactics to counter an amphibious assault. Rundstedt, commander-in-chief in the west, advocating the classic view, argued that the defenders should be held back, ready to deliver a concentrated counter-attack. Rommel, commanding in Northern France, held that allied air supremacy would check the counter-attack, and that therefore the beaches themselves should be held. He planned to overcome the danger of dispersion by building coastal defences. However, these were still incomplete on 6 June, and the German response was therefore divided. It was further weakened by the second dilemma facing Rommel and Rundstedt. The allies could choose between two possible landing points – one was in Normandy, and the other, following the most direct cross-Channel route, was the Pas de Calais. During the course of May, the allies led the Germans to believe that 85–90 divisions and 7 airborne divisions were assembled in Britain. In reality the total was less than half that. But the result was that, even after the landings in Normandy, the Germans held back troops, ready to counter what they conceived would be the main attack in the Pas de Calais. By 16 June four of the ten available Panzer divisions had still not been committed to the battle.

The first few weeks of fighting were extremely hard. The *bocage* of Normandy, while impeding the movement of German tanks, also aided a stubborn defence. The thrust of the widening bridgehead was dictated by the problem of supply. An armoured division required 600 tons of supplies a day. At the outset the allies constructed artificial harbours which were code-named 'Mulberry'. On 1 July, they captured Cherbourg, but its docks remained unusable until August. Meanwhile the Germans tenaciously held Lorient and St Nazaire to the south, and Le Havre to the north. The landing in the South of France on 15 August opened a fresh avenue of supply, but the problem still continued. Montgomery's failure in September to clear the Scheldt and so free Antwerp was an enormous constraint to his plans to drive rapidly on a narrow front into the heart of Germany. Indeed, an examination of the supply problem supports Eisenhower's advocacy of an attack on a broad front. Montgomery's narrow thrust, even if fast, would have been in danger of out-running its supplies. A broad front allowed the allies to build up their strength. They could apply their enormous material superiority to mount a number of concentric and related attacks from different directions. Eisenhower reflected the American strategic tradition established by Grant in the final stages of the Civil War. Moreover, this reliance on a style designed to exploit the allies' resources did not make for ponderousness. On the contrary, the advance after the break-out from Normandy was very fast. The American and British armies were highly motorised in all arms, and, once they had effected a breakthrough their movement sustained it.

Similar features can be found in the Russians' continuous offensive, beginning with the counter-attack at Kursk in July 1943 and ending with the fall of Berlin in April 1945. The Russians followed their success at Stalingrad with a thrust in the direction of Kursk and Kharkov. Although German counter-strokes drove them back out of Kharkov, a Russian salient remained around Kursk. To knock it out, the Germans planned a limited offensive, using seventeen Panzer divisions. The battle opened on 4 July 1943, and at its height 3,000 tanks were simultaneously on the move. But this was not the German army of *Blitzkrieg* any more than it was the enemy of 1940. The Germans completely failed to achieve surprise. Indeed the Russians were so well prepared that they had three levels of defence, forty miles deep in all. When the Germans broke in, the Russians held close to the sides of the breach, and thus the Germans found themselves battling to widen a wedge with a broad apex rather than driving fast and deep on a narrow front. The ultimate Russian stroke was to counter-attack from a prepared position in the rear, the so-called 'Steppe front'. Thereafter, for nigh on two years, until the fall of Berlin, the Germans were almost continuously on the defensive in the east. The Russians mounted simultaneous and related attacks all along the front. The Germans would move to meet a thrust in one sector, only to be threatened by a fresh advance in another. Their reserves were rapidly exhausted. Each Russian attack was so related to the next that it prevented the creation of exposed salients, and thus, once the line had become fluid, it was given no opportunity to stabilise again. The rate of advance was set at 20–40 kilometres a day. The USSR's industrial recovery gave her overwhelming local superiority at the point of attack. The Soviets regularly outnumbered the Germans in a ratio of four or six to one, and this strength itself constituted the element of surprise in an offensive. The leading idea in the attack was to envelop, to encircle and then finally to annihilate.

On neither the western nor the eastern fronts was the tank the dominant arm of the offensive. Instead, it became but one component in a combined arms team. Anti-tank defences were never again as weak as they had proved in 1939 or 1940. The tank's moral impact declined, while its opponents learned more flexible methods of countering it. They abandoned linear defence for area defence. They held the flanks at the point of break-in, as the Russians had done at Kursk, or they formed deep pockets of resistance, as the Americans did in the Ardennes. The terrain, particularly in Italy and Normandy, often provided less favourable going for armour. Anti-tank guns became more effective: in 1941, the Germans adapted the 88 mm from its anti-aircraft role, and the British replaced 2-pounders with 6-pounders. Minefields toughened the outer crust of the defence. Thus the tank alone could no longer hope independently to break in to a defensive system. That had to be achieved primarily by infantry and artillery, with the principal role of the tank lying in the later phase of break-out and exploitation.

The advocates of the independent use of armour were thus routed. In Germany, their position was never as entrenched as Guderian's advocacy or the image of *Blitzkrieg* has suggested. The infantry component of the Panzer division, in any case never low, was increased. In June 1940, the ten Panzer divisions mustered a total of thirty-five tank battalions; a year later an increase to twenty-one divisions was accompanied by the creation of only eleven more tank battalions. The effect was to halve the tank establishment of a Panzer division (to 140 tanks, and in practice battle casualties brought actual strengths considerably lower), and to leave the division with two tank battalions as against four infantry battalions. In addition, the German army boasted 14 motorised divisions and 163 other infantry divisions. Its main weight, therefore, lay in the infantry. In North Africa, the Panzers relied on their artillery to break up the enemy tanks and artillery before themselves counter-attacking against the infantry. This trend became more evident in the east from 1943. Mobile defence was supplemented by greater firepower. In the air, *Stukas* directly attacked Soviet armour. On the ground, the Tiger had an 88 mm gun and the Panther a high velocity 75 mm. Moreover, by the end of the war self-propelled assault guns outnumbered conventional tanks in the German army.

In Russia itself, the massive armoured formation, the mechanised corps of 1940–1 (which had in any case contained sizeable artillery and infantry components), did not outlive the equipment losses of Operation Barbarossa. The gaps were made good by large numbers of highly effective T34s. Late in 1942 the tank corps and the mechanised corps (comparable to divisions in Western armies) became the basic formations. The belated nature of these developments and the fluidity of the eastern front meant that the role of the tank in the Russian army was still expanding in 1945. However, to cope with the German defences, the calibre of the T34's gun was increased to 85 mm and its firepower was supplemented with self-propelled artillery and the 122 mm gun of the Stalin tank.

In 1940, the British idea of an armoured division consisted of two (or later three) lorried infantry battalions, two artillery battalions and six tank battalions. It was thus much more weighted in favour of the tank than its German or Russian counterparts. The pure armour idea met its nemesis in Operation Crusader in North Africa in the winter of 1941. The British attempted to fight a pure tank battle with an independent armoured division, and in the process left their infantry without armoured support. Auchinleck concluded that the distinction between armoured and infantry divisions should go and that each division should have its own ratio of tanks, guns and infantry. The 1942 armoured division consisted of four infantry, three tank and four artillery battalions. The basic tank of this division was the American Sherman, which, with its 75 mm gun, was the first in British use with adequate firepower. From a projected target of eleven armoured divisions in 1940, the British army actually possessed five in 1944.

At the outset of the war, the United States planned to create 213 divisions by June 1944, fifty or sixty of which would be armoured. In the event she had a maximum of ninety-one, of which sixteen were armoured. The standard US infantry division of twenty-seven rifle companies had three artillery battalions and, in practice, one tank battalion. Equally each armoured division had its own infantry component. From 1940 to 1942 the establishment was six tank, three armoured infantry and three armoured artillery battalions. In 1943, the division was restructured with three of each. The doctrine that underpinned this organisation was the integration of tanks and infantry down to battalion level. In the battle for penetration, the tank regained its First World War role; it became a mobile gun to support the infantry in the breaking of the main enemy resistance. General McNair, the commander of the US Army Ground Forces, expressed the new-found balance: 'An armoured division is of value only in pursuit or exploitation. For plain and fancy slugging against an enemy who is unbroken or at least intact the tank battalion or group is adequate.'

Therefore, the unsung hero of the war became the artillery. The Russian superiority over the Germans was particularly pronounced in this arm. By the end of 1943, the USSR had 80 artillery divisions, 90,000 guns and 73 independent artillery brigades. At the end of the war, almost half the Red Army was artillery. For the final attack on Berlin, the Russians had 41,600 guns to the Germans' 8,000, giving them 670 guns for each kilometre of front. It was used increasingly *en masse*, in reserve, to prepare for the attack. It was supported by Soviet aerial superiority, which concentrated over the battlefield rather than on long-range bombing, and which was also treated as a *Stavka* reserve. The Western allies' emphasis on artillery was never of this order, but for them too it became the agent of break-in. In 1942 the arrival of the 6-pounder anti-tank gun and of the Sherman tank, with its 75 mm gun, supplemented the independent firepower of the infantry and armour. Therefore the artillery no longer had to compensate for the under-gunning of other formations and was able to concentrate. On the eve of Alamein, Montgomery had collected almost 1000 field and medium guns, and on 23 October 456 of them opened 30 Corps's attack with a massive hurricane bombardment. With field guns capable of firing at high elevations, such as the American 105 mm and the British 25-pounder, artillery was kept well forward and used with aggression.

The lubricant of all these independent but interdependent arms was the radio. Its significance has already been indirectly touched on: the value of signals intelligence to the shaping of British strategy is offset by the defeats of Crete and Arnhem, both in part attributable to problems with wireless. But its real importance lay on a regular, more mundane and daily basis. Wireless sets were distributed to forward units, to artillery batteries and to tank squadrons, in the late 1920s. They became the agents of tactical flexibility. They conquered time. An infantry platoon could call up artillery or aerial support; a tank commander could talk directly to the pilot overhead. The big problem of the First World War had not been the break-in, but the break-through and the break-out. The internal combustion engine, in the shape of the tank, the aircraft or the lorry, was vital in the recovery of mobility at that stage. But the radio was also essential: it enabled rapid concentration against weakness and thus ensured that the momentum of the advance could be sustained.

Neither the advocates of the bomber nor those of the tank had been proved right in the Second World War. The independent use of any one arm in the long run was inadequate. But in collaboration with each other and with infantry and artillery, both bomber and tank achieved much. Each arm, each service and each nation developed a specific approach. Those traits of independence did not become divisive and ultimately self-defeating because of the effectiveness of allied communications. From the major tripartite conferences, through the staff talks, down to wireless conversations on the battlefield itself, communications ensured coherence. Thus the allies could attack on a broad front, allowing the full deployment of their economic superiority.

Guide to Further Reading

The main, readily available general histories of the Second World War are Calvocoressi and Wint, Michel, and Liddell Hart (1970). The first is the most objective, the second is good on the French perspective, and the last concentrates disproportionately on military operations (and specifically those of the British). The most stimulating accounts – Lukacs and Wright – are more concerned with the impact of war on European society. So much is this the case with Lukacs that he stops in December 1941.

The broad lines of allied grand strategy have now been explored, and the Davis-Poynter series, the *Politics and Strategy of the Second World War*, edited by Noble Frankland and Christopher Dowling, provides a succession of guides to key areas. But little has been done to analyse the main tactical developments, or to relate them to the social or economic aspects of the war. Perhaps too much remains in a state of flux. The British official history is now in the process of being supplemented with an account of intelligence (by F. H. Hinsley and others) which has already caused some major reappraisals. Both East and West Germany have recently undertaken the publication of official histories. The latter's, entitled *Das Deutsche Reich in der Zweite Weltkrieg*, is a project of the *Militärgeschichtliches Forschungsamt* in Freiburg (Vol. I by W. Deist and others, Stuttgart, 1979). From the Soviet perspective, the second volume of John Erickson's account of Stalin's war with Germany is still awaited.

Literature on Germany was mentioned at the end of chapter 10. Seaton (1971) is the best book on the eastern front, but Erickson's first volume

(1975) is essential for the Russian perspective. Garthoff (1954) analyses Soviet tactics. Van Creveld (1972) tackles the vexed question of the timing of Operation Barbarossa.

Brief guides (albeit in French) to the strategy of the Western allies by authorities in the subject are Howard (1975) and Pogue. A similarly short general account, in this case of codebreaking, is given by Kahn, while Lewin assesses the significance of the contribution of 'Ultra'. Overy (1980) is the best guide on the air war, and is particularly strong on the economic dimension. Tugwell discusses airborne operations and Bidwell (for the British alone) artillery. Barnett's (1960) analysis of British operations in North Africa is still highly contentious. On American tactics, begin with Weigley (1968), chapters 18 and 19, and Weigley (1973), chapter 24. Two recent accounts of the Normandy fighting are by Weigley (1981) and Keegan (1982).

Chapter 12

The Revolution in Strategy

The Second World War marked two distinct breaks in the declared subject matter of this book. First, it was no longer (if it ever had been) realistic to consider Europe in isolation: the United States emerged as one of the two dominant arbitrators in European military affairs. Secondly, it finally became impossible to consider the operations of armies independently of those of air forces or even of navies. Both these trends were confirmed after 1945. Politically, the creation of the North Atlantic Treaty Organisation in 1949 tied America's defence policy to that of Western Europe. Militarily, the challenge to the pre-eminence of armies by the theorists of strategic bombing seemed finally to have succeeded with the advent of nuclear weapons. A discussion of warfare that centred on European armies was in danger of deliberately excluding the major issue.

On the morning of 6 August 1945, the first atom bomb was dropped at Hiroshima. Its explosive force was equivalent to 20,000 tons of TNT, and the temperature at its centre was 150 million degrees centigrade, ten times the temperature of the sun. Most of the city, an area of four and a half square miles, was destroyed. Eighty thousand people were killed, and the survivors still suffer the longer-term effects. Three days later, on 9 August, a second bomb was dropped at Nagasaki.

The strategic bombing of Japan had already destroyed an area thirty times greater than that obliterated by the two atomic bombs. A quarter of a million Japanese had been killed, almost half a million wounded and 40 per cent of the buildings in sixty-six cities had been smashed. The number of bombs and the period of the raids (begun in January 1945, and intensified from March) were fractions of those in the bomber offensive against Germany. The success was due to the use of incendiary bombs in preference to high explosive. Directed against highly inflammable targets (particularly wooden houses), they created great fire storms. Japan had been brought to the brink of surrender before 6 August. Eight days later, she surrendered without being invaded. The joint chiefs, extrapolating from the fighting at Okinawa, had expected a landing to cost up to a million casualties. Therefore, the effect of the atomic bombs, in the eyes of the American Air Force, was to clinch the arguments for the independent use of strategic bombing.

However, the case for the effectiveness of either strategic bombing or of the atom bombs was not so clear cut. On 8 August 1945 the Russians finally entered the war against Japan. The effect was twofold. For the joint chiefs the desire to exclude the Russians from the peace settlement in the Far East added to the demand for a swift victory. For the Japanese it was – like the atom bomb – one of a succession of major blows against an already grievously weakened structure. Japan surrendered as the result of a succession of blows, not because of any one in isolation.

Although the atomic bombs used against Japan were not in themselves decisive, they have provided the only practical example for all the theory which is discussed in the rest of this chapter and which has underpinned much of postwar international relations. If the blows against Hiroshima and Nagasaki have served to keep the peace since 1945, then perhaps some good has come from the suffering the names of those cities evoke. But such reasoning is not without its problems. Japan was already weakened by war, its resolve to fight had slipped and it had no means of retaliation. The world since 1945 has been dominated by two more equal adversaries, both strong but geographically well separated. The relevance of the atom bomb to both sets of circumstances is insufficient to produce a symmetry.

The simultaneity of independent developments in nuclear weaponry is an instructive commentary on the nature of scientific research. In 1938–9 parallel work in many countries, principally France, Germany, Britain and the United States, suggested the possibility of nuclear fission. The overrunning of Europe by Germany had the effect of congregating nuclear expertise in Britain. Fearing that the Germans would be the first successfully to develop an atom bomb, the Maud Committee in July 1941 urged that nuclear research become a priority. The United States was anxious to collaborate, and her relative security, coupled with her prosperity, caused the project to be focused in North America. Under the Quebec agreement of 1943, the British and the Americans agreed to exchange information. None the less, the Americans shut the British out in 1946, when Congress passed the MacMahon Act. The British reaction was to press ahead with the development of their own bomb, which they tested successfully in 1952. Far more unnerving for the Americans was the speed with which Russia responded. Predictions for the first Russian atomic bomb picked 1951 as the earliest date, and ranged as late as 1955. In the event, Russia tested a nuclear weapon in 1949. However, the United States was afforded some respite by Russia's lack of delivery systems and by the slowness with which she subsequently developed a doctrine for her new weapon. The victories of 1945 had been achieved by her ground forces, and strategic bombing on the eastern front had no rhetoric of success into which the atom bomb could be dovetailed.

However, the lag between the technological breakthrough and the formulation of doctrine was also evident in the United States. Those who saw the atomic bomb as inaugurating a fresh departure in strategy were exceptional. For many, and particularly for the air force, the virtues of the bomb were its cheapness (since fewer would be required) and its increased range (since the load per aircraft was less). Thus it was adopted more as a super bomb to supplement an existing arsenal than as a forerunner of a new way in warfare. American thinking about the next war was dogged by the experience of the last. On the analogy of Pearl Harbor, it would begin with a surprise attack launched by an unprincipled enemy against the cities of the United States. This would be the preliminary to a long war dominated by conventional operations. In the immediate term such thinking was not unreasonable. The United States did not possess a stockpile of atomic bombs and not until 1955, with the advent of the B52, did she have a long-range bomber with which to deliver them.

The deepening of the Cold War provided a context in which to assess the significance of the bomb. The concerns of Western Europeans for their own defence, coupled with the conduct of the USSR in Eastern Europe, led to the signature of the North Atlantic Treaty in 1949. To begin with, the apparent importance of conventional forces obscured the fact that the United States nuclear contribution would become the primary feature of NATO's defence. At the Lisbon conference of 1952, NATO reckoned it needed 96 divisions by 1954 to match the 175 Russian divisions aligned against it. The financial and political implications of parity in conventional defence promised to become unacceptable. At the same time, the United States was licking its wounds after its first attempt to contain communism. Fighting in Korea had brought 33,000 casualties for no decisive result. Containment suggested a future dominated by protracted and inconclusive wars, while the driving force in communist expansion, the USSR, remained snug and inviolate. Russia, surrounded by buffer states, was only really vulnerable to nuclear bombs, and from 1947–8 the plans of the United States Air Force included targeting against Russian urban and industrial centres.

In 1952–3 both the United States and the USSR tested a hydrogen or fusion bomb. The yield of the H-bomb was measured not in kilotons (thousands of tons) of TNT, as the A-bomb had been, but in megatons (millions of tons). One hydrogen bomb had an explosive force greater than all the bombs dropped on Germany in the Second World War. It was a thousand times more powerful than the bombs dropped at Hiroshima and Nagasaki. A further development of the mid-1950s confirmed its significance: the miniaturisation of inertial guidance systems produced a missile that was accurate to 5,000 metres. The harnessing of explosive power to an effective delivery vehicle had transformed war more fundamentally than had the atomic bomb itself. The compulsion to consider the strategic import of nuclear weapons was now overwhelming.

In 1953, Eisenhower, as President of the United States, and John Foster Dulles, his secretary of state, embodied these strands in their so-called 'New Look'. American possession of a stockpile and of the means of delivery combined with the economic arguments against conventional forces. In addition, the USSR's growing ability to respond to the use of nuclear weaponry in kind had the effect of separating nuclear from conventional forces. With the United States itself vulnerable to nuclear attack, American leaders could not see nuclear weapons simply as supplements to operations in a general war. The Eisenhower/Dulles strategy, dubbed 'massive retaliation', was first expounded in October 1953. It emphasised the ability to hit the USSR with nuclear weapons in order to deter the Russians from embarking on a major war. It assumed that eventually the Russian nuclear arsenal would be on a par with that of the Americans, and that stalemate would follow. Although 'massive retaliation' put the weight of US defence policy behind nuclear weapons, it was seen as primarily relevant to Europe and it did not exclude the possibility of conventional operations, particularly in other theatres. It thus made some attempt to render the means employed proportionate to the political objectives. However, in January 1954 Dulles said he wanted 'a great capacity to retaliate, instantly, by means and at places of our own choosing.' He thus fed a caricature of 'massive retaliation' as a ponderous bludgeon, designed to invoke nuclear war against communism anywhere in the world. It was a caricature that could be supplemented by one interpretation of America's traditional attitudes to war: isolationist by temperament, she was slow to anger, but once roused she would fight with every means at her disposal in order to ensure absolute victory. Global responsibilities since 1945 had brought continuing, irritating and expensive military obligations. 'Massive retaliation' had apparently been adopted to remove these.

What 'massive retaliation' had acknowledged was that nuclear weapons had rendered war so awful as to be unthinkable. War had ceased to be an instrument of policy. By emphasising that nuclear weapons would be used in retaliation, Dulles regained for them some political effectiveness. Their purpose was not to conduct war but to maintain peace. The idea of deterrence was not a new one. British thinking between the wars had seen the bomber as a means of discouraging aggression. In the 1950s, the 1930s seemed additionally relevant as a cautionary tale on the dangers of weakness in peacetime diplomacy. The threat of war should be a continuous element in the spectrum of foreign policy options.

The implications of the theory of deterrence, and its role in bringing stability to international relations, were fully explored between the mid-1950s and early 1960s. The principal writers – men such as Bernard Brodie, William Kaufmann, Herman Kahn, Albert Wohlstetter, Henry Kissinger, Richard Osgood and Thomas Schelling – were academics, with their focus in a USAF-funded research organisation, the RAND Corporation. They were stimulated in part by the breakthroughs of the hydrogen bomb and the missile. They were also prompted by the exaggerated image of 'massive retaliation': it seemed inflexible and unsubtle, threatening a punishment which was far greater than the possible crime and which had dire implications for the United States itself.

It was in these years that the vocabulary of deterrence was established. Subsequent thinking has in some cases overturned what was then said, but more often it has refined and confirmed. The consensus argued that, for deterrence to be effective, the threat must be credible. It had to be of a nature that rendered it likely to be used, or else deterrence would seem to be no more than bluff. Above all, a power needed to be sure that it could deliver nuclear weapons, and increasingly it has been delivery systems rather than warheads that have eaten into defence budgets. Secondly, the threat had to be communicated to the potential enemy. Secrecy was no longer a necessary feature of peacetime military preparation. Moreover communication was not confined to the publication of capabilities: a power could threaten specific actions in response to specific circumstances (as the United States did over the Russian siting of missiles in Cuba in 1962) or it could take limited military action, such as putting its troops on alert, in order to demonstrate resolve. The willingness to publish intentions was, however, confused by a simultaneous need. By stating particular threats, the strength of deterrence in that area was enhanced, but its range and effectiveness in other areas were correspondingly diminished.

Therefore some argued that an opponent should be left uncertain as to a nation's likely actions. Its published force strengths would demonstrate what it was able to do: what it might actually do could in some circumstances be better left to the imagination of the enemy. All this logic, developed in particular by game theory, made the enormous assumption that conduct in a crisis would remain rational. It tended to assume that the USSR saw the impact of nuclear weapons on international affairs in terms similar to those of the USA.

A basic requirement of deterrence was that the nuclear weapons should themselves be invulnerable. If they were susceptible to attack, they could provide an inducement to a pre-emptive strike which could be profoundly unsettling. American fears of pre-emption, originating with Pearl Harbor and fostered by the USAF's own thinking on strategic bombing, were further heightened by the development of Soviet doctrine. Freed from the shackles of Stalin's baleful influence, Russian theorists stressed the value of surprise. Conscious of the USSR's own exposure and imagining that the war would be long, they pointed to the effectiveness of an initial disabling blow. The Russians gave greater priority to the development of ballistic missiles than to that of long-range bombers, and by 1957 they appeared to have the lead in this particular area. Their technological competence was confirmed on 4 October 1957, when they launched the world's first satellite, Sputnik I. American airfields and missile sites were now directly observable by the Russians. The possibilities of pre-emption loomed ever larger in American minds. They provoked a crucial article from Albert Wohlstetter, published in 1959 under the title, 'The Delicate Balance of Terror'. Wohlstetter distinguished between what he called a first-strike capability and a second-strike capability. A first-strike capability was the ability to initiate a nuclear war. Its forces were aimed against military targets in order to minimise the enemy's power to retaliate. However, these weapons would be rendered useless if the other side attacked first. Therefore, a nation needed a second-strike capability. This Wohlstetter defined as an ability to survive an enemy attack and still retaliate. Its forces would exact a punishment from the enemy's cities, and sufficient weapons must emerge from a first strike to guarantee a level of destruction unacceptable to a potential enemy. Thus a second-strike capability could provide a check against a surprise attack. It was the true deterrent.

A number of methods were available to ensure that second-strike forces survived an enemy first strike. They could be hidden. Given the underdeveloped state of anti-submarine warfare, the concealment provided by the oceans favoured the submarine-launched ballistic missile. Submarines also had two other qualities: they were mobile and they could disperse. Ground-launched systems could be protected by hardened silos invulnerable to all but direct hits. Air-launched systems were (in 1961) put on a fifteen-minute alert, and thus could be airborne before enemy missiles arrived. The proliferation of methods was itself an insurance, since – whatever the pace of technological change (and this was itself exaggerated) – not all were likely simultaneously to become vulnerable.

Further props were added to the edifice of deterrence. Civil defence underlined the seriousness with which a power prepared for nuclear war:

it demonstrated that the threat to use nuclear weapons was genuine. During the 1960s and 1970s increasing stress was laid on the need for command and control systems also to be invulnerable. Speedy decision-making would add to the credibility and firmness of the response. However, solutions here had to settle for a compromise. Fully centralised control was incompatible with the requirements of invulnerability: on the other hand, forces that were dispersed, mobile and concealed were also harder to co-ordinate. In addition the West faced a range of political problems which did not encumber the Warsaw Pact: the nature of a voluntary alliance and the domestic structure for taking decisions in a democratic state were potentially unwieldy. One solution to this problem of decision-taking was to resort to an automatic response, the so-called 'launch on warning'. Particularly when in the late 1970s and early 1980s the American ground-launched force seemed so vulnerable to Russian attack as no longer to have a secure second-strike capability, the answer for some was to fire before being hit. This indeed would be a 'doomsday machine'.

What such options highlighted was the problem of credibility. Posing an excessive threat for a minor danger was incredible. 'Massive retalia-tion' seemed an inappropriate level of violence for many possible world crises. It was particularly incredible when its employment might call down a response on the American homeland. American policy therefore needed more alternatives at a lower level which would thus simultaneously strengthen deterrence. The availability of conventional forces, theatre or tactical nuclear weapons, and limited nuclear options would allow the Americans to employ a threat suitable to the crisis. Critics of 'massive retaliation' were proposing what came to be called 'graduated deterrence'.

The Eisenhower administration responded to many of these prescriptions. The apparent Soviet superiority, highlighted by Sputnik, was offset by accelerating the programme for ground- and sea-launched systems, dubbed respectively Minuteman and Polaris. None the less J. F. Kennedy, the Democratic candidate, fought much of his presidential campaign in 1960 on the issue of defence, and in particular on the weaknesses of 'massive retaliation' and on the existence of a Soviet superiority in missiles. Duly elected, Kennedy appointed as his secretary of defense an executive of the Ford Motor Company, Robert McNamara. By incorporating the advice of the academic critics McNamara restored the centre of the strategic debate to the Pentagon. At the same time an expanding defence budget doused service rivalry. He stressed the need for a second-strike capability: invulnerability was served by the Minuteman and Polaris programmes and by putting half the Strategic Air Command on a fifteen-minute alert. But the Soviet superiority proved a figment of American imaginations. The Russian missile programme had fallen behind, and in 1961 satellite intelligence confirmed that there was a 'missile gap', but that it was to the disadvantage of the USSR, not of the USA.

Equipped with this knowledge, McNamara gave a speech in June 1962 in which he adopted the principles of 'graduated deterrence'. He urged that nuclear war should be considered in terms more akin to those of conventional operations. The main initial targets should be the enemy's forces, and the enemy himself should be encouraged to reciprocate by refraining from striking cities. At the same time the United States should retain sufficient nuclear forces to hit the enemy's population if it proved necessary. McNamara was trying to extend the principles of deterrence into the conduct of war itself. The advocates of 'graduated deterrence' rested their case on an extreme presentation of 'massive retaliation'. 'Massive retaliation' was incredible. It had usurped policy by tying the United States to a simple but devastating military response. With the introduction of the possibility of escalation, policy and the employment of force were once again integrated. Bargaining could continue through ascending levels of violence. Limited war became a possible option in foreign policy. The US army saw its chance. 'Massive retaliation' had placed the emphasis on its rival services, the navy and the air force. The corollary of 'flexible response', as Kennedy saw full well, was an increase in conventional armaments. However, his first application of the new strategy – in Vietnam – proved even less happy than the tests of containment in Korea. What had remained unclear was whether limited war would cause more violence below the nuclear threshold, or whether the possibility of escalation would introduce greater prudence. The answer in South-east Asia proved to lie in the second for the Americans and in the first for the North Vietnamese. The limits were confined to one side only. Furthermore they were, unlike those under which the armies of the eighteenth century had laboured, primarily self-imposed. The Americans restricted themselves in their use of weapons and in their theatre of operations. But the political objectives revolved around conflicting ideologies and – for the North Vietnamese at least – remained open-ended.

It was the attempt to persuade NATO to adopt the principles of 'graduated deterrence', rather than the failure of those principles in Vietnam, which aroused most controversy. Europe, led by the British in 1957, had embraced 'massive retaliation'. In 1962, Kennedy's expectation of a renewed conventional effort from his allies promised little but rising costs. Even more seriously, it highlighted doubts about the degree of American support in the event of a Russian attack in Europe. Increasing Soviet missile strengths exposed the vulnerability of American cities: deterrence was becoming mutual. The incentive for the United States to protect its own cities by fighting outside America at lower levels of violence was therefore seen to be great. However, such a war would be total in its impact for the Europeans themselves, and Russia would certainly not fight it under self-imposed restraints. McNamara's insensitivity in handling European reactions only exacerbated the problem. He stressed that stability lay in a bipolar world, with states grouping themselves round the two nuclear superpowers. None the less, in 1967 NATO adopted the strategy of 'flexible response'. It was a triumph of political manoeuvre. For a European 'flexible response' never meant quite the same thing as 'graduated deterrence' did for an American: the former still carried as its major threat the use of nuclear weapons, the latter was a policy which could consider the application of conventional weapons as an end in itself. However the fact that the European theatre was the focus gave a semblance of unity. In that context, 'graduated deterrence', like 'flexible response', carried the idea of escalation up to and beyond the nuclear threshold. The difference lay in the timing of each step in the ascent. For the Europeans the conventional phase had to be seen as short; for the Americans the possible employment of nuclear weapons – although still present – lay further in the background. The German defence white paper of 1975–6 phrased the policy with marvellous tact: 'The initial use of nuclear weapons must be timed as late as possible but as early as necessary'.

However, not all Europeans were (or had to be) as trusting of the Americans as the Germans. For some the solution seemed to be for Europe to have its own deterrent, so that it could once again be sovereign in its attitudes to war. McNamara was predictably appalled: the sin of proliferation was coupled with the destabilising consequences of divided command in a crisis. However, in order to retain some measure of political control, he proposed a joint NATO nuclear deterrent, the multilateral force. The proposal was unrealistic. The basic problem was that no one state could reasonably expect any other state to incur the devastation of a nuclear strike on its behalf. The problems of command for a multilateral force were insuperable. National nuclear forces were the logical alternative. Both Britain and France possessed such forces, and in the 1960s they pressed ahead with their expansion – the former with American aid, the latter without. The penalty of the USA's move from 'massive retaliation' was that it fed Gaullist ideas of France's leading role in an autonomous Europe, and in 1966 France withdrew from the military line-up of NATO. She could defend her actions with impeccable logic: the credibility in nuclear deterrence could only run to national self-defence.

The differing views on the length of the conventional phase of a war in Europe highlighted the contrast between deterrence and defence. Logically put, pure deterrence would present nuclear war as so awful that recourse to it was unimaginable. But then deterrence – as the critics of 'massive retaliation' had argued – became incredible. Nuclear weapons therefore had to be integrated with the rest of the defence forces in order to endow the threat of their use with conviction. The extreme presentation of this argument roused the fear of an excessive readiness to resort to nuclear weapons, and in particular that in a crisis military necessity would overcome political sense.

This dilemma was accompanied by a second. Powers with small nuclear forces, such as Britain or France, did not have sufficient weapons to engage in the various levels of response suggested by escalation. They had to argue from the position of extreme deterrence: any release of nuclear weapons would result in unacceptable levels of damage. In order to ensure credibility, the logical corollary of the minimalist position was that nuclear weapons would only be employed in the defence of national sovereignty. France accepted this argument. Britain, by remaining a full member of NATO, settled for compromise. The protective range of her deterrent was thus extended to other states, but its plausibility was simultaneously limited.

The United States has thought rather harder about how it could fight a nuclear war, if deterrence failed. Late in 1959 the RAND Corporation and the USAF began to integrate the targeting policies of the navy and air force. The consequence was the Single Integrated Operational Plan, drawn up in 1961 and adopted in 1962. The plan identified three possible tasks for a nuclear strike – the pre-emption of the enemy's nuclear forces, an attack on other military targets or the destruction of cities and industrial centres. The emphasis in the plan fell on the last group. The purpose of such an attack would be to inflict unacceptable damage after a Russian first strike. (McNamara subsequently defined 'unacceptable' as the killing of 30 per cent of Russia's population and the destruction of 75 per cent of her industrial capacity.) However, the other two categories of target were still included in the plan. The United States therefore retained the option of launching nuclear weapons first, particularly in the event of there being insufficient troops to restore stability in a war in Europe.

None the less McNamara's initial emphasis lay on high-yield, accurate weapons for striking military targets. The second-strike force would be kept in reserve. Thus the damage to cities would be limited, and victory in the traditional sense would remain a possibility. This strategy, dubbed 'counter-force', added to credibility since it made the use of nuclear weapons more likely. But it posed many technical and doctrinal problems. Its emphasis on a first strike smacked of pre-emption and therefore seemed destabilising. It was not calculated to reassure the densely populated continent of Europe, for which a distinction between civilian and military targets was not very meaningful. But, even more decisive, it was technologically fallible. Only very few Russian missiles needed to survive a first strike for the USSR to be able to reciprocate with devastating effect against the cities of the United States. Buttressed by the need to ensure an effective first strike, the services' demands for weaponry became open-ended. At the same time, however, the increasing invulnerability of missile systems and the growth of the Russian nuclear forces made the likelihood of a successful disarming first strike increasingly remote.

By 1963, McNamara had concluded that his war-fighting doctrine lay in ruins. Instead he swung in favour of a strategy of 'mutually assured destruction', better known by the unfortunate acronym, MAD. The targeting base was to be 'counter-city' or 'counter-value', not 'counter-force'. The prevention of war should rest on the fear of its horrors. With both sides in possession of invulnerable forces, the temptation to pre-empt was removed and a cap seemed to have been placed on the arms race. In practice, however, American doctrine remained a blend of 'counter-city' and 'counter-force'. The former was a way of stressing the dangers of nuclear war in peacetime: it ceased to be valuable the moment when war broke out. The latter remained a strategy for fighting a war. US plans deterred the Russians by aiming for their soft targets, and prepared for war by simultaneously taking in their military installations. MAD became a device for setting force strengths, not for the employment of nuclear weapons.

In October 1962 the two superpowers found themselves locked in crisis over Cuba. The successful resolution of the confrontation reassured faint hearts. In practice, however, deterrence theory had played almost no part in the negotiations. Certainly the American response owed nothing to the idea of escalation. The statesmen had endeavoured to avoid using force at all rather than advocate its controlled application. It was the possibility of total war that guided their actions. Prudence had dominated. Moreover, the crisis was misleading in another way. Its issues were clear-cut. America's interests were threatened when those of the USSR were not; the territorial integrity of neither was at stake; and there were no allies to confuse the issue. The time was available for careful and considered decision-making.

Both sides were sufficiently shaken to inaugurate a period of *détente*. In 1963 the 'hot-line' was established between the heads of state. They signed the Test Ban Treaty to indicate their joint opposition to nuclear proliferation. They recognised a mutual interest in freezing their own nuclear superiority. However, those not embraced in this framework for international relations were impatient of the American and Russian advantage. France and China denounced the Test Ban Treaty, and many nations – including Israel, South Africa and Pakistan – have not signed the 1970 Non-Proliferation Treaty. The superpowers endeavoured to control their own arms as well as those of others. They both wanted to limit the economic damage wrought by the arms race, and in 1969 began the strategic arms limitation talks (or SALT). With satellite intelligence to verify the good behaviour of the other side, SALT I was agreed in 1972. It set a total of 2,400 strategic nuclear delivery vehicles for each power for a five-year period. In 1974 the Vladivostok accords established the framework for a new treaty and, even if SALT II has subsequently foundered, these talks and others like them (the mutual balanced force reductions or MBFR and, most recently, the strategic arms reduction talks or START) have become the focus for diplomacy between East and West. Therefore by the mid-1960s a stable system of bipolar international relations seemed to have been inaugurated. Its basis was deterrence. Both sides had mutually balancing forces which threatened each other with terrible destruction.

However, in time the edifice began to look less secure. It was above all the creation of American imaginations. It supposed that Russian attitudes to nuclear weapons were similar. There were really only two pieces of evidence to support this view. At Helsinki in 1969 the USSR accepted that both sides would incur losses in a nuclear war, and in 1972 the SALT I agreement rested on a Russian acceptance that defence against a massive nuclear attack was impossible and that mutual deterrence therefore relied on parity. In practice Russian thinking was developing on very different lines. Krushchev had taken considerable interest in the missile programme. He had seen it as a way of running down conventional forces and putting the weight on a 'minimal' deterrent. Therefore McNamara's emphasis on a secure second-strike capability and on increases in conventional troops had left the USSR feeling vulnerable. The service chiefs, anxious for their own domains, argued instead that each weapon system should be part of an interlocking whole. The all-round material strength of the Soviet ground forces of the Second World War was carried forward into the postwar era. In 1964, the USSR began to increase her nuclear and her conventional forces. By the 1970s she had more intercontinental and submarine-launched ballistic missiles than the United States. The West, guided by the SALT talks and the idea of balance, looked on aghast. It judged this build-up in terms of capability, not of doctrine. It tended also to overlook the American lead in bombers and technology: in the middle of the decade the United States was just completing the adoption of multiple independently-targetable re-entry vehicle (MIRV) warheads, when the Soviet Union was only beginning.

Soviet doctrine was based not on the writings of academics or of politicians, but on those of soldiers. The early missile programme had been in the hands of artillery officers. The ideas of superiority and of victory therefore remained present in nuclear strategy. The acceptance of mutual vulnerability seemed insane, since it put the security of the USSR in the hands of its principal political opponents. The emphasis lay less on deterrence, and more on defence. Since the USSR was not bound by the political sensibilities of her allies, her military doctrine did not have to gloss over the more unacceptable features of war-fighting. The theme of a nuclear war was to be damage-limitation, through air defence (which became a separate command), through civil defence and through preventive strikes against American nuclear systems. Thereafter Russia would fight until it gained a position of relative advantage.

American observers were appalled. It seemed that, having suffered 20 million casualties in World War II, the Soviet Union had concluded it could do so again in World War III. In practice the reverse was true: those very losses made Russia even more determined to avoid such devastation again. Her leaders were under no illusions as to the appalling consequences of nuclear war. But they also looked at war in political terms. They differentiated between wars according to the socio-political characteristics of the belligerents. The military theorists at any rate rejected the idea that the nature of war had fundamentally changed because of a development in weapons technology. The level of violence in a war was determined by the purposes of the war. By contrast, nuclear weapons caused the United States to define war according to the level of violence – strategic nuclear war, tactical nuclear war, conventional war – rather than according to its objectives. In the Soviet view, American deterrence theory had confused the means of war with its ends. Nuclear weapons made less impact on the Soviet armed forces than they did on those of the West: the principles of mass and of defence remained enthroned. But, looked at without the vocabulary of deterrence, the Soviet build-up could appear less threatening.

The tension between defence and deterrence, between military and political demands, has proved most acute at the levels of tactical and theatre nuclear weaponry. Tactical nuclear weapons were introduced into the arsenal of NATO between 1954 and 1956 as a bid to create limited options within the framework of 'massive retaliation'. The logic was almost entirely military. They seemed to compensate for the Soviet superiority in manpower, they gave the army a role in the nuclear age and they augmented the firepower of the defence. NATO used its technical lead to enhance its capability without thinking through the political or strategic ramifications. Subsequently, however, it was held that the ambiguity of tactical nuclear weapons increased the strength of deterrence. On the one hand, intermediate types of weaponry reduced the danger of automatic escalation to strategic weapons and were therefore more likely to be used. On the other hand, if they were used, the process of escalation would have been inaugurated. Thus they increased the likelihood of escalation and so enhanced the strength of deterrence.

But problems soon emerged. The requirements of deterrence and defence conflicted. The logic of deterrence suggested that tactical nuclear weapons should be invulnerable and under centralised command; tactical sense urged that they be scattered, with the command delegated well forward. The best military use, given NATO's numerical weakness, would be early in a battle for Europe, particularly because if the conventional armies were defeated NATO would have to resort to strategic weapons. However, in that case escalation would not come into operation at all.

Russia, when she responded to the NATO initiative with the introduction of her own theatre nuclear weapons, was not hamstrung by the same considerations. She held that the use of any nuclear weapon, however small, constituted the beginning of nuclear war, and she refused to acknowledge the continuance of deterrence or the relevance of escalation beyond that point. Furthermore she integrated the use of tactical nuclear weapons far more closely with the exercises of her ground forces, implying that she would be prepared to employ them from the outset. On reflection the logic of the military arguments did indeed seem to support the Warsaw Pact, not NATO. The higher casualty rates would favour the Soviet numerical superiority. Troops concentrated in static defensive positions, as those of NATO would be, would present better targets than dispersed, mobile attack formations.

NATO had introduced a tier of weaponry whose military advantages proved illusory and whose political implications widened the rift between Europe and America. In an exercise based on the imagined unrestricted use of tactical nuclear weapons in Germany in 1957, 335 were fired, with the consequence that 1·7 million people were killed and 3·5 million wounded. The collateral damage of such weapons meant that the distinction between their use and that of strategic nuclear weapons was meaningless for all except the citizens of the United States themselves. Tactical and theatre nuclear weapons created dangers for international stability. The problems of definition dogged arms control talks and varied according to a nation's geographical position: the British Polaris force was a theatre nuclear weapon for the United States (because it was stationed within Europe), although its range and 'counter-city' role made the British regard it as strategic. In 1979–80 a fresh generation of NATO theatre nuclear weaponry renewed fears that the United States would fight a nuclear war confined to Europe. Thus such weapons fostered tensions between allies, while at the same time creating confusion at the fringes of deterrence.

A fourth source of instability to nuclear deterrence – after proliferation, Russian doctrine and theatre nuclear systems – is the introduction of new weaponry. In 1966 Alastair Buchan reckoned that 20 per cent of scientific research was concentrated on defence related projects. The consequent technological advances have not occurred simultaneously in both East and West. Thus they limit the success of arms control to those areas where a balance already exists. However, some of these developments reinforce stability rather than undermine it: SALT itself would not have been possible without the satellite to ensure its enforcement. The main trends within the framework of nuclear weaponry since the 1960s have been towards mobility, in order to ensure invulnerability for second-strike forces, and towards accuracy, in order to enhance a first-strike capability. The intercontinental ballistic missile of the 1960s, the Minuteman, had accuracy, while the submarine-launched system, Polaris, had mobility: their replacements of the 1980s – MX and Trident respectively – each enjoy both attributes. Increased accuracy clearly raises once again the fear of pre-emption. The other problems are those of definition. Does a MIRVed warhead count as one weapon or several weapons for SALT purposes? Is the Cruise missile a tactical or a strategic system? Should the neutron bomb be subsumed within the panoply of theatre nuclear weaponry when its purpose is to enhance conventional capabilities? The fear of a whole generation of weapons which would fall outside the vocabulary of nuclear deterrence has so far proved illusory. But the destabilising consequences of a breakthrough in, say, lasers are self-evident. A nation might be tempted to capitalise on its fleeting superiority in a new technology with a pre-emptive attack. However, one major cause for concern has, at least for the moment, been stilled. The prospect of an anti-ballistic missile defence promised to destroy the mutual vulnerability on which deterrence rested. But the cost and effort of erecting such a system would be valueless unless it was completely effective. The superpowers therefore agreed in 1972 to limit themselves to two defensive networks, and in 1974 to one. In the event only the Russians have completed the installation of such a system, around Moscow.

The consequences of technological innovation have been far more limited than might have been expected. The foundations built for US strategic policy by McNamara have, broadly speaking, remained in place. MAD has been attacked, but no practicable alternative, particularly in view of the increase in Russian capabilities, has been forthcoming. The rhetoric of deterrence still concentrates on stability – or, as President Nixon and his secretary of state, Kissinger, put it, 'sufficiency'. Kissinger himself disliked MAD because it limited the value of nuclear weapons in the conduct of foreign policy. He wanted to be able to use nuclear weapons more flexibly in order to support specific diplomatic stances. James Schlesinger, as secretary for defense, developed Kissinger's thinking in 1973–4. He argued that massive nuclear attacks were unlikely because a first strike could not disarm either side and the damage from a second, retaliatory strike would be enormous. Attacks against Russian cities would not protect American cities from devastation. Once again the problem was that of credibility. Schlesinger therefore planned a number of limited options to allow a rapid and more flexible reaction. Improved command and control permitted retargeting during the course of a nuclear war, and the targeting itself could be more precise thanks to the improvements in guidance systems and in satellite intelligence. Schlesinger proposed to blur the distinction between theatre and strategic systems by targeting the latter on military concentrations in Europe. Technological innovation, in the shape of the neutron bomb and of enhanced accuracy in theatre nuclear weaponry, also permitted more effective aid for the conventional forces in Europe while at the same time lessening collateral damage. In July 1980 President Carter embodied Schlesinger's targeting policy in his Presidential Directive 59.

However, the change was largely cosmetic. It is true that technological improvements had widened the options for limited nuclear war. But, because Russian missiles were positioned close to cities, the distinction could never be particularly significant. The additional flexibility gained by Schlesinger and Carter was minimal. Moreover the 'counter-force' strand had been present in American targeting ever since the Single Integrated Operational Plan of 1961–2. The change in emphasis was part of the continuing dialectic between deterrence and defence, and the need to stress the latter in order to enhance the former.

The emergence of contradictions between deterrence and defence was one of the ways in which nuclear weapons could be seen as marking a fundamental break in strategic evolution. Their capabilities were such that, unlike their predecessors, their value lay more in their non-use than their use. They fulfilled their function by avoiding war, not fighting it. And, if they did have to be used, not only were the moral restraints of proportionality and non-combatant immunity definitively overthrown, but so was the more prosaic military concept of victory. The war in which nuclear forces were used might begin as a political act but its course would probably destroy the political identity of the states who waged it. The professional role of the armed forces was challenged on two further counts: in peacetime strategic theory was evolved by civilian academics and in wartime the military policy was implemented by civilian heads of state. For soldiers, therefore, nuclear weapons constituted a revolution in strategy. The creation of a fully prepared peacetime arsenal capable of instant employment promised such a speedy resolution in war as to end the Moltkean distinction between war and peace. The validity of the 'principles of war', the hackneyed catch-phrases of military academies, seemed lost for ever.

However, the professional soldier's vocation had never really been concerned with strategy. His tasks were those of tactics, administration or at best operations. The tendency to assess force strengths in terms of equipment and capabilities and not of doctrine and intentions reflected a desire to reduce the imponderables of nuclear strategy to a more familiar shape. But strategy was not a list of rules or a quartermaster's inventory; it was rather a way of thinking about the problems of war. In the past most of the thought, it is true, was done by soldiers. One of them was Clausewitz. His method was to question and to provoke, so as to encourage rigour in thinking. He also stressed that war was an instrument of policy. Many of the problems of nuclear strategy, and in particular the friction between NATO allies, have arisen because procurement decisions have been removed from their political context. Another abiding conundrum in deterrence has also been political, that of the credibility of the use of nuclear weapons. Moreover, deterrence itself is but a means to a political end, that of better Russo-American relations. The main function of nuclear weapons since 1945 has been as an instrument of diplomatic bargaining.

None the less the reiteration of Clausewitzian maxims remains insufficient. Nuclear strategy cannot ignore the potential effects of nuclear weapons. The means for waging war have now outstripped the objectives war can achieve. Even in the pre-nuclear era there was no necessary correlation between means and ends. The First World War was fought as a total war when only limited ends could thereby be achieved. Colonial operations were often limited wars fought for much wider ends. The global threat of nuclear weapons is so great as to make simple reliance on rationality an insufficient security. Political restraint cannot guarantee restraint in war itself. Weapons systems, not political ends, could determine whether a war is total or not. Restraints must therefore be applied to the means as much as to the ends of war. To the realist the future of arms control may appear pessimistic, but equally no realist can afford to neglect it.

Guide to Further Reading

Freedman's account of the evolution of nuclear strategy is comprehensive. However, Mandelbaum is briefer and puts the theory more firmly in the context of US politics. Harkabi, although older than Freedman or Mandelbaum, is particularly lucid on deterrence. Friedberg provides a short, stimulating account of American policy, stressing the 'war-fighting' aspects. Pipes is a hard-hitting, hawkish but valuable look at Russia: Garthoff (1966) is more moderate.

Brodie (1959) is a good representative work of the era, and his later book (1973) reveals why he was regarded as one of the most balanced and wise postwar strategic thinkers. The concepts that he and others refined have not dated as much as might be expected. Buchan's two books (1966 and 1970) are good departure points. Relatively recent surveys over the whole field of defence are Martin, and Baylis, Booth, Garnett and Williams. To update these volumes consult the publications of the International Institute for Strategic Studies – its bi-monthly journal (*Survival*), its annual résumés (*Strategic Survey* and *The Military Balance*) and its periodic analyses of specific issues (*Adelphi Papers*).

Epilogue

Since 1945 the difficulty of relating the theory of warfare to its practice has become more pronounced than ever before. Doctrine has focused on the problems posed by nuclear weapons. However, the experience of the armies of Europe and the United States has been exclusively conventional. Britain, France, Belgium, Portugal and Spain have been involved in the protracted and bitter campaigns of colonial withdrawal. The United States' sense of global responsibility has drawn it into Korea and Vietnam, and most recently the Soviet Union has saddled itself with a similar incubus in Afghanistan. Industrialised states may train their armies to fight a conventional war against each other, but the actual experience of those armies is in fighting the guerrillas and insurgents of peasant societies. Therefore the problem is a double one. It is not simply a question of harmonising conventional and nuclear capabilities; there is also the historically more familiar task of analysing colonial operations and assessing their relevance to the European battlefield.

Thinking about the likely form of a battle in Europe is consequently dogged by imponderables. The major tank battles since 1945 have taken place not in Europe but on the frontiers of Israel. Although these wars have provided a laboratory for NATO and Warsaw Pact equipment, they have been fought in a climate and by armies that are both very different from those of Europe. It is therefore not surprising that the experience of the Second World War still looms large in the European military mind. The masses of Russian armour and the suggestion that they could break through to the Channel in forty-eight hours evoke the imagery of *Blitzkrieg*. The popularity of Liddell Hart's 'indirect approach' in Israeli thinking has helped keep alive the memory of 1940. In Russia, the veterans of the 'Great Patriotic War' still direct the affairs of the Soviet Union, and it is therefore easy (perhaps too easy) to conclude that the victories from Kursk to Berlin shape their thinking. In the West, although those who fought in the break-out from Normandy no longer serve in the armies of Britain and America, their achievements remain the subject of battlefield tours for their successors.

The oft-heard jibe that peacetime armies prepare to refight the last war would seem to hold good. It is difficult to break an army's mould. Branches and services that are created to meet a genuine need can begin to feed that need and thus supply their own *raison d'être*. The lead times in research and development ensure that current equipment tends to reflect outdated technology. Armies, like other institutions, are caught by what they have become rather than what they might be. But, if the lesson of Kursk and of Normandy is one of the co-ordination of different arms, then the continuing force of that experience may not be deleterious. The main technological development in the conventional land battle since 1945 has been the advent of precision-guided munitions. Anti-tank guided weapons and surface-to-air missiles – many of them man-portable – have certainly limited the offensive roles of the tank and the aeroplane. Indeed the 1973 Arab-Israeli War was loudly hailed as heralding the demise of both. But by 1982 more cautious counsels have prevailed. The 1973 war has served to refine, not to overthrow, the verdicts of 1943 to 1945. Each arm is complementary; no one weapon in isolation can dominate the battlefield for long.

The biggest relative change since 1945 has afflicted air forces, not armies. The long-range bomber has lost its strategic role to the missile. The tactical roles of fighter and bomber have now been combined in one aircraft, and in truth (although this is not yet reflected in NATO force structures) both may be obsolete. In 1973, only 4 of the 115 Israeli aircraft lost were the casualties of aerial combat: the principal enemy of the aeroplane is not the fighter but the surface-to-air missile. Although the manned aircraft is now fitted with counter-measures to help it evade ground fire, its cost (and the cost of training its pilot) has made men wary of using it offensively. Therefore its principal task is not in bombing, but in reconnaissance and close air support. Flying over its own territory, and therefore free from the threat of ground fire, it can concentrate on countering the intrusions of the enemy. Both the fixed-wing aircraft and the more vulnerable helicopter are designed as highly mobile anti-tank gun platforms.

The dramatic fate of the 190th Israeli Armoured Brigade on 9 October 1973 tended to overstate the challenge to the tank. Egyptian infantry, firing wire-guided anti-tank missiles from prepared positions, knocked out 85 tanks in three minutes. Five days later, over 1,600 tanks were engaged as the Egyptians endeavoured to gain control of the Sinai passes, and the Israelis – who this time had the advantage of the defensive – claimed that they accounted for 250 Egyptian tanks. However, in both cases tanks were attacking prepared positions with insufficient support from other arms. The Israelis, in particular, after their successes in 1967, had put too much faith in the initiative and capacity for improvisation of their armour. Certainly neither NATO nor the Warsaw Pact has concluded that it should eliminate the tank from its inventory: in 1982 the Warsaw Pact deployed 26,300 main battle tanks in Eastern Europe, and NATO possessed 17,000. However, what NATO has done is to augment its anti-tank arsenal: in 1982 alone it planned a 60 per cent increase in its holdings of heavy and medium anti-tank missiles. The point therefore remains: the tank cannot operate on its own but is part of an all-arms team. The infantry has its own defensive firepower, but the tank still possesses the mobility and protection for the counter-attack. Co-operation between arms and between ground and air forces is being evolved at progressively lower levels of command. Battle groups and combat teams are replacing the single-arm brigades or battalions of the Second World War.

The main area of technological interest and innovation is centred on the application of electronics and of computers to warfare. At a strategic and a tactical level, one focus is on efficient communications: their importance is intensified by the multiplication of tri-service, multi-national formations. Reconnaissance and intelligence are particularly crucial for NATO, whose role is explicitly defensive: early warning can be given by satellite, but also by airborne warning systems (AWACS) and –

over the battlefield – by pilotless vehicles or 'drones'. In battle itself the main problem is one of target acquisition. The effectiveness of precision-guided anti-tank weapons is curtailed by a number of factors: poor light or adverse weather conditions can limit visibility; broken terrain or housing can obscure the target; the suppressive fire of the attacker can upset the steadiness of the aimer. While the operator is guiding the weapon onto its target, the target itself is probably moving. In some parts of Europe, there is only a 0·7 probability that a tank travelling at 15 kilometres per hour 2,000 metres away will still be visible to the aimer when the weapon arrives in the target area. Image intensification and thermal imagery are therefore important means of improving target acquisition. The potential sophistication of this equipment, which includes the use of lasers, is well-illustrated by the fact that 20 per cent of the total cost of a modern tank could be devoted to target acquisition.

Cost is a major problem for NATO. The two biggest demands on contemporary defence budgets are the procurement of equipment and the maintenance of manpower. The advent of precision-guided munitions has threatened to increase the attrition rate of precious stocks of highly complex tanks and aircraft. Therefore, many service thinkers are beginning to reject the pressure to acquire increasingly sophisticated and temperamental technology at prices which escalate faster than inflation, and instead favour large quantities of less expensive items. The most direct way to obtain large numbers of men – and historically the dominant method in Europe since Napoleon – is to conscript. But the practical difficulties of training conscripts and reservists in the use of new generations of arms have been important factors in limiting the effectiveness of Western European armies. Those armies that have not practised conscription have not had this problem. The United Kingdom and the United States, both powers with limited experience of European war and traditionally protected by maritime defence, reverted to voluntary enlistment in 1960 and 1972 respectively. But for them enlistment rates have fluctuated, and pay and pensions have taken up an increasing proportion of the defence budget. Therefore, the pressures on both regular and conscript armies have helped to curb any increase in NATO conventional capabilities. These problems of procurement and manpower seemed to be resolved by the Egyptian success with man-held anti-tank weapons in 1973: such weapons require little training to use and they can be fired from defensive positions. On the one hand, therefore, precision-guided munitions have been presented as convenient tools for large reserve armies committed to a static defence.

On the other hand, however, if the lessons of 1973 are in favour of many small and highly mobile combined arms teams, fighting a dispersed defensive battle in depth, then the demands of training and sophistication will not diminish, but increase. There are a number of supporting arguments in favour of regular and professional armies. If NATO opts for quantity rather than quality, it may forfeit the technological advantage which has given its conventional forces compensation for their numerical inferiority when compared with those of the Warsaw Pact. Moreover, the armies of Europe are confronted with two broad but different categories of possible war. One is the threat of a clash between NATO and the Warsaw Pact in Europe. Many would contend that such a war is likely to escalate to the nuclear threshold very quickly, and that therefore the creation of effective conventional defences is superfluous. (As a rider, it can be said that this argument feeds the inevitability of the war being nuclear, even if it simultaneously makes it more remote.) The second possible application of military force is in theatres outside Europe. Since 1945 this has been the sole area of actual operations, and there is no immediate likelihood of the trend being reversed. The West's dependence on Gulf oil has encouraged the United States to create a Rapid Deployment Force, and both France (in Africa) and the British (in the Falkland Islands, Belize and – by extension – Northern Ireland) have found their military commitments still bound by imperial legacies. Extra-European operations can require the political detachment and the immediate readiness, as well as the professional competence, of the trained regular.

The functions of European armies within Europe itself have therefore arguably become less decisive since 1945. The main burden in deterrence rests with nuclear forces, and armies justify their existence as steps on a ladder of escalation. Crudely put, that ladder represents a compromise between two extreme positions – deterrence that rests on nuclear weapons or defence that relies on massive conventional armies. The former is provided largely by the United States, and efforts to minimise the consequent reliance on America by producing an independent West European deterrent have so far failed. A European deterrent would resolve many ambiguities in strategic doctrine, but it is hardly likely to evolve while the political framework for its direction and deployment is lacking. But, as successive American administrations have learnt, the political resolution to accept the costs of the second option – massive conventional forces – is also absent.

Select Bibliography

Addington, Larry H., *The Blitzkrieg Era and the German General Staff* (New Brunswick, 1971).

African History, Journal of, vol. 12, nos 2 and 4 (1971), Papers on firearms in sub-Saharan Africa.

Andolenko, C. R., *Histoire de l'Armée Russe* (Paris, 1967).

Arnold, Joseph C., 'French tactical doctrine 1870–1914', *Military Affairs*, vol. 42, no. 2 (1978), pp. 61–7.

Aron, Raymond, 'Clausewitz's conceptual system', *Armed Forces and Society*, vol. 1, no. 1 (1974) pp. 49–59.

Aron, Raymond, *Penser la Guerre, Clausewitz* (Paris, 2 vols, 1976).

Atkinson, C. T., *Marlborough and the rise of the British Army* (London, 1921).

Badsey, S. D., 'Fire and the Sword. The British Army and the *Arme Blanche* controversy 1871–1921' (Cambridge University Ph.D. thesis, 1982).

Bailes, Howard, 'Patterns of thought in the late Victorian Army', *Journal of Strategic Studies*, vol. 4, no. 1 (1981), pp. 29–46.

Bailes, Howard, 'Technology and Imperialism: a case study of the Victorian Army in Africa', *Victorian Studies*, vol. 24, no. 1 (1980), pp. 82–104.

Baker, R. H., 'The Origins of Soviet Military Doctrine', *Journal of the Royal United Services Institute for Defence Studies*, vol. 121, no. 1 (1976), pp. 38–43.

Barnett, Correlli, *The Desert Generals* (London, 1960).

Barnett, Correlli, *The Swordbearers* (London, 1963).

Baylis, John, Ken Booth, John Garnett, Phil Williams, *Contemporary Strategy. Theories and Policies* (London, 1975).

Bellamy, Christopher, 'Seventy years on: similarities between the modern Soviet Army and its Tsarist predecessor', *Journal of the Royal United Services Institute for Defence Studies*, vol. 124, no. 3 (1979), pp. 29–38.

Bergounioux, A., and Polivka, P., 'Clausewitz et le militarisme allemand', *Revue d'histoire moderne et contemporaine*, vol. 23 (Oct. – Dec. 1976), pp. 501–27.

Bernhardi, Friedrich von, *On War of Today*, (2 vols, London, 1912).

Bertaud, Jean-Paul, *La Révolution Armée* (Paris, 1979).

Best, Geoffrey, *Humanity in Warfare. The modern history of the international law of armed conflicts* (London, 1980).

Best, Geoffrey, *War and Society in Revolutionary Europe 1770 – 1870* (London, 1982).

Best, Geoffrey, and Wheatcroft, Andrew, (eds), *War, Economy and the Military Mind* (London, 1976).

Bidwell, R. G. S., 'The Development of British Field Artillery Tactics 1920–1943', *Journal of the Royal Artillery*, vol. 94 (1967), pp. 13–24, 83–93, and vol. 95 (1968), pp. 1–12.

Bien, David D., 'The Army in the French Enlightenment: Reform, Reaction and Revolution', *Past and Present*, no. 85 (Nov. 1979), pp. 68–98.

Bloch, I. S. [J. G.] *Modern Weapons and Modern War* (London, 1900).

Bond, Brian, *British Military Policy between the Two World Wars* (Oxford, 1980).

Bond, Brian, *Liddell Hart. A study of his military thought* (London, 1977).

Bond, Brian, *The Victorian Army and the Staff College 1854–1914* (London, 1972).

Bond, Brian, (ed.), *Victorian Military Campaigns* (London, 1967).

Bourgin, Georges, 'Bugeaud Social en Afrique', *Revue Historique de l'Armée* (April–June 1948), pp. 38–49.

Broad, C. N. F., 'The development of artillery tactics 1914–18' *Journal of the*

Royal Artillery, vol. 49 (1922–3), pp. 62–81, 127–48.

Brodie, Bernard, 'On Clausewitz', *World Politics*, vol. 25 (Jan. 1973), pp. 288–308.

Brodie, Bernard, *Strategy in the Missile Age* (Princeton, 1959).

Brodie, Bernard, *War and Politics* (London, 1973).

Brodie, Bernard, and Brodie, Fawn M., *From Crossbow to H-Bomb* (Indiana, 1973).

Buchan, Alastair, (ed.), *Problems of Modern Strategy* (London, 1970).

Buchan, Alastair, *War in Modern Society* (London, 1966).

Caemmerer, Lt.-Gen. von, *The Development of Strategical Science during the Nineteenth Century* (London, 1905).

Callwell, C. E., *Small Wars. Their principles and practice* (3rd edn, London, 1906).

Calvocoressi, Peter, and Wint, Guy, *Total War* (London, 1972).

Carrias, Eugène, *La pensée militaire allemande* (Paris, 1948).

Carrias, Eugène, *La pensée militaire française* (Paris, 1960).

Challener, Richard D., *The French Theory of the Nation in Arms 1866–1939* (New York, 1955).

Chandler, David, *The Art of Warfare in the Age of Marlborough* (London, 1976).

Chandler, David, *The Campaigns of Napoleon* (London, 1967).

Charles, Archduke, *Principes de la Stratégie*, translated by A. H. Jomini (Brussels, 1842).

Clarke, I. F., *Voices Prophesying War 1763–1984* (Oxford, 1966).

Clarkson, Jesse D., and Cochran, Thomas C., *War as a social institution. The historian's perspective* (New York, 1941).

Clausewitz, Carl von, *On War*, translated and edited by Michael Howard and Peter Paret (Princeton, 1976).

Colin, J., *The Transformations of War* (London, 1912).

Collier, Basil, *A History of Air Power* (London, 1974).

Corvisier, André, *Armies and Societies in Europe 1494–1789* (Bloomington, 1979).

Craig, Gordon A., *The Battle of Königgrätz* (London, 1965).

Craig, Gordon A., *The Politics of the Prussian Army 1640–1945* (London, 1955).

Creveld, Martin van, 'The German attack on the U.S.S.R: the destruction of a legend', *European Studies Review*, vol. 2, no. 1 (1972), pp. 69–86.

Creveld, Martin van, *Supplying War. Logistics from Wallenstein to Patton* (Cambridge, 1977).

Creveld, Martin van, 'War Lord Hitler: some points reconsidered', *European Studies Review*, vol. 4, no. 1 (1974), pp. 57–79.

Cruttwell, C. R. M. F., *A History of the Great War 1914–1918* (2nd edn, Oxford, 1936).

Curtiss, John Shelton, *The Russian Army under Nicholas I, 1825–1855* (Durham NC, 1965).

Deist, Wilhelm, *The Wehrmacht and German Rearmament* (London, 1981).

Delbrück, Hans, *Geschichte der Kriegskunst im Rahmen der politischen Geschichte* (7 vols, Berlin, 1900–36); a translation is now in progress, *History of the Art of War* (vol. 1– , Westport Conn., 1975–).

Denison, George T., *A History of Cavalry* (2nd edn, London, 1913).

Donald, David, *Lincoln Reconsidered* (New York, 1959).

Duffy, Christopher, *The Army of Frederick the Great* (Newton Abbot, 1974).

Duffy, Christopher, *The Army of Maria Theresa* (Newton Abbot, 1977).

Duffy. Christopher, *Russia's Military Way to the West* (London, 1981).

Dupuy, R. Ernest, and Dupuy, Trevor N., *The Encyclopedia of Military History* (2nd edn, London, 1977).

Earle, Edward Mead, (ed.), *Makers of Modern Strategy* (Princeton, 1943).

Elting, John R., 'Jomini; disciple of Napoleon?', *Military Affairs*, vol. 28, no. 1 (1964), pp. 17–26.

Erickson, John, *The Road to Stalingrad. Stalin's War with Germany, volume 1* (London, 1975).

Erickson, John, *The Soviet High Command. A Military–Political History* (London, 1962).

Esposito, V. J., and Elting, J. R., *A Military History and Atlas of the Napoleonic Wars* (New York, 1964).

Falls, Cyril, *The Art of War* (London, 1961).

Falls, Cyril, *A Hundred Years of War* (London, 1953).

Feldman, Gerald, D., 'The Political and Social Foundations of Germany's Economic Mobilization, 1914–1916', *Armed Forces and Society*, vol. 3, no. 1 (1976), pp. 121–45.

Ferro, Marc, *The Great War 1914–1918* (London, 1973).

Foch, Ferdinand, *The Principles of War* (London, 1918).

Freedman, Lawrence, *The Evolution of Nuclear Strategy* (London, 1981).

French, David, 'The military background to the "shell crisis" of May 1915', *Journal of Strategic Studies*, vol. 2, no. 2 (1979), pp. 192–205.

Friedberg, Aaron L., 'A History of the U.S. Strategic "Doctrine" – 1945 to 1980', in *Strategy and the Social Sciences*, ed. Amos Perlmutter and John Gooch (London, 1981), pp. 37–71.

Fuller, J. F. C., *British Light Infantry in the Eighteenth Century* (London, 1925).

Fuller, J. F. C., *The Conduct of War 1789–1961* (London, 1972).

Fuller, J. F. C., *Sir John Moore's System of Training* (London, 1924).

Garthoff, Raymond L., *How Russia Makes War* (London, 1954).

Garthoff, Raymond L., *Soviet Military Policy* (London, 1966).

Glover, Richard, *Peninsular Preparation. The Reform of the British Army 1795–1809* (Cambridge, 1963).

Goltz, Colmar von der, *The Nation in Arms* (English trans: London, 1906).

Gooch, Brison D., *The New Bonapartist Generals in the Crimean War* (The Hague, 1959).

Gooch, John, *Armies in Europe* (London, 1979).

Gooch, John, *The Plans of War, The General Staff and British Military Strategy c. 1900–1916* (London, 1974).

Gorce, Paul-Marie de la, *The French Army. A Military–Political History* (London, 1963).

Görlitz, Walter, *The German General Staff* (London, 1953).

Gray, J. Glenn, *The Warriors. Reflections on Men in Battle* (New York, 1970).

Greenhous, Brereton, 'Evolution of a Close Ground-Support Role for Aircraft in World War I', *Military Affairs*, vol. 39 (Feb. 1975), pp. 22–8.

Griffith, Paddy, *Forward into Battle. Fighting Tactics from Waterloo to Vietnam* (Chichester, 1981).

Griffith, P. G., 'Military Thought in the French Army 1815–1851' (Oxford University D. Phil. thesis, 1975).

Guderian, Heinz, *Panzer Leader* (London, 1952).

Guibert, J. A. H. de, *A General Essay on Tactics* (2 vols, London, 1781).

Hagermann, Edward, 'The tactical thought of R. E. Lee and the origins of trench warfare in the American Civil War 1861–62', *The Historian*, vol. 38, no. 1 (1975), pp. 21–38.

Hamley, E. B., *The Operations of War* (Edinburgh, 1866).

Hardach, Gerd, *The First World War 1914–1918* (London, 1977).

Harkabi, Y., *Nuclear war and nuclear peace* (Jerusalem, 1966).

Hart, B. H. Liddell, *The Ghost of Napoleon* (London, 1933).

Hart, B. H. Liddell, *A History of the World War 1914–1918* (London, 1934).

Hart, B. H. Liddell, *History of the Second World War* (London, 1970).

Hart, B. H. Liddell, *Strategy. The Indirect Approach* (London, 1967).

Headrick, Daniel R., 'The Tools of Imperialism: technology and the expansion of European colonial empires in the nineteenth century', *Journal of Modern History*, vol. 51, no. 2 (1979), pp. 231–63.

Henderson, G. F. R., *The Science of War* (London, 1905).

Higginbotham, Don, (ed.), *Reconsiderations on the Revolutionary War* (Westpoint Conn., 1978).

Higginbotham, Don, *The War of American Independence* (New York. 1971).

Higham, Robin, *Air Power. A Concise History* (London, 1972).

Hittle, J. D., *The Military Staff. Its History and Development* (Harrisburg Penn., 1961).

Holmes, E. R., 'The Road to Sedan: the French Army 1866–70' (Reading University Ph.D. thesis, 1975).

Houlding, J. A., *Fit for Service. The training of the British Army 1715–1795* (Oxford, 1981).

House, Jonathan M., 'The Decisive Attack: a new look at French infantry tactics on the eve of World War I', *Military Affairs*, vol. 40 (Dec. 1976), pp. 164–9.

Howard, Michael, *The Continental Commitment* (London, 1972).

Howard, Michael, 'The forgotten dimensions of strategy', *Foreign Affairs*, vol. 57, no. 5 (1979), pp. 975–86.

Howard, Michael, *The Franco-Prussian War* (London, 1961).

Howard, Michael, 'L'Angleterre dans la guerre. La pensée stratégique', *Revue d'histoire de la deuxième guerre mondiale*, no. 90 (April 1975), pp. 1–9.

Howard, Michael, (ed.), *Restraints on War* (Oxford, 1979).

Howard, Michael, *Studies in War and Peace* (London, 1970).

Howard, Michael, (ed.), *The Theory and Practice of War* (London, 1965).

Howard, Michael, *War in European History* (Oxford, 1976).

Hughes, B. P., *Firepower: weapons' effectiveness on the battlefield, 1630–1850* (London, 1974).

Hunt, Barry, and Preston, Adrian, (eds), *War Aims and Strategic Policy in the Great War 1914–1918* (London, 1977).

Huntington, Samuel P., *The Soldier and the State* (Cambridge Mass., 1957).

Hutchison, G. S., *Machine Guns: their history and tactical employment* (London, 1938).

Irvine, Dallas D., 'The French and Prussian Staff Systems before 1870', *Journal of the American Military History Foundation*, vol. 2, no. 4 (1938), pp. 192–203.

Irvine, Dallas D., 'The French Discovery of Clausewitz and Napoleon', *Journal of the American Military Institute*, vol. 4, no. 3 (1942), pp. 143–61.

Irvine, Dallas D., 'The Origin of Capital Staffs', *Journal of Modern History*, vol. 10, no. 2 (1938), pp. 161–79.

Jervis, Robert, 'Deterrence theory revisited', *World Politics*, vol. 31 (Jan. 1979), pp. 289–324.

Jomini, A. H., *The Art of War*, translation of *Précis de l'art de la guerre* by G. H. Mendell and W. P. Craighill (Philadelphia, 1862; reprinted Westport Conn., 1971).

Jones, Archer, 'Jomini and the strategy of the American Civil War: a reinterpretation', *Military Affairs*, vol. 34 (Dec. 1970), pp. 127–31.

Josselson, Michael, *The Commander. A Life of Barclay de Tolly* (Oxford, 1980).

Kahn, David, 'Codebreaking in World Wars I and II', *Historical Journal*, vol. 23, no. 3 (1980), pp. 617–39.

Keegan, John, *The Face of Battle* (London, 1976).

Keegan, John, *Six Armies in Normandy* (London, 1982).

Kennett, Lee, *The French Armies in the Seven Years' War* (Durham NC, 1967).

Kiernan, V. G., 'Conscription and society in Europe before the war of 1914–18' in *War and Society*, ed. M. R. D. Foot (London, 1973), pp. 143–58.

Kiernan, V. G., *European Empires from Conquest to Collapse 1815–1960* (London, 1982).

Kitchen, Martin, *A Military History of Germany* (London, 1975).

Lauerma, Matti, *L'artillerie de campagne française pendant les guerres de la révolution* (Helsinki, 1956).

Lefebvre, Georges, *Napoleon* (2 vols, London, 1969).

Léonard, Emile G., *L'Armée et ses problèmes au XVIIIè siècle* (Paris, 1958).

Lewin, Ronald, *Ultra goes to War* (London, 1978).

Lloyd, E. M., *A Review of the History of Infantry* (London, 1908).

Lloyd, Henry, *The History of the Late War in Germany* (2 vols, London, 1766–81).

Lukacs, John, *The Last European War* (London, 1977).

Lupfer, Timothy L., 'The Dynamics of Doctrine: the changes in German tactical doctrine during the First World War', *Leavenworth Papers*, no. 4 (Fort Leavenworth, Kansas, 1981).

Luvaas, Jay, *The Education of an Army* (London, 1970).

Luvaas, Jay, *Frederick the Great on the Art of War* (New York, 1966).

Luvaas, Jay, *The Military Legacy of the Civil War. The European Inheritance* (Chicago, 1959).

Lynn, John, 'Esquisse sur la tactique de l'infanterie des armées de la république', *Annales Historiques de la Révolution Française*, no. 210 (Nov.–Dec. 1972), pp. 537–66.

MacDougall, P. L., *The Theory of War* (London, 1856).

Mackintosh, Malcolm, *Juggernaut. A History of the Soviet Armed Forces* (London, 1967).

Mandelbaum, Michael, *The Nuclear Question. The United States and Nuclear Weapons 1946–1976* (Cambridge, 1979).

Marshall, S. L. A., *Men against Fire* (New York, 1947).

Martin, Laurence, *Arms and Strategy* (London, 1973).

Mellenthin, F. W. von, *Panzer Battles 1939–1945* (London, 1955).

Messenger, Charles, *The Art of Blitzkrieg* (London, 1976).

Messerschmidt, Manfred, 'La stratégie allemande (1939–1945)', *Revue d'Histoire de la Deuxième Guerre Mondiale*, no. 100 (1975), pp. 1–26.

Michel, Henri, *The Second World War* (London, 1975).

Millis, Walter, *Armies and Men. A Study of American Military History* (London, 1958).

Milward, Alan S., 'The End of Blitzkrieg', *Economic History Review*, 2nd series, vol. 16, no. 3 (1964), pp. 499–518.

Milward, Alan S., *The German Economy at War* (London, 1965).

Milward, Alan S., *War, Economy and Society 1939–1945* (London, 1977).

Mitchell, Allan, 'A Situation of Inferiority: French military reorganization after the defeat of 1870', *American Historical Review*, vol. 86 (1981), pp. 49–62.

Munholland, J. Kim, 'Collaboration strategy and the French pacification of Tonkin 1885–1897', *Historical Journal*, vol. 24, no. 3 (1981), pp. 629–50.

Murray, Williamson, 'The Luftwaffe before the Second World War: a mission, a strategy?', *Journal of Strategic Studies*, vol. 4, no. 3 (1981), pp. 261–70.

Nef, John, U., *War and Human Progress* (New York, 1950).

Neimanis, George J., 'Militia vs the Standing Army in the History of Economic Thought from Adam Smith to Friedrich Engels', *Military Affairs*, vol. 44, no. 1 (1980), pp. 28–32

Nelson, Paul David, 'Citizen Soldiers or Regulars: the views of the American General Officers on the military establishment, 1775–1781', *Military Affairs*, vol. 43, no. 3 (1979), pp. 126–32.

Nickerson, Hoffman, *The Armed Horde 1793–1939* (New York, 1940).

Nove, Alec, *An Economic History of the U.S.S.R.* (London, 1969).

Ogorkiewicz, R. M., *Armoured Forces. A History of Armoured Forces and their Vehicles* (London, 1970).

Oman, C. W. C., *Wellington's Army* (London, 1912).

Osgood, R. E., *Limited War. The Challenge to American Strategy* (Chicago, 1957).

Overy, R. J., *The Air War 1939–1945* (London, 1980).

Overy, R. J., 'From Uralbomber to Amerikabomber: the Luftwaffe and Strategic Bombing', *Journal of Strategic Studies*, vol. 1, no. 2 (1978), pp. 154–78.

Overy, R. J. 'Hitler's War and the German economy: a reinterpretation', *Economic History Review*, 2nd series, vol. 35, no. 2 (1982), pp. 272–91.

Pakenham, Thomas, *The Boer War* (London, 1979).

Papke, Gerhard, and Petter, Wolfgang, (eds), *Handbuch zur deutschen Militärgeschichte 1648–1939* (6 vols, Munich, 1964–81).

Paret, Peter, *Clausewitz and the State* (Oxford, 1976).

Paret, Peter, 'Colonial experience and European military reform at the end of the eighteenth century', *Bulletin of the Institute of Historical Research*, vol. 37, no. 95 (1964), pp. 47–59.

Paret, Peter, 'Education, politics and war in the life of Clausewitz', *Journal of the History of Ideas*, vol. 29, no. 3 (1968), pp. 394–408.

Paret, Peter, *Yorck and the era of Prussian reform 1807–1815* (Princeton, 1966).

Pargellis, Stanley, 'Braddock's defeat', *American Historical Review*, vol. 41, no. 2 (1936), pp. 253–69.

Parish, Peter J., *The American Civil War* (London, 1975).

Paskins, Barrie, and Dockrill, Michael, *The Ethics of War* (London, 1979).

Pipes, Richard, 'Why the Soviet Union thinks it could fight and win a nuclear war', *Commentary*, vol. 64, no. 1 (1977), pp. 21–34.

Pogue, Forrest C., 'La conduite de la guerre aux Etats-Unis (1942–45) – ses problèmes et sa pratique', *Revue d'histoire de la deuxième guerre mondiale*, no. 100 (1975), pp. 67–94.

Porch, Douglas, 'The French army and the spirit of the offensive', in *War and Society*, ed. Brian Bond and Ian Roy (London, 1975), pp. 117–43.

Porch, Douglas, *The March to the Marne. The French Army 1871–1914* (Cambridge, 1981).

Pratt, Edwin A., *The rise of rail-power in war and conquest 1833–1914* (London, 1915).

Preston, Adrian, 'Wolseley, the Khartoum Relief Expedition and the Defence of India, 1885–1900', *Journal of Imperial and Commonwealth History*, vol. 6, no. 3 (1978), pp. 254–80.

Preston, A. W., 'British military thought, 1856–90', *Army Quarterly*, vol. 89, no. 1 (1964), pp. 57–74.

Preston, Richard A., Wise, Sydney F., and Werner, Herman O., *Men in Arms* (London, 1956).

Quimby, Robert S., *The Background of Napoleonic Warfare* (New York, 1957).

Regnault, Jean, 'Les campagnes d'Algérie et leur influence de 1830 à 1870', *Revue historique de l'armée*, vol. 9, no. 4 (1953), pp. 23–37.

Reid, Brian Holden, 'J. F. C. Fuller's theory of mechanized warfare', *Journal of Strategic Studies*, vol. 1, no. 3 (1978), pp. 295–312.

Ritter, Gerhard, *The Schlieffen Plan* (London, 1958).

Ritter, Gerhard, *The Sword and the Sceptre* (4 vols, London, 1970–3).

Robson, Eric, 'British light infantry in the mid-eighteenth century', *Army Quarterly*, vol. 63, no. 2 (1952), pp. 209–22.

Ropp, Theodore, *War in the Modern World* (New York, 1974).

Rosinski, Herbert, 'Scharnhorst to Schlieffen: the rise and decline of German military thought', *U.S. Naval War College Review*, vol. 29, no. 1 (1976), pp. 83–103.

Ross, Steven T., 'The development of the combat division in eighteenth-century French armies', *French Historical Studies*, vol. 4, no. 1 (1965–6), pp. 84–94.

Ross, Steven, *From Flintlock to Rifle. Infantry Tactics 1740–1866* (Cranbury NJ, 1979).

Rothenberg, Gunther E., *The Army of Francis Joseph* (Indiana, 1976).

Rothenberg, Gunther E., *The Art of Warfare in the Age of Napoleon* (London, 1977).

Rothenberg, Gunther E., 'The Austrian Army in the Age of Metternich', *Journal of Modern History*, vol. 40, no. 2 (1968), pp. 155–65.

Rothenberg, Gunther E., 'The Habsburg Army in the Napoleonic Wars', *Military Affairs*, vol. 37 (Feb. 1973), pp. 1–5.

Rothenberg, Gunther E., *Napoleon's great adversaries. The Archduke Charles and the Austrian Army* (London, 1982).

Russell, Peter E., 'Redcoats in the wilderness: British officers and irregular warfare in Europe and America, 1740 to 1760', *William and Mary Quarterly*, 3rd series, vol. 35, no. 4 (1978), pp. 629–52.

Saxe, Maurice de, 'My reveries upon the art of war', in *Roots of Strategy*, ed. T. R. Phillips (London, 1943).

Scott, Samuel F., *The Responses of the Royal Army to the French Revolution* (Oxford, 1978).

Seaton, Albert, *The German Army* (London, 1982).

Seaton, Albert, *The Russo-German War 1941–45* (London, 1971).

Shanahan, W. O., *Prussian Military Reforms 1786–1813* (New York, 1945).

Shaw, G. C., *Supply in Modern War* (London, 1938).

Showalter, Dennis E., 'Infantry weapons, infantry tactics, and the armies of Germany, 1849–64', *European Studies Review*, vol. 4, no. 2 (1974), pp. 119–40.

Showalter, Dennis E., 'The influence of railroads on Prussian planning for the Seven Weeks' War', *Military Affairs*, vol. 38 (April 1974), pp. 62–7.

Showalter, Dennis E., 'Prussian Cavalry 1806–1871' *Militärgeschichtliche Mitteilungen*, vol. 19, no. 1 (1976), pp. 7–22.

Showalter, Dennis E., *Railroads and Rifles. Soldiers, technology and the unification of Germany* (Hamden Conn., 1975).

Showalter, Dennis E., 'Soldiers into postmasters? The electric telegraph as an instrument of command in the Prussian Army', *Military Affairs*, vol. 37 (April 1973), pp. 48–52.

Shy, John, *A People Numerous and Armed* (Oxford, 1976).

Silberner, Edmund, *The Problem of War in nineteenth-century economic thought* (Princeton, 1946).

Sked, Alan, *The Survival of the Habsburg Empire: Radetzky, the imperial army and the class war* (London, 1979).

Spiers, Edward M., *The Army and Society, 1815–1914* (London, 1980).

Spiers, Edward M., 'Rearming the Edwardian Artillery', *Journal of the Society for Army Historical Research*, vol. 57, no. 231 (1979), pp. 167–76.

Spiers, Edward M., 'Reforming the infantry 1900–1914', *Journal of the Society for Army Historical Research*, vol. 49, no. 238 (1981), pp. 82–94.

Spiers, Edward M., 'The use of the Dum Dum bullet in colonial warfare', *Journal of Imperial and Commonwealth History*, vol. 4, no. 1 (1975), pp. 3–14.

Stolfi, Russell H. S., 'Equipment for victory in France in 1940', *History*, vol. 52, no. 1 (1970), pp. 1–20.

Stone, Norman, *The Eastern Front 1914–1917* (London, 1975).

Strachan, Hew, 'The early Victorian army and the nineteenth-century revolution in government', *English Historical Review*, vol. 95, no. 377 (1980), pp. 782–809.

Strachan, Hew, 'The pre-Crimean origins of reform in the British army' (Cambridge University Ph.D. thesis, 1977).

Strachan, Hew, 'Soldiers, Strategy and Sebastopol', *Historical Journal*, vol. 21, no. 2 (1978), pp. 303–25.

Tate, James P., (ed.), 'The American military on the frontier', *Proceedings of the 7th Military History Symposium, U.S.A.F. Academy, 1976* (Washington, 1978).

Taylor, Philip M., 'Clausewitz in Nazi Germany', *Journal of Contemporary History*, vol. 16, no. 1 (1981), pp. 5–26.

Taylor, William L., 'The debate over changing cavalry tactics and weapons 1900–1914', *Military Affairs*, vol. 28 (1964–5), pp. 173–83.

Travers, T. H. E., 'The offensive and the problem of innovation in British military thought 1870–1915', *Journal of Contemporary History*, vol. 13, no. 3 (1978), pp. 531–53.

Travers, T. H. E., 'Technology, tactics, and morale: Jean de Bloch, the Boer War, and British military theory, 1900–1914', *Journal of Modern History*, vol. 51, no. 2 (1979), pp. 264–86.

Trebilcock, Clive, 'War and the failure of industrial mobilisation: 1899 and 1914', in *War and Economic Development*, ed. J. M. Winter (Cambridge, 1975), pp. 139–64.

Trevor-Roper, H. R., (ed.), *Hitler's War Directives 1939–1945* (London, 1964).

Trumpener, Ulrich, 'The Road to Ypres: the beginnings of gas warfare in World War I', *Journal of Modern History*, vol. 47, no. 3 (1975), pp. 460–80.

Trythall, Anthony John, *'Boney' Fuller. The Intellectual General* (London, 1977).

Tugwell, Maurice, *Airborne to Battle. A history of airborne warfare 1918–1971*, (London, 1971).

Tulard, Jean, *Napoléon ou le mythe du sauveur* (Paris, 1977).

Vagts, Alfred, *A History of Militarism* (London, 1959).

Walzer, Michael, *Just and Unjust Wars* (London, 1978).

Ward, S. G. P., *Wellington's Headquarters* (Oxford, 1957).

Warlimont, Walter, *Inside Hitler's Headquarters 1939–45* (London, 1964).

Watt, Donald Cameron, *Too Serious a Business. European armed forces and the approach to the Second World War* (London, 1975).

Weigley, Russell F., *The American Way of War* (New York, 1973).

Weigley, Russell F., *Eisenhower's Lieutenants: the campaigns of France and Germany 1944–1945* (London, 1981).

Weigley, Russell F., *History of the United States Army* (London, 1968).

Westwood, John, *Railways at War* (London, 1980).

Whitton, F. E., *Moltke* (London, 1921).

Wilkinson, Spenser, *The Defence of Piedmont 1742–1748* (Oxford, 1927).

Wilkinson, Spenser, *The French Army before Napoleon* (Oxford, 1915).

Wilkinson, Spenser, *The Rise of General Bonaparte* (Oxford, 1930).

Wilkinson, Spenser, *War and Policy* (London, 1910).

Williams, T. Harry, 'The Military Leadership of North and South', in *Why the North won the Civil War*, ed. David Donald (New York, 1962), pp. 33–54.

Williams, T. Harry, 'The Return of Jomini – some thoughts on recent Civil War writing', *Military Affairs*, vol. 39, no. 4 (1975), pp. 204–6.

Winter, Denis, *Death's Men* (London, 1978).

Wright, Gordon, *The Ordeal of Total War 1939–1945* (New York, 1968).

Wynne, G. C., *If Germany Attacks. The battle in depth in the West* (London, 1940).

Young, Robert J., *In command of France: French foreign policy and military planning, 1933–1940* (Cambridge Mass., 1978).

Young, Robert J., 'Preparations for defeat: French war doctrine in the inter-war period', *Journal of European Studies*, vol. 2, no. 2 (1972), pp. 155–72.

Zaniewicki, Witold, 'L'impact de 1870 sur la pensée militaire française', *Revue de Défense Nationale* (Aug.–Sept. 1970), pp. 1331–41.

Supplementary Bibliography

Alger, John I., *The quest for victory: the history of the principles of war* (Westport Conn., 1982).

Arnold, James R., 'A reappraisal of column versus line in the Napoleonic Wars', *Journal of the Society for Army Historical Research*, vol. 59, no. 244 (1982), pp. 196–208.

Aron, Raymond, *Clausewitz. Philosopher of War*, translation of *Penser la Guerre. Clausewitz* by Christine Booker and Norman Stone (London, 1983).

Ashworth, Tony, *Trench Warfare 1914–1918. The live and let live system* (London, 1983).

Ball, Desmond, *Politics and force levels: the strategic missile program of the Kennedy administration* (London, 1980).

Berghahn, Volker R., *Militarism: the history of an international debate 1861–1979* (Leamington Spa, 1981).

Bidwell, Shelford, and Dominick Graham, *Fire-Power: British army weapons and theories of war 1904–1945* (London, 1982).

Blanning, T. C. W., *The French Revolution in Germany: occupation and resistance in the Rhineland 1792–1802* (Oxford, 1983), ch. 3 'Military exploitation'.

Bond, Brian, *War and Society in Europe, 1870–1970* (London, 1984).

Childs, John, *Armies and Warfare in Europe 1648–1789* (Manchester, 1982).

Creveld, Martin van, *Fighting Power. German and U.S. army performance, 1939–1945* (London, 1983).

Erickson, John, *The Road to Berlin. Stalin's War with Germany, volume 2* (London, 1983).

Graham, Dominick, 'Sans Doctrine: British army tactics in the First World War', in Timothy Travers and Christon Archer (eds.), *Men at war: politics, technology and innovation in the twentieth century* (Chicago, 1982).

Hahlweg, Werner (ed.), *Freiheit ohne Krieg? Beiträge zur Strategie – Diskussion der Gegenwart im Spiegel der Theorie von Carl von Clausewitz* (Bonn, 1980).

Headrick, Daniel R., *The Tools of Empire: technology and European imperialism in the nineteenth century* (Oxford, 1981).

Holloway, David, *The Soviet Union and the Arms Race* (New Haven, 1983).

Howard, Michael, *The Causes of Wars* (London, 1983).

Howard, Michael, *Clausewitz* (Oxford, 1983).

Hughes, B. P., *Open Fire: Artillery Tactics from Marlborough to Wellington* (Chichester, 1983).

Jones, David R. (ed.), *The Military-Naval Encyclopedia of Russia and the Soviet Union* (vol. 1–, Gulf Breeze, Florida, 1978–).

Keep, John L. H., 'The Russian army's response to the French Revolution', *Jahrbucher fur Geschichte Osteuropas*, vol. 5, no. 28 (1980), pp. 500–23.

McNeill, William H., *The Pursuit of Power: technology, armed force and society since AD 1000* (Oxford, 1983).

Menning, Bruce W., 'Russian military innovation in the second half of the eighteenth century', *War and Society*, vol. 2, no. 1 (1984), pp. 23–41.

Murray, Williamson, *Strategy for Defeat: the Luftwaffe 1933–1945* (Alabama, 1983).

Murray, Williamson, 'The strategy of the "Phoney War": a re-evaluation', *Military Affairs*, vol. 45, no. 1 (1981), pp. 13–17.

Pearton, Maurice, *The Knowledgeable State: diplomacy, war and technology since 1830* (London, 1982).

Pintner, Walter M., 'Russia's military style, Russian society, and Russian power in the eighteenth century', in A. G. Cross (ed.), *Russia and the West in the Eighteenth Century* (Newtonville Mass., 1983).

Porch, Douglas, *The Conquest of Morocco* (New York, 1983).

Robbins, Keith, *The First World War* (Oxford, 1984).

Rosenberg, David Alan, 'The origins of overkill. Nuclear weapons and American strategy, 1945–1960', *International Security*, vol. 7, no. 4 (1983), pp. 3–71.

Snow, Donald M., *Nuclear strategy in a dynamic world. American policy in the 1980s* (Alabama, 1981).

Strachan, Hew, *Wellington's Legacy. The reform of the British army 1830–54* (Manchester, 1984).

Summers, Harry G., Jr, *On Strategy. A critical analysis of the Vietnam War* (Novato, 1982).

Sweet, John J. T., *Iron Arm: the mechanization of Mussolini's army* (Westport Conn., 1980).

Woodward, David, *Lloyd George and the Generals* (Newark, 1983).

Index